The Oratory of Negro Leaders:
1900–1968

The Oratory
of Negro Leaders:
1900–1968

Marcus H. Boulware

Department of Speech / Florida A & M University

Negro Universities Press
Westport, Connecticut

Dedication

To those individuals who are aware
that the lines of communication between the races
within the United States can best be mended
by leaders who can speak not only effectively,
but with some measure of artistry.

Contents

Foreword

There are three reasons why I am intrigued by a book on "black oratory." Black orators were major boyhood heroes of mine; they were 1930s southern black preachers. Secondly, as something of a black historian myself, I am perhaps more aware than most people of how, in this country in the last century, one or another form of black oratory has been the keel of the black experience. Thirdly, in very recent years, it has been my privilege to interview in depth, to hear and see repeatedly, the two men whose spell-binding abilities unquestionably place them first among the modern-era black orators whom Professor Boulware includes: the late Dr. Martin Luther King, of whom I wrote an in-depth magazine portrait; and the late Malcolm X, with whom I spent two years in collaboration writing *The Autobiography of Malcolm X*.

This book is needed not only by students of rhetoric and oratory, but also by students of history. The latter in particular will find satisfaction in the wide sampling, sensitively selected, that Professor Boulware offers here. The reader will become acquainted not only with the black preachers and politicians, but with statesmen, scholars, and demagogues, both the saints and the sinners.

This book, too, will give its readers more insight into why and how the history of American blacks has witnessed a progression from the sheer survival attitudes of most slaves to the growing present black attitude either to assimilate fully in American society or, at least psychologically, to reject and separate from it.

The white perspective toward black voices has undergone almost as vast a change. In the past, those few whites who were exposed to any black oratory at all appraised it, generally, as an amusement—with rare exceptions, such as, of course, Booker T. Washington, Dr. W. E. B. Du Bois, and a handful of others, who came to be limelight figures for whites. At best, whites considered black oratory to be a curiosity, very much as if some few simians had been trained remarkably. This is well put by my friend and colleague here at Hamilton College, Professor Charles Todd: "The black orator was regarded by most white men as someone who had accidentally stumbled onto a clever parlor trick. Today, however, the white man is no longer amused."

The amusement ceased at about the time of the Malcolm X stance of "I'm Talking To You, White Man!", along with the development of Dr. Martin Luther King's forthright brand of nonviolence.

So, while whites laughed at black orators for being largely illiterate or poorly trained, ironically one reason why those black speakers played such a strong role in black history is something which history itself has proved most amply: that great orators need not be educated. In fact, traditionally oratory has been a natural gift among even the most unliterate peoples.

Says Carter G. Woodson, in *Negro Orators And Their Orations,* a volume that preceded Professor Boulware's work: "Oratory in the broad sense requires no other equipment than fluency of speech and self-confidence." Massachusetts Senator George

F. Hoar, himself a powerful orator of the 1890s, said, "The orator must be able to play at will on the mighty organ, his audience, of which human souls are keys."

The really special value of Professor Boulware's book lies in the fact that it gives us, as a corrective, a wide range of sundry types of black orators, of both the past and the relative present. These untutored earlier black orators were not merely articulate beings; they were physically and psychically one with their audiences. In their own everyday lives they shared fully their audiences' trials and despairs. They emerged from among their people to provide a motivation for further endurance and sustained hope.

When we speak of the earliest black orators, we must begin with the black preachers whose model and precedent has spawned virtually all other facets of black oratory. The black preachers, Sunday after Sunday, brought new life to their tired people. They graphically presented promise and deliverance. "Their tones were beautiful, their gestures natural," says Woodson. "They could suit the word to the action, and the action to the word. Using skillfully the eye and voice, they reached the souls of man."

For a true appreciation of the early black orators one actually had to see and hear them, as I did as a boy. For only thus could one savor the sheer flavor and charisma of these elocutionary artists. Yea! Those who, thundering from their pulpits, would part the Rea Sea or stir the Eagle's Nest! Perhaps their apex was reached with that black preacher whom the great black poet James Weldon Johnson has described: "—so sure of his power . . . that banging shut his Bible and jerking off his glasses, and glaring at his parishioners, who had come to feel his confidence that particular Sunday morning, he announced, 'This mornin', Brothers and Sisters, I 'tends to 'splain the inexplainable, to fin' the indefinable, to unscrew the inscrutable!' "

I can hear them now out there in those worn pews, "Yay-*man*, brother!" And how I wish I might have been in that church that morning! For hasn't it been said that not only should the orator instruct, but he should move, and he should delight? Did not Cicero say, "The object of oratory alone is not truth, but it is persuasion"? And Marlowe: "The heart must glow before the tongue can gild"?

My point is that this preacher whom Johnson describes—in fact, all of those largely untutored historical black voices—fueled, with their raw eloquence, the hopeful emotions of black men down through their long history in this country. What were they engaged in if not pure art, giving their people more by far than all of the known "-ologies" gave them, more than all of the rest of the society in which they lived gave them? For, the point is, their black listeners believed—and they *did* find endurance and hope!

Few will deny that black Christianity has been more fervently articulate in America than white Christianity has been—due in part to the patterns of exultant audience feedback that history's unheralded black preachers sought and demanded of their congregations. Dr. Martin Luther King, standing before three hundred thousand people drawn to the March on Washington, echoed that earlier sound in his "I Have a Dream" speech. It was a more polished performance than was ever achieved by his predecessors; nonetheless, it brought back memories of all black yesterdays, and the black dreams that filled and buoyed them. From the slave orators to Dr. King and Malcolm X, and on into the present shifting hierarchy of articulate black militants, only the words and phrases have differed, dictated by the social forces of the changing times. But through it all runs one central theme: the black man petitioning for human rights.

Professor Boulware here offers us a wider range of oratory and orators than have hitherto been recognized. Naturally, he has not included all of *my* particular favorites—among them Richmond, Virginia's Reverend ("De Sun Do Move") John M. Jasper, of post-Civil War fame, along with Mississippi's Senator Blanche K. Bruce (1841–1898). But all this says is that the anthologist will never live who will not omit some of his readers' favorites. Professor Boulware's feat, to me, is that his sensitive selection has made available to us so many of them.

This is a splendid beginning to the critical search we must conduct into all facets of black life and history in America. We have been given here a much-needed book, an important book, and one that richly deserves to be used widely.

Alex Haley

July, 1969

Preface

Many years ago I was invited to deliver a short speech during Negro History Week sponsored by a local historical society. The assigned topic was "Spokesmen for an Oppressed People." To secure materials for this address, I went to the local library to assemble a bibliography. Surprisingly, there was only one anthology—*Negro Orators and Their Orations* by Carter G. Woodson, the noted historian. While this book was inadequate, it supplied the bulk of materials for the address.

Later interest in the subject of Negro oratory led me to review the literature in search of what had been done. In 1946, I spent some time thumbing through Knower's *Index* to theses and dissertations in the area of speech and found Winfred Bennett, "A Survey of American Negro Oratory, 1619 to 1925," an unpublished M.A. thesis which was submitted to George Washington University in 1935. The work traced Negro oratory from its African origin through the career of Booker T. Washington. Further investigation revealed that William W. Pipes did a doctoral dissertation at the University of Michigan in 1942 under the title, "An Interpretative Study of Old-Time Negro Preaching." In 1914, Mrs. Alice Dunbar Nelson published a volume carrying the title *Masterpieces of Negro Eloquence.* A chapter on the public addresses of Booker T. Washington appears in a *History and Criticism of American Public Address,* two volumes, edited by William Norwood Brigance and prepared under the auspices of the Speech Association of America. During various stages of the research, I visited numerous libraries having outstanding Negro collections. Two of these deserve special mention. At Hampton Institute in 1946, I was assigned a place in one corner of the room housing the Negro collection. Much of the research was done during the summer of 1947 in the extensive collection of the Wisconsin State Historical Society at Madison. Between 1962 and 1965, I made use of the Negro collection housed in the Coleman Library of Florida A and M University.

The paucity of materials on Negro oratory in histories revealed a need for a book of this kind. Hence, I prepared this history, which has been limited to the twentieth century. It will tell the story of Negro oratory in the United States from the rise of Booker T. Washington in 1900, as a finished public speaker, through June, 1968, of the Great Society made popular by President Lyndon B. Johnson. Considerable emphasis will be placed upon the Negro revolt which has been symbolized in the leadership of the orator, Martin Luther King, Jr., as well as through the civil-rights activities of college students who affiliated themselves with CORE, SNCC, and SCLC.

No particular standard of literary criticism had to be determined, because this history is primarily chronological. A strict rhetorical criticism of Negro public speaking is a task for another investigator. On the other hand, one cannot easily separate criticism from history, for often what an orator says must be interpreted before the historian can make judgment concerning the orator's influence. Therefore, some critical evaluation has been given concerning the platform oratory of the individuals included in this book. This history is not exhaustive;

neither could all sources be examined. I did, however, select basic materials from American histories, narratives, literary and historical anthologies, memoirs, books on the subject of the Negro, political advertisements, mimeographed and printed matter, newspaper clippings, sketches, and letters from speakers or persons who knew the orators.

The reader will observe that in some ways each orator has been a success; in some ways, each speaker was, or is, a product of his childhood environment and immediate habitat; and, in some ways, each orator has espoused a special plan for advancing the Negro's cause.

I encountered many difficulties. First, the Negro press generally has not made accessible reports on the speeches of orators during the last sixty years. Second, space limitations have prevented many Negro newspapers from publishing detailed accounts of addresses delivered by black leaders. In earlier days, a reporter leisurely filled in several columns with details of what was said, who was there, what was eaten, what was worn, and the like. Stage management and mannerisms were often described. Today a similar speech might rate only three or four paragraphs—often written from advance copy. Modern newspapers, for instance, publish only the highlights of a banquet speech, deleting all else unless a significant dramatic incident occurred. Third, I had to rely considerably upon correspondence. Frequently, no amount of persuasion could influence many individuals to send information regarding themselves or others. Fourth, after combing hundreds of sources, I found very little information about women speakers.

This volume is the first history of Negro oratory in the United States during the twentieth century. I am very much aware that I must assume full responsibility for the contents of this book. It is hoped that the information in this work will influence the reader to conclude that effective public speaking is one of the gateways to leadership.

MARCUS H. BOULWARE

Acknowledgments

Generous help has been given by many people in the course of preparation of this work. I wish especially to express thanks for the kind assistance and cooperation of other people and many organizations:

The late Professor Henry L. Ewbank, my adviser at the University of Wisconsin, whose guiding hand, sincere criticism, and constructive suggestions helped me with the material covering the period 1900–1953;

Dr. Frederick Haberman, Professor of Speech at the University of Wisconsin;

The historical societies, organizations, agencies and orators who have furnished materials;

The librarians of the following association and institutions, who went beyond the call of duty to give assistance: The State Historical Association of Wisconsin, Madison; University of Wisconsin, Madison; Hampton Institute, Hampton, Virginia, and Johnson C. Smith University, Charlotte, North Carolina;

Mrs. Alverta N. Morris, circulation librarian at Florida A

and M University, Tallahassee, for assistance in finding materials on the oratorical activities of Negroes during the presidential administrations of the late John F. Kennedy and Lyndon B. Johnson.

Grateful acknowledgment should be made to my wife, who has been a patient sufferer and an encouraging companion throughout the entire labor—to her a special debt of gratitude must always stand. My thanks go also to Mrs. Bessie E. Harris, a dauntless typist, who made the manuscript readable.

Special mention should be made to J. M. Simmons, Chicago *Daily News* librarian, for supplying an abundance of photocopy material relating to the late Roscoe Conkling Simmons, Chicago orator.

NEGRO ORATOR

A black ruby sparkles
On a silvery circlet
Of song and rebellion
His words are shining ships
I hoard for secret hunger.

—Laura Tanne

1 / Nature and Styles of Oratory

MEANING OF ORATORY

It has been said that the day of oratory has passed. This notion is erroneous: first, because oratory will be with us as long as there is a cause to advance; second, oratory is immortal, and in one form or another, it will live and influence mankind; and, third, oratory will not die, because it is the parent of liberty. Henry Hardwicke made this point clear when he declared: "By the constitution of things it was ordained that eloquence should be the last stay and support of liberty, and that with her she is destined to live, flourish, and die. It is to the interest of tyrants to cripple and debilitate every species of eloquence. It is, then, the duty of free states to foster oratory."[1] Voicing a somewhat similar opinion, together with the belief that eloquence is the greatest force on earth among men, Henry Ward Beecher once said that not until human nature changes from what it is, will the function of the living voice cease.

In this history, oratory means effective public speaking. The term is broad enough to include both the classical style of the ancient orators and the conversational manner of modern speakers. Conversational speaking can be eloquent, concrete, clear, concise, elegant, and simple. It can contain the characteristic earmark of the natural orator[2] who often rises from the common ranks to fight verbally the battles of his people. Conversational speaking can also be the medium of expression of the educated, polished, gentleman orator[3] who has a "better chance of securing a hearing than one unable to express himself" according to the best prevailing usage.

It was Wendell Phillips, antislavery proponent, who was the first orator of note to employ the conversational style of platform speaking. His mode of delivery raised conversation to the highest power. Never before had any American orator spoken with so little effort. His biographers reported that his delivery had no element of display or bombast. He spoke as one might talk in conversation, where the voice modulates naturally in response to the changing thought or emotion, wholly without aim for effect or display of any kind. Friends said he was a gentleman conversing while his enemies observed that he was "an infernal machine set to music." In brief, Phillips' addresses were "normal conversation made louder and stronger to meet the needs of his larger audiences."

Most modern public speakers have followed the pattern of the conversational mode set by Wendell Phillips but we still have many politicians who employ special ministerial tones and cadences for the purpose of "orating to" instead of "conversing with" their audience. But, at long last, politicians are discovering that by "straining out loud sonorous monotones," they misuse their voices and fatigue easily. Yet, many pastors will not change their theological delivery unless their congregations demand that they get rid of their Sunday voices.

To be an orator in bygone days, a speaker did not need "to show superiority in power of thought, logical consistency in reasoning, quickness and brilliancy of conception and abundance of knowledge."[4] Yet these are the most desirable attributes. An orator may be illiterate or unlettered. This very fact sometimes makes it possible for him to be successful in

behalf of certain local groups, because the local people understand his language. The gospel writers would have said, "And
the common people heard him gladly."

Oratory embraces a number of fine arts. John P. Altgeld
expressed this idea in these words: "In music, tradition fur-
nishes the ideas. The poet clothes them in words. The com-
poser sets these to music, and the singer renders them into
song. The orator must do all of these things. He must furnish
the ideas, he must clothe them in words, he must give them a
rhythmic arrangement, and he must deliver them with all the
care with which a singer renders a song."[5] It must be emphasized that each of these elements is of supreme importance. The ideas must be bright and seem alive. The language
must be logical, simple, and effective. There must be a logical
unfolding of the subject matter.

THE *How* AND THE *What*

For many centuries, oratory was considered a natural gift.
Even the most civilized people held this notion. This natural
gift of the orator has been demonstrated best in platform
delivery. In many circles, there exists the belief that a person
need not have an education to be an orator, for in most
instances delivery counts more than the information given.
Similarly impressed, James Weldon Johnson, Negro orator and
poet, said in his biography:

So I come back to my theory that the inner secret of sheer oratory
is not so much in the *what* is said as in the combination of the *how,
when,* and *where.* The how is the most important of these factors
and its chief virtues lie in the timing; that is, in the ability of the
speaker to set up a series of vibrations between himself and his
hearers. I have witnessed the accomplishment of this feat by old-
time Negro preachers using pure incoherencies.[6]

The late Lord Rosebery once said that few speeches that
once electrified audiences can bear the colorless photography

of a printed record. While modern audiences demand that a speaker have ideas, it must be admitted that the voice, general appearance, the character and gestures of the speaker are what make a deeper impression upon the minds of the listeners.

CHANGING STYLES OF ORATORY

Oratory today is not the kind used by Phocion of the Greeks, or Cicero of the Romans. In the United States, it has differed in method and character as it was influenced by changing events, inventions, and circumstances. The "art-view of oratory" has been influenced by the physical necessities of the pre-electronic age. It must be recalled that Demosthenes, Cicero, Daniel Webster, and William Jennings Bryan did not have to speak with friendly directness into a public-address system. They were forced to hurl their words across vast outdoor meadows, down the length of barnlike halls and make themselves heard above myriad distracting sounds. Therefore, their inflections, their postures, and their gestures all reflected the demands of heroic projection. When a speaker[7] did not supplement his content with these devices he was likely to fail—even with as great a text as Lincoln's Gettysburg Address.

In the ancient Greek outdoor theaters, actors, standing in highheeled boots and with heads covered with facial masks that served as sounding-board resonators, had to hurl their words at audiences in order to be heard. Tragedy, often through soliloquies, gave the protagonist an opportunity to rise to the majesty of the occasion with a resonant, orotund, and sonorous voice.

With the advent of radio and television came another change in American oratory. Bishop William J. Walls said:

Oratory has changed in our radio age, is circumscribed and rendered cut and dry by radio practice. It is more subdued and reflective. The exhibitionary and heroic features have been modified, particularly as to gestures and flexibility, variability, and enunciation. In a word, oratory is less free and more stilted than in former days when the orator always stood before the 'sea of upturned faces,' whether in the pulpit or in the political arena or in the lecture lyceum.[8]

ORATOR AND LECTURER

There is a difference between the lecturer and the orator. The lecturer appeals primarily to the intellect, while the orator influences both the emotions and the mind. Speakers today cannot, however, contend that audiences do not like emotional speaking. The reason why we don't have more of it is that many speakers of the present century have no convictions on the great moral issues. In this connection, a man who is fired by a great conviction will surely develop some emotion on the subject. The lecturer does not always have a great conviction, since it may be his purpose merely to impart knowledge to students. He must, however, motivate those students to seek the truth that makes men free.

The ancients described the orator as a good man skilled in speaking. This good man had to possess certain convictions which he wished to impart to his listeners. Everyone knows that if a speaker can throw over his message the spell of personal magnetism, character, and prestige, he will captivate and move his hearers.

THE PRESS AND THE ORATOR

There is a growing opinion that the press is overshadowing the orator and his speechmaking. The task of the newspaper is to present facts, evolve ideas, combine ideas into judgments, compare truths or contrast them, so that readers may draw conclusions. But when the press does this, it merely develops an informed audience for the orator. The press, therefore, has not usurped the place of the speaker, but it has given him a new task and responsibility. Mabel Platz described this new function as follows:

The orator now approaches an audience, enlightened or prejudiced through agencies of the press and radio. The highest attainment of an orator is to deal with the convictions of the audience in such a way as to emphasize what is already in their minds. All who today seek to influence the public by oratory must present common forms of knowledge in such a way as to hold the attention and impress judgment of those who hear.[9]

Sometimes the press publishes speeches of our national leaders in full text, so that we may weigh the speakers' words with a more objective attitude. The public has a chance, therefore, to study a speech stripped of the personal magnetism of the orator who, on the previous day, had won the audience by popular acclamation. What is more, radio, television, and other modern inventions have not outmoded the art of public speech. In fact, these technical advances in the communication of the human voice have intensified people's interest in oratory and greatly enlarged the opportunity and obligation of the orator.

AN ART OF CONSEQUENCE

People of primitive communities were united by custom and tradition. But to unite them for collective action, it was necessary for them to have a leader. The primitive leader was also a fighter, but he depended upon persuasive words to get people to follow him so that he might make that *enviable* record as a fighter. Therefore, leadership, in a large measure, is dependent upon effective speaking. Oratory,[10] in this sense, becomes an art of consequence.

An unskilled worker in a trade union may lead his fellow

workers in a strike if he has some skill in public speaking. His eloquence can become powerful in influencing group action, such as striking for higher wages, paid holidays and vacations, and pensions benefits. He must be able to persuade other workers to follow him. If this trade union worker cannot move men by reaching their emotions through oral descriptions of their needs and feelings, he can never attain the role of leadership. It must be added that though public speaking is a gateway to leadership, training in public speaking will not necessarily make one a leader. Alan H. Monroe[11] said that if a man has character and intelligence, careful training in speaking will help him become more forceful, useful, and influential regardless of his proposed career. Most of us have observed that persons with average ability, who speak fluently, move more quickly up the ladder of success than some gifted individuals who have not learned the art of platform speaking.

Footnotes, Chapter 1

1. Henry Hardwicke, *History of Oratory and Orators.*
2. An individual who has no special training but who has by his own efforts developed certain speaking skills.
3. *Negro History Bulletin* 2 (October, 1938): 1.
4. Ibid.
5. John P. Altgeld, *Oratory and the Public.*
6. James Weldon Johnson, *Along This Way.*
7. William Muehl, *The Road to Persuasion.*
8. William J. Walls, *Joseph Charles Price,* p. 307.
9. Mabel Platz, *The History of Public Speaking,* 1935.
10. *Negro History Bulletin* 2 (October, 1938): 1.
11. Alan H. Monroe, *Principles and Types of Speech.*

2 / The Negro Orator and His Mission

Twentieth-century Negro oratory began with Booker T. Washington, heralded as the "Apostle of Racial Goodwill." After his death in 1915, there came upon the scene a new group of orators who, regardless of their spheres of activity, felt impelled to right existing wrongs and were driven by a messianic urge to reshape the American society. They were prophets of a new democracy and advocates of radical social reforms. Another wing of speakers were conservatists who helped to smooth over the antagonism created by militant leaders.

THE NEGRO ORATOR

The eloquent Negro speaker has long been in existence, and the late Benjamin Brawley painted this picture of him:

The Negro is peculiarly gifted as an orator. To his magnificent gift of voice, he adds a fervor or sentiment and an appreciation of the possibilities of a great occasion that are indispensable in the work of one who excels in this field. Greater than any of these things, however, is the romantic quality that finds outlet in vast outreaches of imagery and singularly figurative power of expression.[1]

Repeatedly, the author has observed in rural communities unlettered speakers who have brought comfort and inspiration to struggling agricultural and rural groups.

Modern black orators are well educated and their quality of speaking has evolved from the unlettered and strictly emotional variety to the logical, refined, and cultured. They combine exposition with argument and persuasion, and their messages are sound and informative. Negro speakers are journalists, lawyers, social scientists, teachers, labor leaders, educators, ministers, and college administrators, "whose speeches shed more light and less heat." Many of them interpret the Negro citizen and his achievements, and call attention to his disabilities in a manner designed to get a favorable hearing.

The tempo of black orators is varied, and no single term can describe the versatility of quality, style, and manner of speaking. Harold F. Gosnell, who has observed many speakers, said:

One speaker is crude in his language, unpolished in his style of delivery, but obviously sincere and forceful. Another is gifted with words, skilled in voice inflections, but lacking in drive and human understanding. A third is learned in history, entertaining, a master of phrases, but too obviously an actor. A fourth is able to work himself into an emotional frenzy, to stir the audience profoundly, to recall vividly examples of race prejudice and persecution. Still a fifth exhibits an extraordinary smoothness, a mastery of Bible history, law and politics, and an ability to arouse his listeners as well.[2]

Negro orators employ language that reflects the aspirations, hopes, interests, and habits of their audiences. Through this medium, they are able to establish with their hearers a rapport that is often astounding.

THE DOUGLASS TRADITION

Vernon Loggins once paid the black orator, Frederick Douglass, a very high compliment. He said, "Frederick Douglass, trained in the tradition of the art when it was at its prime in America, remained until his death in 1895, the unrivaled orator of his race. And his successor has never arisen."[3] Loggins further stated that oratory was the field in which the Negro made no advancement after 1865. Voicing a similar opinion, Winfred Bennett said, "We must look to the past to find the great speakers among the Negro race."[4]

Modern audiences would probably disagree with Loggins. For instance, Booker T. Washington was in every way an able successor to Douglass. While the two men carried different messages to the people, they were alike in that they appeared before large audiences of both races—black and white. Not only is this true, but Negro oratory has advanced and kept pace with those modifying influences of new inventions, the radio and television.

NEGRO VERSUS WHITE SPEAKERS

There is a sharp line of demarcation between the leading black and white orators of the present century. This difference cannot be observed readily in such matters as education, vocal effectiveness, religion, and the like, but rather on the basis of the far-reaching influence of the orator's message upon a national audience. The lightest utterances of topflight white orators often become official statements of the United States government. Many daily newspapers print their speeches in full text. Television and radio carry their messages over large broadcasting systems. Movie newsreels give significant excerpts from the most important addresses of the week.

The Negro orator, however, is a special pleader, an advocate for minority rights; and since he holds very few high army and governmental positions, the black speaker talks chiefly to small and more intimate groups. His speeches are seldom broadcast by radio or television. Even Negro newspapers scarcely devote more than five paragraphs to a speech story, and almost never print speeches in full text.

MISSION OF THE ORATOR

More than stirring speeches will be needed to raise the Negro citizen to first-class status. Grievances may be expressed through many channels of publicity—speeches, sermons, poems, petitions, resolutions, news reports, editorials, radio broadcasts, movies, civil-rights demonstrations and marches. Many of these find a sympathetic clearinghouse in Negro newspapers.

No one leader or orator directs the black man's fight for complete equality. Chance, as much as anything else, determines the site of the next skirmish. But what the Negro leader lacks in a "grand design for equality" is supplemented with fervor, zeal, and dedication. His followers stand behind him united, even if they are not well disciplined and organized. On one occasion, the author heard Whitney Young say that Negro leadership is locked into a course of action by the militancy of the rank and file. In this predicament, the world has noticed that the church has been the tactical headquarters and sanctuary where, even southern "police bullies" are reluctant to interfere with the Negro's right of assembly so long as he is in the church. Within these walls, the Negro leader or orator has assumed the role of a great fighter who helped Negro congregations gather strength, courage, and responsibility to moral and legal principles. Convinced that God marches with them, church members have followed their ministers from the church into the streets to use the most visible, if not annoying, of their revolutionary weapons.

The guerrilla tactics of "striking the enemy" in least expected places have aggravated white segregationists unmercifully.

These annoyances have stirred diehard southerners to employ mud-slinging devices, claiming that Negroes are Communist-inspired. Symbolically, the affray is a sort of a hand-to-hand encounter much like that of Jacob wrestling with the angel. The Negro won't let the enemy go "until he blesses him" with the promise of a new freedom.

The Negro has made oratory a multichannel through which he expresses his discontent. Thus, the Negro orator's mission is many-fold: (1) to protest grievances, (2) to state complaints, (3) to demand rights, (4) to advocate racial cooperation, (5) to mold racial consciousness, and (6) to stimulate racial pride. And in protesting grievances, stating complaints, and demanding rights, the orator warns his listeners that they must not submit in silence to injustice and oppression. The idea of protest is not a Negro invention; men have used this medium for centuries, for example, the early American colonists who petitioned, drafted resolutions, and threatened open rebellion.

The plight of the Negro "phantom army" has been best described by Richard Wright, in his *Twelve Million Black Voices*:

Again we say, of the North as of the South, that life for us is a daily warfare and that we are hard like soldiers. We are set apart from the civilian population; our kitchenettes comprise our bar-racks; the color of our skin constitutes our uniform; the streets of our cities are our trenches; a job is a pillbox to be captured and held; and the unions of white workers for a long time have formed the first line of resistance which we encountered. We are always in battle, but the tidings of victory are few.[5]

At once, the Negro speaker becomes a sort of safety valve for the boiling protest and resentment, an agency for group con-trol, a criterion for how Negroes should think and feel, a persuader to assist the audience in disciplining its resentment. Yet, there is no definite planning of protest techniques and strategy among Negro leaders and orators. However, the auth-or has outlined a program for a unified high command of Negro leadership in the July, 1967, issue of *Quarterly Review*

of Higher Education Among Negroes, published at Johnson
C. Smith University.

Negro speakers have been criticized for making racial complaints a "swan song." Booker T. Washington, recognizing
this, praised both Negroes and whites for their worthwhile
contributions to racial progress. This praise was usually followed by his plea for eradication of the shortcomings of both
groups. Perceiving how easy it was for the Negro press and
orators to become greatly immersed in the expression of
grievances, Dr. Ralph Bunche, former UN mediator, when
addressing the Fortieth Alpha Kappa Boule in Washington,
D.C., in January, 1949, advised his audience to prepare and
take advantage of every opportunity when it arises. He
denounced Negro leaders who resisted programs of progress
simply because they were too busy making complaints. Most
orators are favorably inclined to racial cooperation and stress
that democracy operates not only under laws, but it also
depends upon certain unwritten rules of honor and decency
impressed upon the consciences of all American citizens.
There is, they plead, no legal punishment that can be inflicted
upon men who violate these unwritten laws or who do not
want to observe them.

The orator finds it easy to arouse racial consciousness, for it
has been the medium by which Negroes have become a
historic group with a future and aspirations, according to
Elizabeth A. Ferguson.[6] The late journalist and author, Roi
Ottley, made this statement, "Negroes may quarrel among
themselves about minor issues, but on the questions concerning their economic, moral, and political rights, they form a
solid block." Black orators have used racial sentiment to great
advantage.[7]

THE NEGRO AUDIENCE

Carter G. Woodson,[8] the historian, said that the Negro
protest orator, with no constructive program for the attain-

ment of the things necessary to compel recognition of his claim, lost his hold on the public during the period of trying out the optimistic program of industrial education as a means of economic sufficiency. The optimistic oratory of men like Booker T. Washington caused the majority of those white people who were kindly disposed to the Negro claim for civic and political equality to abandon the Negro. By the time new Negro protest orators had replaced the conservative optimists, their national audience was "so reduced as to render their appeal hopelessly ineffective, . . . a voice crying from afar." Then, Negro speakers were forced to appear before small audiences among minority groups that had no power to redress their grievances. Since the passage of the 1964 Civil Rights Bill, the Negro orator has been speaking to national television audiences.

Audiences generally assemble in churches, school auditoriums, on public squares, and in stadiums. The educated audience exists mainly on college campuses, but they may be found in some large cities where the population is continually exposed to educational and cultural influences. The listeners demand that speakers have something to say in choice diction and acceptable English. Before these people, the speaker must make his appeal primarily to the intellect.

Because of the importance of religion in rural communities, audiences assemble mostly in churches. These hearers respond with emotional vigor to a "Sunday preaching style," and the minister seeks primarily to transpose the emotional congregation into forceful psychological responses. An educated person attending these services is generally moved by the eloquence of the man of God. He, too, feels like joining the congregation in shouts of "Amen!"

In cities with large concentrations of Negro voters, like Chicago, New York, Philadelphia, and Los Angeles, numerous political meetings are held during election campaigns. Gosnell[9] reported that these meetings are well staged and provide entertainment features, instruction, and incentives for political action. Entertainment is necessary to draw large crowds. Singing, dancing, and music help to polarize audiences into unified wholes which are made ready at the appropriate time for an address from a political speaker. Then, when the orator strikes a popular chord, the listeners clap, shout, and throw hats and programs into the air.

The general audience is a fusion of the educated, rural, and political audiences. It responds to both emotional and intellectual appeals. This audience is attentive, enthusiastic, patient, good-natured, and it will sit many hours whether or not the seats are comfortable. It responds to the speaker in a manner similar to the cheering of crowds at a football game. This audience will brook no foolishness, because, as Joseph Bibb said: "They want speakers who are able to meet their foes and bring them to task by the presentation of cold facts. Screwballs, fanatics, and wild-eyed agitators are not getting to first base. Colored Americans need to speak with conviction, comprehension, and purpose."[10]

LEADERSHIP AND ORATORS

A number of Negro speakers are called leaders whether or not so designated by whites or Negroes. They have been severely criticized for the deficiencies of black people, while extended praise is neglected. In his Prague address, Paul Robeson allegedly said that 95 percent of Negro leadership is corrupt. In rebuttal, J. A. Rogers, newspaper columnist, denied the charge on the grounds that Negro leadership does not have the chance to be corrupt. When Julius J. Adams, in *The Challenge,* charged Negro leaders with the employment of ineffective techniques, the late P. B. Young, Sr., in the January 20, 1951, issue of the *Journal and Guide,* defended them in these words: "There are no techniques that Negro leaders have not employed that they could have used, except, perhaps, the technique of revolution, and everyone knows that this action would have been fatal."

Writing under the headline, "Does Negro Leadership Need a Unified High Command?" Lem Graves, Jr., newspaper correspondent, called upon Negro leaders to organize a full-scale offensive against prejudice. In part, he said:

The enemies of Negro progress and integration are united. There are, in this country, organized hate groups with imposing mailing lists. This reporter receives weekly poison notes from these hate-mongers. The Army general staff has a unified high command in its operation of army posts. The Dixiecrats are organized and hold regular caucuses in the United States Congress. Industrial corporations plan by day and night how to keep Negroes and poor whites at each other's throats.

Against this united front, Negro leaders are still acting like guerrilla chiefs, when the combined resources, planning concepts, and fire-power are urgently needed for strategic concentration at vulnerable targets and in such sequence as will achieve the most good with the least racial dislocation.

That is why this writer dares to challenge Negro leadership to devise a system of unified command, a system of priorities and the machinery for softening the blow of integration upon the Negro community. Small private autonomies must be liquidated for the general good.[11]

The American economic system has given Negroes a great deal of freedom and opportunity, but considerable handicaps still exist to frustrate them. To succeed in spite of handicaps, Negroes have devised many methods to solve their own problems in an effort to help the black man make significant contributions to our civilization. They have established banks, insurance companies, building and loan associations, credit unions, schools and colleges. The Negro church, for instance, has furnished more effective leadership than have other types of organizations. The church has trained ministers, physicians, teachers, businessmen, and skilled craftsmen. Graduates from church schools have assumed roles of leadership in the fields of science and mathematics, medicine and allied arts, music and art, education, business, politics, and industry.

Footnotes, Chapter 2

1. Benjamin Brawley, *The Negro in Literature and Art.*
2. Harold F. Gosnell, *Negro Politicians.*
3. Vernon Loggins, *The Negro Author.*
4. Winfred DeWitt Bennett, "A Survey of American Negro Oratory" (Master's thesis).
5. Richard Wright, *Twelve Million Black Voices.*
6. Elizabeth A. Ferguson, "American Slave Insurrection Among Negroes," *Journal of Negro Education,* p. 32.
7. Roi Ottley, *New World A-Coming.*
8. Carter G. Woodson, *Negro Orators and Their Orations.*
9. Gosnell, *Negro Politicians,* p. 147.
10. Joseph D. Bibb, *Pittsburgh Courier,* February 3, 1951.
11. Lem Graves, "Washington Notebook," *Pittsburgh Courier,* November 12, 1949, p. 3.

3 / Historical Background

Six presidents have dominated the affairs of the United States since 1900. Because of their dynamic leadership, these men rose above the common level. They were the half dozen presidents, who, from 1900 to 1968, deserve to be called great. These men gave of themselves unstintingly and gained eternal influence. They kept the currents of human progress moving forward; attractive psychological labels enhanced their national prestige. They were: Theodore Roosevelt, Woodrow Wilson, Franklin D. Roosevelt, Harry S. Truman, John F. Kennedy, and Lyndon B. Johnson.

THE ROOSEVELTIAN ERA

Because Theodore Roosevelt was such a forceful leader of public opinion during the first part of this century, his administration, 1901-1909, was labeled "the Rooseveltian Era." A strong bond of friendship existed between Roosevelt and Negroes during the Spanish-American War. Colonel Roosevelt praised the Negro troops with his famous Rough Riders. Apparently "Teddy" was not always consistent in this praise, because Professor John Hope Franklin said, "The reaction of the President to the performances of Negro troops was varied."[1] In his farewell speech to the Rough Riders, the Colonel had unqualified praise for Negro soldiers; and while campaigning for governorship of New York in October, 1898, Roosevelt lauded Negroes who served in the Spanish-American War. But in *Scribner's Magazine,* April, 1889, he wrote: "They are, of course, peculiarly dependent upon their white officers. . . . None of the white regulars of Rough Riders showed the slightest sign of weakening; but under the strain the colored infantrymen began to get a little uneasy and drifted to the rear." The explanation of this alleged retreat was supplied by Sergeant Preston Holliday of the Tenth Cavalry on May 11, 1889. The sergeant wrote in the *New York Age* that Negro soldiers were ordered to retreat to bring up supplies.

By 1900, the lot of Negroes had become more unbearable in the South, and the election of Roosevelt to the Presidency brought them a new hope. Black people were disappointed in Roosevelt's article discrediting Negro soldiers, but he regained their confidence by urging the equality of all men. Before he had been in office two months, the President invited Booker T. Washington to the White House and dined with him during an interview. This incident outraged southerners, but the President ignored the criticism, since it was not unusual for Washington to dine with white leaders of American finance, such as Andrew Carnegie, H. H. Rogers, and Julius Rosenwald. When Washington was not giving counsel to whites on the Negro question, he filled lecture engagements for Negroes and spoke on the need for self-improvement.

The appointment of a Negro, William D. Crum, to the collectorship of the Port of Charleston caught the fancy of the Negro press despite the fact that President William McKinley had appointed twice as many Negroes as did Roosevelt. Near the end of his second term, Negroes found that Roosevelt's friendship was not always reliable;[2] and this led Negro orators to call attention to Roosevelt's hypocrisy.

Searching for better jobs, black people migrated northward. By 1900, ten thousand Negroes were moving from the South annually. This condition led Booker T. Washington to urge Negroes to remain in the South to assist in resolving the racial problem. He envisioned a new prosperity in Dixie, but few people heeded his request to remain at home. The arrival of Negroes in the North created housing and employment problems and increased racial prejudice. Beginning in 1904, a wave of race riots swept the country and black citizens felt insecure because innocent people were beaten, tortured, and killed. The worst riots occurred in Statesboro and Atlanta, Georgia; Houston and Brownsville, Texas; and Springfield, Ohio. These outrageous happenings created themes for Negro speakers.

THE NEW FREEDOM PERIOD

The two administrations of Woodrow Wilson, 1913 to 1921, have been identified as "the New Freedom Period." President Wilson urged the "fitting of a new social order to the happiness and prosperity of the people." which was never intended for Negroes. When Asa Philip Randolph criticized the President, he was branded as a Bolshevik. Once when Randolph was speaking in Cleveland, Ohio, during 1918, the Department of Justice arrested and jailed him. Some newspapers branded Randolph as the most dangerous Negro in America.

The 1912 presidential campaign of Woodrow Wilson marked the return of Negroes to politics in great numbers. Therefore, Wilson made a strong bid for the Negro vote by expressing his "earnest wish to see justice accorded colored people and emphasized that, if he were elected, minority groups could rely upon him for fair dealing." When Wilson assumed office, he disappointed the Negro rank and file. The orator Archibald Grimke, in an address entitled "Shame of

America," said that when Wilson was elected he forgot straightway those fair promises and professions and began within a week after he entered the White House "to put in office men filled with colorphobia, the better to finish the work of undoing the citizenship of the Negro in the government."

President Taft would not appoint a Negro to office in the South if white people objected. Wilson went even further, and no Negro was assigned work in any office in the government if whites objected. Racial segregation became the fixed pattern during the Wilson administration. Yet, in the 1916 campaign, Wilson reasserted his original promise to Negroes, and this led *Crisis* in 1916 to print an editorial that remarked, "We need scarcely to say that Mr. Wilson disappointed us."

When Negroes first tried to volunteer for the Army in 1917, they were generally not accepted; but then the Selective Service Act of May 18, 1917, made Negroes between twenty-one and thirty years of age eligible to enter the armed forces. The first registration listed more than 700,000 Negroes. In 1918, a group of Negro ministers went to Washington to confer with the President at the White House on March 14. President Wilson told them:

I have always known that the Negro has been unjustly dealt with; your people have exhibited a degree of loyalty and patriotism that should command the admiration of the whole nation. In the present conflict, your race rallied to the nation's call, and if there has been any evidence of slackerism by Negroes the same has not reached Washington. With thousands of your sons in camps and in France, out of this conflict you must expect nothing less than the enjoyment of full citizenship rights—the same as are enjoyed by every other citizen.

Negroes asked for a hearing at the Paris Peace Conference, but to no avail. Then, three national Negro organizations presented to the United States Foreign Relations Committee of the Senate on August 28, 1918, several proposed amendments to the Peace Treaty for the purpose of securing equality and protection. To place the cause of black people before the world, Dr. W. E. B. Du Bois called a Pan-African Conference, which met at the Grand Hotel in Paris in February, 1919, simultaneously with the Peace Conference. Fifty-seven delegates attended the conference, including 16 Americans, 20 West Indians, and 12 Africans. Negroes all over the world showed great interest in this conference where black men sought democratic status for which thousands had spilled their blood in battles.

Near the end of the war, it was reported publicly that Negro soldiers were criminally assaulting French women in large numbers. Robert R. Moton, successor to Booker T. Washington at Tuskegee Institute, was sent abroad to France to investigate the rumors concerning Negro soldiers. Doctor Moton found that among 12,000 Negro soldiers of the Ninety-second Division, only seven had been charged with rape, and two had been found guilty. Speaking to Negro soldiers in France, Moton urged them to be contented with their prewar status when they return to the United States, and, in part, said:

You have been tremendously tested. . . . Your record has sent a thrill of joy and satisfaction to the hearts of millions of black and white Americans, rich and poor, high and low. You will go back to America heroes, as you really are. You will go back to America as you have carried yourselves over here . . . in a straightforward, manly, and modest way. If I were you, I would find a job as soon as possible and get to work. I hope no one will do anything in peace to spoil the magnificent record you have made in war.[3]

Negro citizens, upon reading the address of Doctor Moton, became indignant, and the Negro press said that Moton did little to prepare Negro army personnel for civilian life in the United States.

When Negro soldiers returned from Europe, they found that their prewar status had not changed. The white press urged Negroes to find the place they had before the war and stay in it. The attitude of the white press brought forth vigorous protest from orators who denounced emphatically the New Freedom myth of Woodrow Wilson. Four years after the Armistice, November 11, 1918, Mordecai W. Johnson, an eloquent orator, called attention to these postwar conditions in his Harvard commencement oration, "Fires of Our American Faith":

We have the world's problems of race relations here in crucible, and by the strength of our American faith we have made some encouraging progress in its solution. If the fires of that faith are kept burning around that crucible, what comes out of it is able to place these United States in the spiritual leadership of all humanity. When the Negro cries with pain from his deep hurt and lays his petition for elemental justice before the nation, he is calling upon the American people to kindle about that crucible of race relationships the fires of American faith.

This oration has been called a classic, comparable to Lincoln's Gettysburg address, Patrick Henry's "Call to Arms," Robert G. Ingersoll's "Funeral Oration at His Brother's Grave," and Christ's Sermon on the Mount.

THE NEW DEAL

In the late 1920s, an acute economic depression gripped the nation. Millions of men were out of work, and the author was among the 3 million unemployed persons. Hoover's administration tried to sound a hopeful note with the slogan, "Prosperity is just around the corner." Theaters endeavored to increase public morale by playing "Happy Days Are Here Again" during intermissions. But this did not fool the millions of men who had no jobs. Although disappointed with the Hoover regime, few black voters deserted the Republican party in the 1932 election campaign, because the Democratic party had very little to offer and commend itself to Negroes. Franklin D. Roosevelt was a target of criticism because he had held office in the administration of Woodrow Wilson, who had segregated civil service employees. Besides, the Democrats ran for the Vice-Presidency "Cactus" John Garner from Uvalde, Texas, a town that allegedly banned Negro residents.

When Franklin D. Roosevelt took office in 1933, our capitalistic system was under severe attack by the Communist party on account of the economic depression. Negro voters were wooed by Communists, but Roosevelt's New Deal program of relief and public works was more appealing, since these provided employment for thousands of Negroes who later voted for the Democratic party. Enemies of the New Deal attacked FDR's program on the grounds that relief, recovery, and reform would cost vast sums of money and cause unbalanced budgets and huge deficits. Negroes liked the way the President answered his critics: "It is more important to balance the human budget than the fiscal one." While the masses of Negroes hailed Roosevelt as the greatest President since Abraham Lincoln, the Negro press and orators focused their criticism on segregation in the army. Oratorical propaganda dramatized the failure of war industries to utilize Negro manpower fully in the war effort. The navy had only ten Negro doctors in its medical division. Negro speakers, therefore, held that it was bad enough to permit discrimination in the production of tanks, planes, and munitions; but must a soldier lose his life because the hand that applied the tourniquet was black?

Strong newspaper opposition beset Roosevelt as he ran for the unprecedented fourth term. This opposition, however, did not shake the faith most Negroes had in the President. Josephus Simpson, *Afro-American* staff writer in Baltimore, in his column "Thinking Out Loud," voiced on one occasion in the 1944 campaign these Negro sentiments:

In spite of the crocodile tears shed by the *Sun* papers (Baltimore) over the pending *fate* of the Constitution, a document that it uses for political purposes and its professed love for tradition, I am not yet convinced I should vote for Dewey.

While the *Sun* papers love traditions, I hate them like the devil hates holy water. Traditions are the chains that have bound me since birth to second-class citizenship. They stand between me and jobs; they restrict my liberties as an American citizen.

Mr. Roosevelt, . . . by action in 1933, . . . broke the back of the Hoover depression which the *Sun* papers and others are trying to pin on FDR.

Personally, I like Dewey and were it possible for him to run for President without taking his tutors and others with him, I might be able to vote for him. This being impossible, I have only one choice left—Roosevelt.

By breaking traditions in 1933, Roosevelt gave our financial structure a shot in the arm, took idle youth out of the streets and put them in camps, drove the money-changers out of the temple and gave hope to the hopeless, jobs to the jobless. It's Roosevelt in 1944 or ruin in 1946.

When plants holding large defense contracts showed few signs of changing their rigid anti-Negro policies, A. Philip Randolph, orator and labor leader, convinced Negroes it was time to take drastic action. In January, 1941, Randolph planned a "March on Washington Movement" in which approximately 50,000 to 100,000 Negroes would participate on July 1, 1941. The purpose was to urge the government to do something to ensure employment for Negroes in defense industries. Fearing unwholesome repercussions from such a demonstration, Roosevelt issued his famous executive order that forbade discrimination against workers on account of race, and it established a temporary Fair Employment Practices Commission to hear complaints presented by workers. Meanwhile, Negro soldiers began to express their concern about what they were fighting for. Typical of the articles and poems submitted by Negro soldiers was one by James M. Rosebrow, published in most weekly newspapers in November, 1944, under the title: "I Died for What?" During the New Deal, Negroes advanced primarily in economic status as employees in thriving ordnance plants and war industries. Many of these benefits were the results of the "all-time record" set by President Roosevelt during the first hundred days of his administration when Congress enacted sweeping legislation dealing with banks, government economy, the legalization of beer, agricultural adjustment, forest camps, direct unemployment relief, security regulations, farm mortgage relief, the Tennessee Valley Authority, loans to homeowners, inflation remedies, railroad reorganization, industrial recovery, control of the oil industry, and gold standard invalidation.

Roosevelt will be remembered for his radio "fireside chats" which set him apart as a great orator. With conversational delivery, a friendly smile, and persuasive voice, the President gained the people's confidence with his talks and led them to believe that their government had the ability to meet the economic, military, political, and social challenges of a world engaged in battle. Near the end of the war, Roosevelt laid plans for a just peace and a universal organization to end all wars. On the domestic scene, he advocated the Four Freedoms with all the eloquence he could command. Death, however, prevented him from viewing the "promised land" that he hoped would be established in the United States and the world.

ERA OF THE COMMON MAN

The term Fair Deal was coined by President Harry S. Truman for his administration. Admiring citizens preferred the phrase Square Deal, because the philosophy of this administration connoted a square deal for everybody who sincerely wanted to share the abundance of the American economy, to vote without restrictions on account of race or color, and to be accorded the rights and privileges that are enjoyed by every other citizen. Truman's noble ideal of human brotherhood struck a responsive chord with the Negro minority, and orators admired the civil-rights pronouncements of the man from Missouri. Somehow the President's name became synonymous with the term Era of the Common Man. This might be attributed to the fact that Truman had had a varied career— clerk, small-town businessman, farmer, politician, and soldier. In the 1944 election campaign, Harry S. Truman was drafted as the running mate of FDR. When Roosevelt died in April, 1945, the responsibility of facing reconversion and peace fell upon the shoulders of Vice-President Truman. Before Mr. Truman had an opportunity to prove his capabilities, Negroes said he was a "near-to-nothing" substitute for the late President Roosevelt. But they did not join the white press in belittling the new President because of his ties with the Pendergast political machine, his provincial background, and his alleged lack of knowledge of international affairs.

Within eighteen days after Truman became President, two other main characters in the World War II drama—Hitler and Mussolini—were dead. On May 7, 1945, Truman was able to announce officially that the war was over. He faced more domestic and national troubles than ever before. In 1946, more than 4 million industrial workers struck, forcing the President to order seizure of railroads by the government. Truman did not invoke the Taft-Hartley Law to deal with such emergencies, since he was antagonistic toward it. Tired of experimentation, war, and expenses, the American people apparently were not in the mood to give Truman the support they had given unreservedly to Franklin D. Roosevelt. Therefore, when it was time for Truman to campaign for reelection in 1948, he was hard put. He had not remained the mild and undramatic individual he was when he began his political career. He was a "100 percent Democrat" of the New Deal persuasion and was bold enough to label his administration the Fair Deal.

Truman's 1948 campaign platform was very unpopular because of his beliefs respecting the poll tax, the Negro, and antilynching. While these were sound and humanitarian, the President made the mistake of trying to resolve on a national scale something which each locality would have to do at its own pace. The polling agencies predicted the defeat of Truman, but the President defied predictions by carrying his campaign directly to the people on a transcontinental tour and won. Having fallen from grace, the polling agencies went to work to study the reasons for their error of prediction. They found that they had not considered "the 4 or 5 percent margin of error factors" which could throw an election one way or another if the voting was close. It was concluded that Truman's victory was traceable to his pronouncements that "every segment of our economy and every person have a right to expect from the national government a fair deal."

The Truman 1948 campaign had the general support of the Negro press and speakers. Because the United States Congress defeated Truman's Civil Rights Bill, Negro orators joined the President in labeling the lawmakers "an assembly of stick whittlers in matters alarmingly out of tune with the problems of the times." The journalist George S. Schuyler in the March 26, 1949, issue of the *Pittsburgh Courier,* lambasted Truman with the statement: "The Civil Rights program is as dead as Crispus Attucks. While Mr. Truman basked on the beach at Key West amidst his cronies, the senatorial strategists slaughtered the program. Not only did they molest the right to filibuster but actually strengthened it." The *Capital Times*[1] blamed the Republicans for their share in the defeat of Truman's Civil Rights Bill: "The issue of civil rights is one which Republicans of this country like to labor during campaign time. But when it is raised in specific legislation after election, they scoot for cover. The Republicans in Congress are playing a deceitful game with Southern Democrats right now in an attempt to kill the civil-rights program. . . ." The

Civil Rights Bill gave Negro orators good reasons for attacking discrimination in every form, while at the same time, they cried out that the United States must practice what it preaches. When the Civil Rights Bill failed to pass in the Congress, a conservative speaker, Dr. Charles Clinton Spaulding, once president of the North Carolina Mutual Life Insurance company in Durham, urged Negroes in November, 1948, to remain in the South and work with white people to iron out their differences. He said, "The South offers the greatest opportunity I have ever known for my people." This kind of counsel made no imprint upon the minds of the Negro masses who felt, at that time, that "the South was a good place to be from."

During the Fair Deal period, several Supreme Court decisions chipped away at the structure of racial segregation in the South without actually abolishing it. Because of the court decisions in the cases of *Herman Sweatt* vs. *Texas* and *G. W. McLaurin* vs. *Oklahoma,* qualified Negro students were admitted to all but a few of the southern state-supported institutions of higher learning. Many white newspaper columnists[5] urged southern states to appropriate enough funds to make educational facilities equal for the races if they hoped to remain segregated. Nevertheless, many southern "diehards" stated that if the government forced their respective states to adopt desegregation, they would close their public schools.

Truman may not have been well prepared to handle most of the problems that faced him upon the death of President Franklin D. Roosevelt, but he applied himself diligently to domestic problems and international politics to make himself more conversant with the issues. He adopted a boldness that was amazing. Thus, when he hit the campaign trails in the 1948 and 1952 elections, Truman was castigated by his enemies as a strutting, cocksure, rabble-rousing machine politician at the precinct level. Evidently he took the advice of a famous British statesman who said, "Let them howl, but get the job done." Upon retirement from the President's office, Truman took uncomplimentary verbal shots at Negro civil-rights demonstrators; his unbecoming language and impetuous utterances made him countless enemies.

THE NEW FRONTIER

When the name New Frontier is mentioned, one thinks immediately of the late President John F. Kennedy, including his Alliance for Progress. This young man's personality was almost as compelling as the winsome smile of Franklin D. Roosevelt. The New Frontier was not a "new deal," and never was there any possibility it could have been. Franklin Delano Roosevelt took over the nation in collapse and panic and enacted a change with speed and dispatch. And with a bewildered and frightened Congress, he won overwhelming support. Conversely, John F. Kennedy, after the 1960 election, began injecting new blood into the political leadership of the nation. Great applause greeted the young President at the inaugural ceremonies on January 20, 1961, when he asked citizens to be willing to defend freedom in case of danger and to support his administration in a "struggle against the common enemies of man: tyranny, poverty, disease, and even war itself."

Negroes were particularly interested in what Kennedy had proposed concerning civil rights, but they were also disappointed when the President toned down his planned course of action and simply called for a continuation of the Federal Commission on Civil Rights, and a Committee on Equal Employment Opportunity, headed by Vice-President Lyndon B. Johnson, who obtained pledges from leading defense contractors that they would hire workers without regard to race, color, or creed. The precipitation of racial incidents in Birmingham and Tuscaloosa, Alabama, and Jackson, Mississippi, as well as in other southern towns, forced the new President into the position of pleading vigorously for a new civil-rights bill. It should be added that a group of Freedom Riders, who were testing the newly passed bill outlawing segregation of passengers traveling interstate, forced the President's hand. Besides, United States troops were deployed in a "power play" to guarantee James Meredith's entrance in the University of Mississippi. Governor Ross Barnett became the out-and-out southerner's symbol at the same time Senator Stennis was broadcasting over the radio and television that "we in Mississippi are God-fearing Christians." In reply, the press implied that perhaps it was the Mississippi Christians who caused more than 70,000 Negroes to leave Mississippi between 1950 and 1960. The Negro migration, however, did not hinder the continual election of "segregationists who have always been the beneficiaries of a 'Solid South' political system—which was glorified in the 'so-called States' Rights.' "

In 1958, just two years before President Kennedy was elected, the Fisk University Institute of Race Relations summarized Negro gains from 1950 to 1958. The list included integration in the armed forces, removal of racial barriers in professional sports, increase in the number of appointed federal and elected state, county, and local officials; the judicial invalidation of racial restrictive convenants, civil-rights legislation of 1957; and, above all, the Supreme Court decision of 1954, decreeing the end of public school segregation. No less extraordinary was the changing attitudes of southern whites, as they conquered old hostilities.

The New Frontier period made men extremely conscious of how deadly the southern disease of white supremacy could be. Howard Seals in the *Negro Digest* for September, 1963, stated, "The social psychoses of white supremacy is not a Negro problem, but one of distortion in the minds of white people. Negroes, at best involvement, can only aggravate the social consciousness of white people into an awareness and confrontation with the illness of white supremacy." All the while, a new Negro was being born and the modern concept of him may be traced to the slowness and resistance with which whites in the South responded to his request for first-class citizenship. The untimely murder of Medgar Evers in Mississippi molded Negroes into a solidarity as strong as the rock upon which Jesus Christ built his church. The black minority was determined more than ever to do battle for freedom. Hence, they engaged in sit-ins, demonstrations. Freedom Rides, and marches. They were always a mark for the sniper's bullet, the police water hose, law enforcement brutality, and targets of white "rowdies" who assembled to make trouble.

Negro orators, most often leaders, became very outspoken and militant whether or not any tangible results accrued from such speaking. Since few Negro goals are attained all at once anyway, the question of an accomplishment schedule was of secondary importance in imputing the reputation of the leader. It was during the New Frontier administration that the new Negro revealed several attributes:

1. He has confidence and can use protest and pressure techniques to improve his status;

2. He constitutes all economic and social classes;

3. He is prepared to make great sacrifices;

4. He has intelligent and militant leaders who play no "Uncle Tom" roles. However, his leaders often get into conflict "jockeying" for prestige and power; and

5. He has leaders who can present his cause or demands not only effectively, but with some measure of artistry and eloquence. However, we have seen, on television, some local civil-rights leaders create a poor image, simply because they use illiterate oral language.

"When many Americans looked at President Kennedy, they saw a glamorous personality not unlike a movie star," said a *Washington Post* release on October 25, 1963, "but they were perplexed about the purpose of his almost perpetual motion." That Kennedy had the best public relations of any President we have seen, was the opinion of Howard W. Kay, a young North Platte, Nebraska, lawyer, who added, "But he'll never catch on in Nebraska the way FDR did. He doesn't have that type of personality." The *New Republic* of May 18, 1963, called upon Mr. Kennedy to bring his sense of urgency to Washington. Richard Rovere, *New Yorker* writer, in one of his "Letters from Washington" said that he was struck by the presence of public apathy that deadened the air, and muffled and muddled controversy. Rovere regarded apathy as an earmark of "Ike," the great tranquilizer. He candidly believed that President Eisenhower didn't want to get this country moving again; Kennedy didn't seem able to. Walter Lippmann, a journalistic sage, felt that President Kennedy was often too cautious, and he added that the public wanted its leader to get into a struggle where somebody got a bloody nose.

Negroes were aware that President Kennedy was cognizant of urgent, even desperate domestic issues and yet he was not able to communicate his feelings. They wanted him, however, to stir up a commotion, show passion, and get involved so that the public could enjoy the scrap. Somehow, people thrive upon sputtering fuses. Perhaps this is why Martin Luther King, Jr., came to the fore as an eloquent leader. King's Montgomery boycott and nonviolent demonstrations across the nation gave the people a kind of circus appeal that might explode into physical clashes even with the nonviolent lid clamped down tightly. The freedom rides offered the suspense of a best-selling mystery novel, for one never quite knew what to expect next.

Even though Kennedy's critics felt he could not get the country moving, Negroes were more impressed by the man's genuine moral purpose, high resolve, and humanitarian credo. Somehow Kennedy measured up to their ideal of a President, and Negroes expressed this sentiment when the assassin's bullet took his life on November 22, 1963. People sat close to their television sets where they were chained in silence; then, for the next four days, television took the nation on a tour with the President's body through a prescribed route to the rotunda in Washington, to the funeral ceremonies, and to the cemetery. It seemed that all business stopped to do this noble man homage. A few weeks later, on December 7, 1963, Al Duckett, a *Chicago Defender* journalist, paid the late President honor in a poetical narrative poem—"The Crucifixion of John the Just." It reads:

On a certain Friday when John the Just went into a certain city known as Dallas, he was wearing on his head a crown of thorns of mocking and hateful criticism—and about the shoulders the purple robe of the scorned.

And in that city, for many days, men had smote him with their harsh words and called out: "Crucify him! Crucify him!"

These men had cried out: "We have a law and by our law he ought to die because he has hailed mankind as the children of God and therefore as brothers."

As he rode through the streets of the city of Dallas, they crucified him.

As John the Just was dying his Mary held his head in her hands and the blood of his head dripped upon her.

And that blood dripped upon the hands of all of those who had sat in the judgment and who had said: "We have a law and by that law he ought to die."

Some of those who had said that were governors of provinces. Some of them were scribes who wrote in newspapers and magazines and books. Some of them were counselors and advocates in political places.

And some of them were housewives and shopkeepers and innkeepers and learned men and ministers and judges and policemen.

They laid him in the sepulcher.

On a not distant day, John the Just will arise in resurrection.

Weep not! He shall rise in resurrection, which will be the day when a nation and a world know that God has a law.

Sleep, John the Just!

Awake from your sleep, oh people of a sinful world.

To dramatize the urgency of the Negro's demand to get equal rights now, to emphasize that gradualism is in trouble and anyone who supports this doctrine will not be heard, certain Negro and white leaders scheduled a March on Washington for Wednesday, August 28, 1963. The chief architects persuaded people from all over the United States and from overseas to come to Washington by automobile, plane, bus, and train. Unique among those who came were twelve youths who walked from Brooklyn, an NAACP member who roller-skated from Chicago, and an old man who rode a bicycle from Ohio. All these people assembled on an 180-acre plot around the Lincoln and Washington monuments to lay their grievances before the public and to demand enactment of a strong civil-rights law. Although the news media were in disagreement, the crowd in attendance was estimated from 100,000 to 150,000 persons.

The ceremonies held by the thousands of marchers indicated that racial Jim Crow, about one hundred years old, was ailing and approaching his death. An essay entitled "The Approaching Death of James Crow" said "that valiant, if ignoble, old man of bigotry is on his last legs and has been advised by his doctor to make his peace with God and man before the final bell tolls."[6] In their quest to destroy Jim Crow, whites have accused Negro leaders of flouting local laws, browbeating Congress and state and local officials by trying to make them knuckle under to their demands. Racial demonstrations have been charged with wrecking the paternal racial friendship which has been slowly carrying Negroes to their destination of first-class citizenship.

THE GREAT SOCIETY

On the way to Washington by plane, Lyndon B. Johnson took the oath of office as President of the United States on November 22, 1963, following the untimely death of President Kennedy. In a sense, the transfer of the leadership of this country was analogous to that of Israel's leadership being changed from Moses to that of Joshua, who led them to the Promised Land. By the time Johnson began his first full term, he had earned the label of "the Gentle Persuader." He put "thumbs down" on governmental conservatism and initiated a counterproposal to start a new era of social advance known as the Great Society. The Great Society, Johnson believed, could be achieved by abolishing poverty and inaugurating a higher value system for the American people, because the logic of American politics, economics, and philosophy powerfully suggested such an evolution. The disadvantaged citizens admired President Johnson when he said poverty was less and less excusable, and therefore less tolerable. He hoped to get the Great Society moving toward its goal by effective persuasion upon people with an understanding heart. The first one hundred days of Johnson's administration saw Congress record major accomplishments without equal or close parallel in the present era. Ten bills became public laws, including a general aid-to-education bill, the Appalachia aid bill, and a $750-million increase in the United States contribution to the Inter-American Development Bank. The strides that President Johnson made toward solving the problems of poverty and education in this country led many Negroes to call him "Mr. Civil Rights."

In appearing before audiences, Negro orators praised LBJ in glowing and eloquent phrases. They gave him good publicity for his courage in backing the Civil Rights Bill and a year later a Voter Rights Bill, because they also knew that the President could subtly use his political whip as a gentle persuader. For instance, in the gigantic march to Selma,

Alabama, under the leadership of Dr. King, a white woman was killed by a sniper as she transported some marchers back to Selma. The Alabama incidents perhaps led the President to nudge Congressmen a little harder to pass his legislative program on civil rights. When the bills were passed, Negro speakers hit the lecture trails to praise the President for attempting to nullify "the shame of Alabama."

Because of certain irresponsibilities and the deliberate concealment of financial facts by many elected and appointed officials in high government positions, the President set a code of ethics, in May, 1965, for top government officials who were directly responsible to the executive branch. Johnson said, "We cannot tolerate conflicts of interests or favoritism, or even conduct which gives the appearance that such actions are occurring, and it is our intention to see that it does not take place in the federal government." The code of ethics followed the resignation on April 22, 1965, of Assistant Secretary of Commerce, Herbert W. Klotz, who had profited from a stock tip. Negroes want government officials with integrity, but they are more vitally concerned with the stark realities of life—food and clothing, shelter, better-paying jobs, registering and casting the ballot without racial restrictions, civil-rights advancement, and a good education to prepare black youths for the new opportunities being rapidly opened to them.

In May, 1965, President Johnson got a $700-million vote of confidence from Congress for his policy in Vietnam. The President tied his request for money to an endorsement of the battle against communism. Enemies of the President, including some southerners, accused him of dragging Congress around "like a dog on a leash." Hence, in early May, 1965, nine southern governors held a conference in Atlanta and reported that they believed the federal government was exceeding its legal authority in the amount of integration it demanded for schools to qualify for United States funds. They said they thought the recent interpretations of HEW went beyond the law and court decisions. On the other hand,

Negroes were not impressed with the meeting of the southern governors and their report, because they expected officials in the South to find ways and means to circumvent their moral and legal duties.

Under Johnson's Great Society, minority groups felt that they had a leader in Washington whose moral commitment was strong and clear. They wanted him to continue being the gentle persuader to prod a negligent United States Congress from sitting on its haunches. The new civil-rights bills have made the Negro legally a first-class citizen, and he feels like somebody going somewhere. He can ride public transportation in peace and comfort without fear of arrest for violating some local segregation laws. He can eat at good restaurants like Howard Johnson and Holiday Inn. He can cast his vote without fear of intimidation in most localities in the South, perhaps with the exception of Alabama and Mississippi. Finally, the Head Start program has been a miracle for underprivileged minority children who need it so badly.

Footnotes, Chapter 3

1. John Hope Franklin, *From Slavery to Freedom,* p. 415.
2. Ibid, p. 416.
3. Robert R. Moton, *Finding a Way Out.*
4. *Capital Times* (Madison, Wisconsin), September 3, 1949.
5. C. A. Knight, editorial, *Charlotte News* (North Carolina), June 7, 1950. Reprinted on January 20, 1951.
6. Marcus H. Boulware, "The Approaching Death of James Crow," *Negro Digest* 11 (July, 1962): 38–39.

4/Era of Booker T. Washington

The Atlanta Exposition speech in 1895 brought into the limelight Booker T. Washington, at that time a small-town school principal. Thereafter, he received hundreds of invitations to speak, and his prestige grew until he became the central figure in the history of American Negro oratory from 1900 until his death in 1915. Millions of Negroes accepted him as their leader, and white people came to him for counsel on questions of racial relations. Washington's influence upon the course of American history in the early twentieth century has led some historians to label the period the Era of Booker T. Washington. Recognizing his influence, Dr. W. E. B. Du Bois wrote in 1903, "Easily the most striking thing in the history of the American Negro since 1876 is the ascendancy of Mr. Booker T. Washington."[1] Du Bois further acknowledged that "he stands as the one recognized spokesman of his ten million fellows, and one of the most notable figures in the nation of seventy millions."

While Washington's prestige as a speaker and educator ran high, the era was marked by complete disfranchisement of the Negro in the South, numerous lynchings, discrimination, and exclusion of Negro laborers from large labor unions, as well as inadequate educational facilities for Negro pupils. During this period, the educator distinguished himself as an effective public speaker. For two decades, 1895 to 1915, he delivered probably 4,000 speeches in the leading cities and small towns in this country. He was called "the Apostle of Industrial Education," and "the Symbol of Racial Goodwill," but oratorical critics remember him as "the Finished Public Speaker."

The life of Booker T. Washington is admirably told in his autobiography, *Up from Slavery.* His oratorical career began when he became principal of Tuskegee Institute in Alabama in July, 1881. At the time, the enactment of segregation laws and the terrorism of the Ku Klux Klan and lynching widened the breach between the races. Consequently their relationships became less friendly. Perhaps this was why Washington was anxious to cement the friendship between the two races in the South.

The practice of segregation in the South helped white people to develop the attitude that "the Negro is all right in his place." If Negroes had been content to remain in a subordinate position, racial antagonism would not have developed to any great extent. But when Negroes sought to enter new fields[2] and occupations already sacred to white people, they met the greatest opposition. The person who outlined most vividly "the place of the Negro" in the South was Henry W. Grady. Approximately a decade before the Atlanta Exposition speech by Washington, Grady stated the terms by which black people might live harmoniously in the South. Grady believed that Negroes should have the opportunity to work; that they should have their own religious, recreational, and educational institutions; that they might expect "friendship" from white people if they did not agitate for civil rights, particularly the right to vote and hold public office. Grady further said, "The whites and blacks must walk in separate paths in the South. As near as may be, these paths should be made equal, but separate they must be now and always."[3] This New South orator outlined a program to control southern Negroes, and to check the protest of white Northerners. Thus spoke Grady, "The men who, from afar off, view this subject through the cold eyes of speculation insist that directly or indirectly the Negro race shall be in control in the South. We have no fear of this; already we are attracting to us the best elements of the race, and as we proceed our alliance will broaden. . . ." According to Horace Mann Bond,[4] the two men referred to as "the best elements of the race" were Booker T. Washington and W. H. Council, both ambitious school principals, who actually vied with each other for material favors from the white ruling class. A study of Washington's Atlanta Exposition speech reveals that he had studied carefully Grady's program for the South; hence, in Atlanta, Washington dramatically affirmed Henry W. Grady's philosophy of the place of the Negro in the South. Washington said, "In all things purely social we can be as separate as the fingers, yet one as the hand in all things essential to mutual progress." After the Atlanta address, Washington became the outstanding ally of southern white leadership and of certain influential northern financial corporations.

In addressing the South, the orator was not content with making a general statement of his objectives. He recommended his program in terms of a competitive economy in which the scheme of Negro advancement coincided with southern interests. His speeches were primarily directed to the influential whites. He rarely spoke to poor whites, except in the immediate community of Tuskegee where he often spoke to white farmers. At any rate, Washington emphasized that in a region imperiled by the production of cotton, Negroes educated in agriculture would permit diversification of crops. By citing testimony of white employers, the orator tried to show that education would fit the Negro for the common tasks of life. He said that in proportion as we get education, "We will be more useful in field and shop, in kitchen and laundry . . . and in every walk of life."[5]

WASHINGTON'S ENEMIES

While Washington exerted considerable influence during this era, he was vigorously opposed by leaders who defined the Negro's cause as a continuous struggle for civil rights. Regardless of the criticism, one is impressed by the businesslike behavior of Washington who first examined the confidential memos placed on his desk each morning. In this manner, it is said that the Tuskegee educator controlled the destinies of American Negroes. His activities included an annual speech to his people, counseling on the appointment of white politicians in the South, and nodding favor for substantial money grants to be given various Negro institutions. He allegedly edited messages of presidentially-approved appointments of Confederate postmasters and federal judges in the South. It would appear that, since then, no Negro has been so sure of himself.

W. E. B. Du Bois summarized his disagreement with Washington in *Souls of Black Folk* in 1903 as follows:

So far as Mr. Washington preaches thrift, patience, and industrial training for all masses, we must hold up his hands and strive with him, rejoicing in his honors and glorifying in the strength of Joshua called of God and of man to lead the headless host. But . . . Mr. Washington's [apology] for injustice, North and South [does] not rightly value the privilege and duty of voting."[6]

Monroe Trotter, editor of the *Boston Guardian,* was most uncompromising in his opposition to the educator. He went so far, on one occasion, as to use stench bombs to prevent Washington from delivering an address in a Boston church. A Harvard debater and Phi Beta Kappa scholar, Trotter's persistent crusading bordered upon fanaticism. When the editor spoke from the platform, he made every nerve of the listeners stiffen against the evil or person he was attacking.

Washington also had to face the prejudice of white men like Cole Blease of South Carolina and J. K. Vardaman of Mississippi. When Vardaman became the governor of Mississippi in

1904, he said in his inaugural address: "As a race they are deteriorating morally every day. Time has demonstrated that they are more criminal as free men than as slaves; that they are increasing in criminality with frightful rapidity, being one-third more criminal in 1890 than in 1880." Newspapers gave Vardaman's speech[7] wide circulation. From this time onward, Booker T. Washington proceeded more cautiously in his speeches by filling his addresses with facts compiled by the Department of Research at Tuskegee Institute. Through the use of statistics, Washington attempted to show how an industrial education would raise the status of the community by producing more thrifty, intelligent, law-abiding, and hardworking citizens.

J. A. Rogers, in the November 10, 1945, issue of the *Pittsburgh Courier,* did not attack Washington as some people did, even though he personally favored the point of view of Du Bois. The historian, Rogers, stated once: "He [Washington] was doing an essential work in the South, and I know that he always had the lyncher's rope dangling before him. [Recorded lynchings in the South then averaged 150 annually, with those not listed as such, including those by law, running into the thousands.] Thus I did not feel that Washington was really an Uncle Tom at heart, though most of what he said was Uncle Tom. It took a man of courage to remain in the South and educate Negroes while Tillman and Vardaman were inciting the mob against Negro education."

The biographer Basil Matthews said that although Negroes felt there was something slavish about Washington's compromise with the whole South, "he didn't deserve the critical coals heaped upon his head. He lacked many of the social graces, but he was not timid." Roy Wilkins, when editor of *Crisis,* described Washington in 1944 as a shrewd man, thoroughly in tune with his time; he appeared to be an appeaser and did his greatest work under that cloak. Washington learned the chords that brought response and eliminated all discord. A few lambasted Washington for accepting a grudging support for his educational work at the cost of segregation and second-class citizenship. They forgot that he was mainly an educator and that he spoke mainly to raise money for his work at Tuskegee. But so impressively did the educator present his program of industrial education that it evoked admiration and praise from both the North and South.

In speaking, Washington had to meet the criticism of certain Negro leaders who said that he was opposed to classical instruction. Responsively, Washington said: "I would set no limit to the attainment of the Negro in arts, in letters and statesmanship, but I believe the surest way to reach these ends is by laying the foundation in the little things of life that lie immediately at one's door. I plead for industrial education for the Negro not because I want to cramp him, but because I want to free him. I want to see him enter the all-powerful business and commercial world." This statement has the tenor of many addresses he delivered and which may be examined in *Selected Speeches,* edited by E. David Washington in 1932.

THE MATURING SPEAKER

Booker T. Washington received some training in speaking in the debating societies at Hampton Institute as a student. His first public address of any importance was delivered in 1889 when he was invited to make the commencement address at his alma mater, and he chose the subject: "The Force That Wins." To raise funds for the construction of Alabama Hall at Tuskegee Institute, General Samuel Chapman Armstrong invited Booker T. Washington to travel with him in the North. The Tuskegee educator spoke in New York, Brooklyn, Boston, Philadelphia, and other cities. Prior to the speaking tour, General Armstrong gave the young man this advice: "Give them an idea for every word." From then on, the young principal put this principle into practice until he became a finished public speaker.

The educator began his speaking career while on a tour with General Armstrong, when the Honorable Thomas E. Bicknell invited him to speak at the annual convention of the National Education Association in Madison, Wisconsin, in 1880. This was the beginning of his oratorical career and he spoke to 4,000 persons. Delegates from Tuskegee expected Washington to abuse the South; but, instead, the orator gave the South credit for all of the praiseworthy things it had done, and it was his first speech on the racial problem. He urged racial friendship and stated that the future of the Negro depended upon an education that could make him invaluable to the community through skill, intelligence, and character.

The first opportunity to speak to a southern audience presented itself in 1893 when Washington spoke at a convention of Christian workers in Atlanta. He traveled 2,000 miles to make this five-minute speech, and one hour later he was on a train going to Boston. Three years later, Washington received an honorary master's degree from Howard University, and the occasion matched another event in 1896 when William Jennings Bryan delivered his "Cross of Gold" address. Washington delivered the Harvard alumni dinner address (1896) in which he paid tribute to the dead sons of Harvard who fought in the Civil War. The orator said: "Tell them that their sacrifices were not in vain. Tell them that by habits of thrift and economy, by way of the industrial school, we are coming. We are crawling up, working up, yea bursting up. Often through oppression, unjust discrimination and prejudice, but through them all we are coming up with proper habits of intelligence and acquisition of property. There is no power on earth that can stop us."

Booker T. Washington was next invited to deliver the dedicatory address during ceremonies held at the Robert Gould Shaw Monument on May 31, 1897. The ceremonies were held in honor of Colonel Robert Gould Shaw, commander of the Fifty-fourth Massachusetts Negro Troops, who fell in battle attempting to take Fort Wagner at Charleston, South

Carolina, in July, 1863. A large number of people assembled in the Music Hall of Boston to witness the exercises. When the orator turned and addressed the Negro soldiers on the platform, including a color-bearer who never let the flag touch the ground, he said:

To you, to the scarred and scattered remnants of the 54th, who, with empty sleeve and wanting leg, honored this occasion with your presence, to you your commander is not dead. Though Boston erected no monument and history recorded no story, in you and in this loyal race which you represent, Robert Gould Shaw would have a monument which time could not wear away. [As the orator sat down, Governor Wolcott, who was master of ceremonies, sprang to his feet and shouted: "Three cheers to Booker T. Washington!"]

As a speaker, Washington used tact, according to Emmett J. Scott, who was once the educator's private secretary. In speaking to segregated audiences composed of blacks and whites, "the educator," said Rebecca C. Barton, "walked the razor's edge between Negro pride and white prejudice." His articulate wisdom brought effective response when he addressed audiences in the North to raise funds for Tuskegee Institute. In the South, he told Negro farmers how much land they had, to what extent it was mortgaged, how many cattle and mules they had, and so on. While talking to farmers, his statistics did not become dull, and he marshaled them in a dynamic manner. Often during these meetings, there was an exchange of wit and repartee between the speaker and the humble farmers who dared to dissent from some established opinion.

ATLANTA EXPOSITION SPEECH

The famous Atlanta Exposition speech was delivered on September 18, 1895, at the Atlantic Cotton States International Exposition. Booker T. Washington was selected to speak on the opening program because it was felt that he would stimulate good feelings between the races. Many southern newspapers were unfriendly to the idea; many prominent Negro leaders discussed among themselves what he ought to say, but he was "caught in the middle of a fix" because he had to address northern and southern whites and blacks.

When the educator reached the exposition grounds, the auditorium was packed from top to bottom, and thousands waited on the outside. Cheers greeted him from Negroes, and a faint applause came from the whites who had come out of curiosity or to see the orator make a fool of himself. After an introduction by Governor Bullock, Washington took the platform with the purpose of saying something that would cement friendship and cooperation between the races in the South. The theme of the address was that both races should cast their lots together in the South and make friends the manly way. To accomplish this aim, the orator assured the white people that segregation would not have to be undermined.

Immediately upon completion of the speech, the presiding officer rushed across the platform and shook Washington's hand. Great and prolonged was the applause as crowds pressed forward to congratulate him. *The Atlanta Constitution* called the speech "a revelation," and the *Boston Transcript* said it "seemed to have dwarfed all the other proceedings." Although white leaders heralded the address as "the sensible approach to the racial problem," a few prominent Negroes thought otherwise. W. E. B. Du Bois felt that the cause for complete freedom of the Negro was given a setback. The Negro rank and file accepted the message as words of immortal wisdom. "But if you analyze it," said J. A. Rogers in the *Pittsburgh Courier* (November 10, 1945), "you will find it one of the worst pieces of tripe ever uttered. How can two individuals, even a man and his wife, or even Siamese twins, be any closer than the fingers on the hand? However, the whites of the South hailed it because in their minds it symbolized Jim Crow through which they could continue to exploit Negro labor." Congressman Adam Clayton Powell, Jr. of New York charged Washington with "delivering the souls of black folk into the hands of the masters." He advised the white South that "the Negro was no longer interested in political opportunities or economic adjustment. This wasn't the worst possible viewpoint to take, but Washington elaborated it into a black economy. . . . His speech once again imposed the caste system on Negroes. It separated them rigidly from poor whites with the results that not only the white upper class but the poor as well turned against them."[8]

PLATFORM DELIVERY

Booker T. Washington's eloquence differed from that of his predecessor, Frederick Douglass, just as a gifted orator differs from a finished speaker. The orator Douglass swayed audiences and himself by the passion of his message. On the other hand, Washington studied every detail and weighed every word, always keeping in mind the final impression, he wished to make. In making that impression, he was aware of the importance of personal contact with his audiences. Thus, at the beginning of his speeches, he was somewhat nervous lest he might fail to achieve this visual directness. He described this feeling in *Up From Slavery:*

There is great compensation, though, for this preliminary nervous suffering, that comes to me after I have been speaking about ten minutes, and have come to feel I have really mastered my audience, and that we have gotten into full and complete sympathy with each other. It seems too that there is rarely such a combination of mental and physical delight in any effort as that which comes to a public speaker when he feels that he has a great audience completely within his control. There is a thread of sympathy and oneness that connects a public speaker with the audience, that is just as strong as though it was something tangible and visible.

Douglass, on the contrary, argued with passion, as for example, in 1857, when he advocated agitation: "If there is no struggle, there is no progress. Those who profess to favor freedom, and yet deprecate agitation, are men who want crops without *ploughing* the ground. They want the ocean without the awful roar of its many waters."

The school principal employed the direct, lively, conversational manner of speaking. Karl R. Wallace[9] stated that Washington was probably the first important Negro speaker in this country to forsake the stilted elocutionary methods of utterance in favor of a direct conversational quality, first made popular by Wendell Phillips.

STORYTELLING TECHNIQUE

Booker T. Washington never told a story for its own sake, but rather used it to drive home a good point. One of his apt figures was, "One cannot hold another in the ditch without himself staying in the ditch." In telling one of his well-known stories in Negro dialect, the orator's voice became guttural, and he lowered his head; his eyes glanced upward and to one side in a manner at once skeptical and trusting; and for a moment he looked the emancipated Negro. Allan Davis, in the *Public Speaking Review* for November, 1911, said, "Washington was hopeful, suspicious, somewhat uncertain of himself, with flashes of shrewdness, yet always striving to please, to put his listeners in good humor, to make them receptive."

When it came to a keen sense of humor and a dramatic way of using it, few orators of his day were quite his equal. He could take the shadow of a story or good joke and tell it so well that his audiences groaned with laughter. The effectiveness of his stories could be traced to the artistic manner in which he told them. He used jokes and the telling anecdote as effectively as did Abraham Lincoln, and every illustration had a point that was useful in his speech.

SPEAKING TOURS

The educator made speaking tours in Delaware, Florida, North Carolina, South Carolina, Tennessee, and parts of Arkansas. Plans to travel over Georgia were canceled by his death in 1915.

The Mississippi tour was arranged by Charles Bank and Isaiah T. Montgomery of Mound Bayou, E. P. Simmons, and Perry Howard, an attorney of Jackson. The tour lasted a week and included the important cities of the state. Dr. Robert R. Moton,[10] who succeeded the orator as principal of Tuskegee Institute, stated that Negro and white people did everything in their power to make the trip successful. Washington and a party of thirty men traveled in a private car and often slept there, especially if they had to make an early morning start to fill some engagement. The keynote of the educator's message in Mississippi was contained in these words:

It is often said that the destiny of the Negro is in the hands of southern whites. I can tell you that the reverse is also true—the destiny of the southern whites is largely dependent upon the Negro. In every white southern home the food is prepared by Negro women. Your health, your very life, depends on their knowledge of how to prepare it. Far more than that—the white youth of the South are being trained in their most tender years by Negro girls. It is of first importance to you that these girls should be women of clean character. You can't have smallpox in the Negro's cabin for diseases will invade the mansion.

When Principal William H. Holtzclaw of Utica Institute learned that Washington would be in the state, he invited him to visit his school. The trustees felt that this would be a dangerous thing. Holtzclaw told them, "But I have already invited him, and to tell you the truth, I would rather abandon my work here than to withdraw the invitation. I do not care to live in a place where Doctor Washington cannot come with perfect safety. Besides, he is already on his way and will be here tomorrow."[11] A great crowd met Washington at the station, and the school's chapel could not hold all who wanted to hear him. In Jackson, a large crowd assembled in the Coliseum. One section of the gallery, which held most of the white people, gave way and several people were injured.

The Louisiana tour, according to V. P. Thomas, in the June, 1915, issue of *Crisis,* carried Washington through New Orleans, St. Bernard, Baton Rouge, Lafayette, Lake Charles, Shreveport, and Bissland, where he spoke mainly on industrial education. The *Crisis* reporter, who accompanied him on this tour, criticized Washington for failure to mention the need for preparation in medicine, law, theology, banking, and teaching.

The orator visited some of the leading cities in Florida and spoke to his largest audience at Ocala where 20,000 people were assembled at the fair grounds. For more than an hour, Washington told his audience that Negroes should practice thrift, industry, and morality. He also outlined the duties of both races toward each other. So effective was his Ocala speech that a reporter wrote that he and his audience seemed transfixed.

ORATORICAL CONTEMPORARIES

The chief contemporaries of Washington who excelled in the art of oratory were Bishop Reverdy G. Ransom, Robert R. Moton, Bishop Alexander Walters, and Roscoe Conkling Bruce. Few orators have surpassed Bishop Ransom, who was convinced that Negroes had a right to first-class citizenship and outlined a way of achieving this goal by progressive methods. He is best known for his panegyric on William Lloyd Garrison, delivered in Faneuil Hall in Boston on December 10, 1905. Bishop Alexander Walters was a social reform orator and pulpiteer. He urged Negroes to divide their vote between the two main political parties rather than adhere with slavish allegiance to the Republicans. For his position on politics, church people criticized him. His gestures were dramatic, and he could turn a phrase as glibly as a stump speaker. Listeners were swept away by his boldness and thrilled by his platform charm.

Another one of Washington's contemporaries was Roscoe C. Bruce, who was born in Washington, D.C., when his father, Blanche K. Bruce, was serving as United States Senator from Mississippi. Roscoe attended Howard University, where he became a popular debater, and when he was graduated he was the class orator. He taught school for a while but resigned to go into business. Bruce believed that education was the proper medium for the Negro to use to obtain his freedom and civil rights. His classical address, "Freedom Through Education," was first given before the Memorial Society of Harvard University on Memorial Day, 1905. The thesis of the speech was that until the fetters fell from the minds and hearts and energies of 9 million black Americans, the blood of their heroic soldiers would "cry aloud from the battlefields and the nation's task would not be done."

Footnotes, Chapter 4

1. W. E. B. Du Bois, *The Souls of Black Folk,* p. 43.
2. *Annals of the American Academy of Political Science* 140 (November, 1928): p. 15.
3. Edna L. H. Turpin, *The New South and Other Addresses,* pp. 144–145.
4. Horace Mann Bond, *Negro Education in Alabama,* p. 205.
5. William Brigance, ed., *History and Criticism of American Public Address,* p. 412.

6. Du Bois, *The Souls of Black Folk,* pp. 13–14.
7. Benjamin Brawley, *Social History of the American Negro,* pp. 325–326.
8. Adam C. Powell, Jr., *Marching Blacks,* pp. 24–25.
9. Brigance, *History and Criticism of American Public Address,* p. 412.
10. Robert R. Moton, *Finding a Way Out,* p. 180.
11. William H. Holtzclaw, *The Black Man's Burden.*

5/ The Marcus Garvey Period, 1916– 1927

From 1916 to 1927, a wave of nationalism and self-determination welded the masses of Negroes into a unique protest movement led by Marcus Garvey, who was its champion until he was reduced to inconsequence as a leader. Garvey's Back-to-Africa movement reached its peak during the early part of the twenties by capturing the imaginations of Negroes who had scarcely been impressed by such organizations as the NAACP and Du Bois's Pan-African Conference. The rank and file of Negroes tended to regard the NAACP as an agency of the intellectuals, upper-class Negroes, and white liberals who did not have the true interest of the race at heart. Millions[1] found in Marcus Garvey a leader who was willing to join hands with them in attempting to rise above the handicaps of color. No other Negro, not even Booker T. Washington, commanded the numerical support of that many people.

The Back-to-Africa movement was designed at first to solve the economic problems of the Negro, but it soon developed into a nationalistic scheme to redeem Africa by leading Negroes back to their fatherland where a nation would be established. Garvey's propaganda agents "dramatized Africa as a promised land to a people sorely beset by discrimination, humiliation and injustice."[2] To carry out this plan, Garvey organized the Universal Negro Improvement Association, not to fight the government of America, but to drive every pale face out of Africa. This organization worked to free Africa from the white man's domination and to open the continent to all blacks as a home and refuge. His critics, looking at the goals he set, wondered how he proposed to drive the white man from Africa in a venture that would cost billions in treasure and large armies.

For the purpose of stimulating economic independence among Negroes, wherever they resided, Garvey organized the Black Star Steamship Line, the Negro Factories Corporation, the Ethiopian Engineering Association, and other enterprises. Garvey was an organizational man par excellence, but he didn't seem to have the managerial staff to operate these enterprises successfully.

Marcus Garvey, according to James Weldon Johnson,[3] was a full-blooded black man who was born in Jamaica, British West Indies, in 1887. He felt keenly the racial restriction that a triple caste system—whites, mulattoes, and blacks—placed upon a person of his color. Perhaps this is why, later in life, he glorified black as a symbol of beauty and strength. Soon after his arrival in Harlem on March 23, 1916, he toured thirty-eight states to study at firsthand the conditions of the Negro. It was Garvey's operation of the Black Star Steamship Line that brought about his downfall. People had invested several millions of dollars in the Back-to-Africa movement, and more than a million was spent to buy and equip ships. In 1923, the United States charged Garvey with using the mails to defraud when he raised funds for his steamship line. Found guilty, a federal judge sentenced him to serve five years in the penitentiary at Atlanta. He remained in prison until he was pardoned by President Calvin Coolidge and later deported in 1927 as an undesirable alien.

ORATORICAL CAREER

Marcus Garvey made his first appearance as a public speaker at a large mass meeting held in Bethel AME Church, Harlem, on June 2, 1917, for the purpose of organizing the Liberty League. More than 2,000 people attended. Hubert Morris, who called the meeting, introduced Garvey to the audience. The impression he made on his hearers was described by James Weldon Johnson as follows: "The man spoke, and his magnetic personality, torrential eloquence, and intuitive knowledge of mob psychology were brought into play. He swept the audience along with him. He made his speech an endorsement of the new movement and a pledge of his support of it."[4] The audience was interested in his proposal to establish a school for underprivileged children of Jamaica. But, as Garvey set forth his Pan-African ideas for the first time in the United States, he was heckled and booed. This startled him to such an extent that he stumbled and fell off the platform, injuring himself slightly. This accident terminated the meeting, and days afterward his enemies said that the fall was deliberately planned to win the sympathy of the audience. Later, Garvey was persuaded to join a group of soapbox speakers who stood on street corners in Harlem haranguing the crowds with very radical ideas.

When Garvey organized the Universal Negro Improvement Association (UNIA) in 1917 in New York,[5] he immediately began a lecture tour that covered almost forty states. He was enthusiastically received almost everywhere, and his audiences contributed large sums of money to his movement. In the South, where northern Negroes had been manhandled and chased out for attempting to hold peaceful meetings, Garvey called together large audiences without incident. Perhaps Southerners regarded him as a harmless crackpot. Northern Negro critics said that the South winked at Garvey because he was not a challenge. Garvey used tact, however, in holding his meetings. He told his audiences that "Africa was for the Africans," and cried out to the white South in a semireligious chant, "Let my people go!"

Under the verbal attack of several Negro orators and the press, Garvey vindicated his movement in a speech delivered at Liberty Hall in New York in August, 1921. He emphasized: "The enemy may argue with you to show you the impossibility of a free and redeemed Africa, but I want you to take as your argument the thirteen colonies of America, that once owed their allegiance to Great Britain, that sovereignty has been destroyed to make the United States of America." In the delivery of this speech, he let his emotions have full range and expressed them fearlessly and flamboyantly. Not only were his techniques effective, but Garvey created oratory through understatement that could turn a word into a righteous indictment. When the moment was big enough to justify effective oratory, Garvey didn't mind pulling out his "oratorical trump" in selling his movement.

The orator's ability to win the attention of listeners on "short exposure" projected him as a man of ability and diligence. When Garvey advocated something, his voice had a sincere ring, and the audience got the impression that he himself was sold upon it. And when he was against something, the listeners thought it must be bad. Like Jesus Christ, he had the voice of authority, and "the people heard him gladly." Garvey's manner and personality begat loyalty and commanded respect.

GARVEY AND OTHER LEADERS

When we compare the aims and methods of Marcus Garvey with those of other Negro leaders, the reason for his meteoric rise to success becomes evident. Booker T. Washington was not a leader of the masses, according to E. Franklin Frazier in *The Nation,* August 18, 1926, because his program "commended itself chiefly to white people and those Negroes who prided themselves on their opportunism." The program of Washington did not appeal to, or captivate, the imagination of the rank-and-file Negroes, simply because he urged them to play an inglorious role. Garvey once said that the world supposed that for generations Negroes would follow the teachings of Booker T. Washington; but, unfortunately, he remarked, "The world is being shocked at the rude awakening of the Negro to a new ideal." Garvey's wife and biographer, Amy Jacques-Garvey, in *Philosophy and Opinions of Marcus Garvey* (1925), said that her husband wrote: "Things have changed wonderfully since Washington's time. His vision was industrial opportunity for the Negro, but the Sage of Tuskegee has passed off the stage of life and left behind a new problem that must be solved, not by the industrial leaders only but by the political and military leaders as well."

W. E. B. Du Bois criticized Garvey's movement as too "bombastic and impractical," but Garvey thought Du Bois's Niagara Movement and Pan-African Congress were "too intellectual to satisfy the masses." The masses of Negroes rejected Du Bois because in his veins was a mixture of Negro, Dutch, and French blood, and because, after returning from study in Germany, he wore spats, a goatee, and carried a cane. Perhaps the goatee reminded many Negroes of the southern white "Colonel," noted for his aristocracy. On the other hand, Garvey's very blackness electrified the masses of Negroes who migrated north at the time. The black orator even taunted and ridiculed the NAACP leaders as "mongrels," since leaders like Du Bois believed that the salvation of the race was in the hands of the "upper tenth" of the Negro population.

In answer to the charge that he was a "fanatic messiah with a fantastic dream," Garvey answered: "The gang thought they would have been able to build up in America a buffer class between whites and Negroes, and thus in another fifty years join the powerful race and crush the blood of their mothers as is being done in South Africa and the West Indies."

APPRAISAL OF GARVEY

When Marcus Garvey was arrested on a federal charge of using the mails to defraud in January, 1922, the leader sought to save his prestige by issuing statements about his arrest. One bulletin stated that "the dishonest ones of our preachers and politicians, believing that I am of their stamp, try to embarrass me by framing me up with the law." Although Garvey's prison term ended his leadership in the United States, he bequeathed to Negroes a consciousness of the power of collective social action. He is remembered for his new and inspiring definition of a black skin. Unlike his contemporary, Robert Abbott of the *Chicago Defender,* who hated the color black in clothes and a wife, Marcus Garvey dramatized and glorified it. He praised black skins and held that the Negro could expect no progress in a country dominated by whites. Upon reflection, it sounds almost ridiculously humorous that Garvey said, "The black man needs his own government, with his own president in the Black House and a Black God in Heaven."

The Back-to-Africa leader, according to his admirers, took the skeleton of a dream to free Africa and gave it flesh and a regalia of showmanship with annual parades of Black Cross nurses, African Legions in bright uniforms, and the Distinguished Order of Ethiopians. Thousands of people read his newspaper, *Negro World,* which was published in English, French, and Spanish. With all the glamour in leadership and parades, it is no wonder that Robert Brisbane, Jr., lamented that "it was like jailing a rainbow" to imprison Marcus Garvey. Because the leader had easy money and was surrounded by many crackpots, it is difficult to find among his remaining followers persons who can give a reliable evaluation of Marcus Garvey. Brisbane,[6] an authority on Negro protest movements, feels that Garvey's star rose and fell so rapidly that little was done to preserve records that would give accurate pictures of the man. Without doubt, however, "Garvey led the largest and richest, as well as most ambitious of all protest movements initiated by Negroes in the United States" up to that time.

ORATORY OF THE PERIOD

The Garvey period was strictly one of protest speechmaking. More Negro orators caught the attention of large audiences, thus becoming targets of attacks by the white South. For example, Ida B. Wells, an effective lecturer, was driven from the South. She settled in Chicago and continued to present the black man's cause to white citizens in Illinois. Monroe Trotter of Boston spoke vitriolically to unfriendly audiences and was forced to relinquish the platform and function solely as an editor. William Pickens and the Grimke brothers were active as protest speakers.

The tenor of William Pickens' oratory is suggested by the title of his oration, "The Kind of Democracy the Negro Race Expects." As field secretary of the NAACP, he gave this speech on many occasions and devoted a large share of his time to organizing branches of the organization. Pickens was born in Pendleton, South Carolina, on January 15, 1881. He attended Talladega College in Alabama; while a student at Yale University, he won prizes in essay and oratorical contests. He held several teaching positions before becoming an official of the NAACP. Pickens was enthusiastic and entertaining on the platform, and was forceful and logical in his messages. He always took a bold and determined stand when defending Negro citizens. Segregation was a subject that aroused his wrath, and he repeatedly spoke to this effect: "To fix the status of a human soul on earth, according to the physical group in which he is born, is the gang spirit of the savage which its own members outlaw to all others."

The Grimke brothers, Archibald and Francis, received top billing as orators during this period. Archibald Grimke was president of the Washington, D.C., branch of the NAACP and espoused the program of this organization in minute detail. His classic oration was entitled, "The Shame of America." Archibald was born in South Carolina in 1849 and moved to the North after the Civil War. He was educated at Lincoln University in Pennsylvania and studied law at Harvard University. As a counselor-at-law, he found time to engage in politics, which was profitable at the time. In voting, Archibald Grimke did not give his allegiance entirely to the Republicans as did most Negroes, but rather supported candidates and platforms.

The Reverend Francis J. Grimke, Archibald's brother, was graduated from Lincoln University in Pennsylvania, where he also studied law. In 1878 he was graduated from the Theological Seminary of Princeton University. He became pastor of the Fifteenth Street Presbyterian Church in Washington, D.C. As a spokesman of Negro rights, he had few equals. His eloquence appealed primarily to the intellect of his listeners, since moving the emotions of the hearers was overshadowed by the principle of having something to say.

The protest speakers of this period, regardless of any extremists like Marcus Garvey, wanted to help humanity to become a loftier race than the world had ever known before. Like Tennyson, they wanted men "to rise with the flame of freedom in their souls and the light of knowledge in their eyes." These men were looking toward a future with hope mingled with apprehension. They thought that progress was possible if men wanted it in order to survive. To survive at that time required harder thinking and nobler behavior than had characterized mankind in the past. There was always the specter of the lyncher's rope and economic slavery on farms where Negroes were tenants.

Footnotes, Chapter 5

1. There is considerable disagreement on the number of Marcus Garvey's followers. The leader boasted of 4 million in 1920 and

6 million three years later. Most historians have estimated the number at no more than 2 million. His severest critics put the number at 600,000.

2. Roi Ottley, *Black Odyssey,* p. 235.
3. James Weldon Johnson, *Black Manhattan,* pp. 251–252.
4. Ibid.
5. Claude McKay, *Harlem Metropolis,* pp. 146–147.
6. Robert H. Brisbane, Jr., "The Rise of Protest Movements Among Negroes Since 1900" (Ph.D. dissertation).

6 / The Early Period of Protest, 1915–1945

Robert H. Brisbane, who studied protest movements of this period, indicated that Negroes manifested two main attitudes toward their environment in the United States: *accommodation* and *protest*.[1] Each attitude had its literature of justification and defense, its prophets and followers. The attitude of accommodation, or collaboration, was first represented by Booker T. Washington, Southern whites said that this attitude was "the diplomatic" approach to the racial problem. The protest attitude, according to Brisbane, was almost wholly confined to the North and East, since the white people in the South had invariably met Negro protest with violence or threats of violence. In the North, Negroes were permitted to exercise their constitutional rights to assemble and petition for almost any cause or purpose, as long as it was done peacefully.

The attitude of protest in this country has been exemplified in three movements: (a) *protest,* symbolized by A. Philip Randolph, labor leader; (b) *nationalism,* carried to an extreme by Marcus Garvey; and (c) *revolt,* probably best typified by Paul Robeson. In the case of each movement, the leader "has been, or is, an effective speaker."[2]

PROTEST ORGANIZATIONS

The Niagara Movement, under the leadership of W. E. B. Du Bois, was organized by a group of young men in Niagara Falls, Canada, in June, 1905, and the platform adopted at this meeting included a program of progressive action. The delegates demanded freedom of speech, manhood suffrage, abolition of distinction on a racial basis, and respect for the laboring man. In 1910, the delegates met with a group of white people to discuss the evils of lynching and riots, as well as to renew the struggle for civil and political liberty. Most of the delegates attended the second conference, but Monroe Trotter, a radical, who was suspicious of the motives of white folk, did not.

From the beginning in 1910, the National Association for the Advancement of Colored People developed a program to increase industrial opportunities for Negroes, to secure more police protection, and to crusade against lynching and lawlessness. As the first publicity director and researcher, Du Bois was commissioned to increase circulation of *Crisis,* which sold only 1,000 copies the first month. In 1919, this organization crusaded for a federal antilynch law. To create public sentiment against this evil, the NAACP published *Thirty Years of Lynching in the United States, 1889 to 1918.* It sent an investigator, Walter White, to the scenes of the crimes to compile data concerning the tragedies of lynching and the reports were published by the NAACP and circulated widely throughout the nation.

The NAACP, about midcentury, went to the courts and attacked the legality and constitutionality of the dual system of southern education. The most significant accomplishments were the Supreme Court decisions ending segregation at the universities of Oklahoma and Texas. These decisions led Dr. Benjamin Fine,[3] education editor of *The New York Times,* to publish that "a thousand Negro students are attending now southern colleges and universities from which they were previously barred." In 1950, the NAACP made an annual report describing the gains of the year as follows: "Compliance of a number of railroads with the Supreme Court decision outlawing Jim Crow arrangement in dining cars, progress in integration of the Air Force and Navy, and defeat of the efforts of the Dixiecrat Congressmen to impose segregation in the nation's armed forces."

In 1911, the National Urban League was established to help open new opportunities for Negroes in industries and to aid migrants from the South in making adjustments in northern cities. The branches of this organization set up programs for welcoming Negro migrants, directing them to jobs and places to live, and distributing information on how to live in the city. For a long time, the National Urban League's national director was Lester Granger. To expand the Urban League, officials traveled over the nation making speeches and setting up new branches. Not all of their speaking, however, was confined to the business of the Urban League.

During the economic depression years, Negroes found it expedient to use whatever force they could to get relief and employment. For instance, in St. Louis and other cities, a jobs-for-Negroes movement got under way. This type of protest was directed at business concerns having a large volume of Negro trade. In cities like Chicago and New York, Negroes formed political organizations and clubs to make the most effective use of the ballot. By means of certain propaganda instruments, black voters were encouraged to shift from the Republican to the Democratic party. Orators told voters that they owed no special allegiance to the party of Lincoln, or any party, if it did not put into action a program to benefit them.

PROTEST ORATORS

One of the earliest founders of the NAACP was William Edward Burghardt Du Bois, whose biographer said of him:

"He breaks every mold into which the average American tries to put the Negro. Born not in the Southern rurals but in New England, educated at Harvard and Berlin, his features not black but finely chiseled in bronze, he is a Boston Brahmin."[4] Du Bois entered Fisk University in Nashville, Tennessee, in 1884, and was graduated four years later. As a student, the young man edited the *Fisk Herald* and delivered orations on the racial problem. His unpublished speeches have been collected by the Fisk University Library. In 1888, Du Bois went to Harvard University on a scholarship, won the Boylston oratorical contest, and was one of the six students chosen to deliver commencement addresses. He chose to speak on Jefferson Davis.

Du Bois was first a rural teacher in Tennessee, but later became a college professor, poet, and NAACP editor and researcher. He founded *Crisis,* which became the medium for all kinds of Negro expression, and helped this magazine to reach a circulation of 100,000 shortly after World War I. Best known as a writer, "for fifty years with pen dipped in gall, he has written what he has deeply felt and studied."

The NAACP editor first attracted public notice when he became engaged in a feud with Booker T. Washington. During the early part of Du Bois's career, he was the chief proponent of the so-called upper tenth of his race who were destined to be leaders of thought and missionaries of culture among the Negro masses. With strong conviction, this leader said: "No others can do this work and Negro colleges must train men for it. The Negro race, like all other races, is going to be saved by exceptional men."

By 1950, Du Bois[5] is said to have entered a period of transition, and his ideas changed from his encounters with Booker T. Washington to the concept that the racial problem is one phase of the working class's struggle for power. Many of his ideas made him unpopular with the Negro masses and the white South. When he died in September, 1963, his eulogy said that he had wanted full economic, political, and social equality among Americans in thought, expression, and action, with no discrimination based on color. After his death in Accra, Ghana, he was given a state funeral and buried outside Christianberg Castle.

By no stretch of the imagination can Du Bois be compared with Frederick Douglass as an orator, but he was one of our outstanding public speakers. He will be remembered for his leadership in the area of ideas where he taught the Negro to recognize exactly what his rights were. Near the end of his career, his convictions led him to take stands far ahead of his peers and finally brought him in conflict with the NAACP and the United States government.

The tone of the voice of Du Bois was that of an articulate scholar, and his vocabulary did not take into consideration the Negro rank and file. His platform posture was dignified, his diction perfect and clear, but he lacked the forceful emotional delivery demanded of an orator. In logical analysis of his subject, he was indeed effective. The intellectual audience appealed to him, for he was not keen on emotional harangue, declamatory intonation, or gymnastic muscle movement and musical tremulo. Du Bois gave the impression of a cultured gentleman conversing on an intellectual plane before a classroom full of learners. He did not indulge in narrating jokes and telling funny anecdotes, since he did not wish to act the buffoon or clown. His training and cultural background would not permit this kind of nonsense. He sought not so much to persuade or compromise, as to expose pretensions and duplicity concerning the attitude of superiority, and this approach put his white enemies on the defensive.

The second protest orator was Paul Robeson who was allegedly the leader of revolt during this period. Oratory was not Robeson's profession but he developed this art through acting and singing. He has sung all the way from the Deep South to Canada, from New York to Paris and Moscow. He has acted in many fine dramatic productions, including O'Neill's *Emperor Jones* and Shakespeare's *Othello*. Somehow

Robeson[6] was dubbed Communist when he mixed speaking on the racial problem, during the intermissions, with concert singing. He aroused public animosity and was barred from holding concerts in many cities in the United States. This action led the singer to label the United States a "police state." While his critics held that his speaking was out of place during his musical concerts, Robeson continued to speak fluently on issues affecting the Negro. He opposed conscription in the army, and membership of Negroes in labor unions.[7] He was probably the only Negro orator who combined singing, acting, and speaking. He said:

Through my singing and acting and speaking, I want to make freedom ring. Maybe I can touch people's hearts better than I can their minds, with the common struggle of the common man. Most of all, I want to help my homeland realize that it will grow only as it lets all its people do their full part in making it rich and strong.[8]

Born in Princeton, New Jersey, on April 9, 1898, Paul Robeson attended Rutgers College on a scholarship and was a four-letter man in athletics, making Walter Camp's All-American football team in 1917. In his junior year, the singer was elected Phi Beta Kappa, and was graduated with the B.A. degree in 1917. Later, he earned the LL.B. from Columbia University, but he gave up a career in law because of racial prejudice. Serving an apprenticeship with the Provincetown Players under Eugene O'Neill, Robeson became an accomplished actor as well as a gifted singer. In this capacity, he traveled "across the world as an example of the humanity and greatness of our democratic heritage."

While at Rutgers, Robeson won the freshman prize in oratory, the extempore speaking prizes during his sophomore and junior years, and was elected student commencement speaker and spoke on "Interracial Relations." He was an important member of the debating team and often represented Rutgers in intercollegiate dates. His father, who was also a fine orator, assisted his son in discovering the weaknesses of his arguments. Therefore, when Paul "actually delivered his speech he knew it was good and he spoke with freedom and confidence because of that knowledge."[9] Robeson took voice lessons from Theresa Armitage, who once taught singing in a school in Chicago. She taught him to relax his throat in order to gain more flexibility of voice, and she insisted that "correct singing oils the chords naturally and rests the voice." The vocal lessons paid off later in Robeson's concerts. The press and the critics bear this testimony regarding his voice: "One of great beauty and power of voice," "voice rich and vibrant like an organ," "a voice in which a deep bell rings," and "a voice with organ-like ease and power."

On July 26, 1949, an editorial in the Hearst newspapers listed Paul Robeson as an "undesirable citizen." It was evident that this editorial stemmed from remarks Robeson made relative to a trip to Russia and the way he was welcomed there. The *Pittsburgh Courier,* in replying to the Hearst editorial, said: "We don't agree with Robeson in all points. But we want America to know that from our viewpoint there are millions of 'undesirable citizens.' "[10] A Catholic magazine[11] called Robeson a self-styled Messiah trying to lead Negroes into Red slavery. Sentiment against him, it is reputed, caused eighty-six of his concerts to be canceled in 1947. "Money isn't everything," said Robeson, "I am willing to make the sacrifice for my people, because I cannot be happy otherwise. I feel I have to speak out against an injustice as I see it."

Paul Robeson, according to an AP dispatch in April, 1949, told a Communist-backed World Peace Conference in Paris that American Negroes would never fight the Soviet Union. Negro enemies at once labeled him "the widely ballyhooed singer" who did not speak officially for Negroes. Quickly, the speech brought a reply from Walter White, executive Secretary of the NAACP, who made public this statement: "In the event of any conflict that our nation has with any other nation, we will regard ourselves as Americans and meet the responsibilities imposed upon Americans." Generally, Negro leaders said that Robeson was not authorized to speak for 14 million Negroes but hundreds of newspaper readers wrote to the editors of Negro weeklies praising Paul Robeson for this speech.

Public animosity caused a riot when Robeson attempted to speak at Peekskill, New York, on August 27, 1949. The blame was placed on local authorities, who did not heed the threats of marching veterans who had announced previously that they would silence him. With special police protection, Robeson held a second meeting without incident. Governor Thomas E. Dewey, commenting on the disturbance, said: "The right of free speech and of assembly are guaranteed to all, regardless of political beliefs. These rights must be respected, however hateful the views of some of those who abuse them."

The publicity given Robeson by the news media led the United States Department of State to revoke his passport unless he agreed to refrain from criticizing the treatment of Negroes and the foreign policy of this country during his travels in foreign countries. The singer carried his case to court to determine the legality of the cancellation of his passport. Judge James A. Cobb declared that such action was a curtailment of freedom of travel, and was in violation of the Fifth Amendment.[12] Some years later, Robeson spent some time in Russia and other foreign countries.

MORDECAI WYATT JOHNSON

In *13 Against the Odds,* Edwin R. Embree created an apt figure when he referred to Mordecai Wyatt Johnson, former president of Howard University, as "The Lord High Chancellor." Johnson will always be conspicuous in the history of American Negro oratory: first, for his scholarly platform speaking against racial injustice; second, for his role as leader of an oppressed people; and, third, for his contribution to higher education in the field of administration. While Johnson was an outstanding orator as early as 1922, his reputation for eloquence reached its climax during the New Deal period. Typical of his utterances was an address delivered at North Carolina College at Durham, in the fall of 1934, at which time the author[13] was in attendance. In this speech, Johnson heralded Franklin D. Roosevelt as "the greatest President since Lincoln" and the prophet of the new democracy. With all the eloquence he could command, Johnson urged Negroes to support the New Deal wholeheartedly. He became most popular as a speaker for special occasions—notably Emancipation Day, commencement, Founder's Day, and conferences.

Mordecai Wyatt Johnson was born in Paris, Tennessee, on January 12, 1890. His father, the Reverend Wyatt Johnson, was a stern, devout, and methodical man. His mother, on the other hand, was very sympathetic. While attending grade school, the boy came under the influence of a teacher, Benjamin Sampson, to whom he is indebted for his first training in public speaking. In 1911, the young man was awarded the A.B. degree from Morehouse College at Atlanta, Georgia. He was employed to teach English at his alma mater, but later enrolled in the Rochester Theological Seminary. Upon graduation, he became pastor of the First Baptist Church in Charleston, West Virginia, where he helped to establish a cooperative grocery store and a branch of the NAACP. Johnson afterward entered the School of Theology of Harvard University and was graduated in 1922. Four years later, he was a member of the Sherwood Eddy American Seminar in Europe. Johnson became president of Howard University at Washington, D.C., in 1926. He received the Spingarn Medal in 1928 for his successful educational administration and for obtaining large annual fedɛral appropriations for the university.

So far as his speech training was concerned, young Mordecai Johnson was more fortunate than most youths of his day, for he received thorough drilling in public speaking. Benjamin Sampson, his elementary school instructor, trained him in "speaking clear, in rolling out his sentences, in driving home his points."[14] To develop effective visual directness, Sampson told Mordecai: "When you speak, pick out a boy in the room and deliver your speech to him. If he is moved, the crowd is moved; if he laughs at your jokes, everybody will be laughing. If he gets bored or looks as if he does not believe you, stretch out your hand, shake a fist at him, walk down and tower over him, do anything to hold and make him believe you." In preparing for debates, young Johnson was encouraged to gather all the possible arguments the opponent might use. Mr. Sampson was impatient with formal and orderly discussion, for he "wanted clash, jokes, even anger if it would add zest and conviction." When Johnson attended college, his speech training enabled him to excel his classmates.

Mordecai Wyatt Johnson developed into a master orator, who has the voice and manner of a true leader—a voice that begets loyalty and commands respect. He admires India's Gandhi, the proponent of passive resistance, and his influence upon the struggles of disadvantaged people all over the world. When talking about passive resistance, the orator is remarkably eloquent. He employs the lively conversational tradition made renowned by the versatile Wendell Phillips, but it is his massive force of argument that gives him his real power upon the platform. In the protest movement for racial freedom, Johnson represents his people with a scholarly harangue that resembles the philippics of Cicero, but with more subdued passion. When listeners attend to the orator's words, they are swayed by both ornament and logic. What counts most is the beauty of truth and the fact that the speaker feels it strongly. The causes of Johnson always stand in urgent need of what he can give. To him, the speaking opportunity is one of those moments when a civil rights force, not yet having found an opening for action, finds salvation in the phrasemaker and the literary artist who can embody its cause in words.

If Johnson's language tends to be lively, descriptive, and erudite, his message rarely runs longer that forty-five minutes or an hour. His ideas are germane and, best of all, he never bores his fellowman. Under the cloak of lively conversation, his eloquence is pulsating. The audience feels his ideas surge forth with the power of a jet airliner. His persuasion is strong and convincing. He is a natural verbal artist when he describes the origin of racial prejudice between the slaves and poor whites who scarcely eked a living from the mountain hills of the South. The description does not astonish his hearers, but with it he engages their emotions and humor. Through the years, Dr. Johnson has become as famous for his pathos as he already was for his brilliance and inflectional agility. The orator arouses positively hysterical enthusiasm by his arguments in behalf of the downtrodden.

When people learn that Johnson is going to speak at some city, they will travel a hundred miles to hear him. It has become a proverbial expression that those who have not heard Johnson speak, or Howard Thurman preach, or Marian Anderson sing, are not qualified to appear in genteel company. One can attest to this fact when he observes the personable appearance of the orator on the platform. By the grace and propriety of his action and gestures, he does honor to the human figure with his platform decorum. He is as effective with his body movements as he is with words made brilliant by his resonant, upper baritone voice. He performs the most ordinary platform action in a manner suitable to the greatness of his character and the causes he espouses.

In describing the evils of prejudice during World War II, Mordecai Johnson once said: "Western civilization, Christianity, decency are struggling for their very lives. In this worldwide civil war, race prejudice is our most dangerous enemy for it is a disease at the very root of our democratic life."[15] He concluded: "I call upon you to bring about a halt and healing of this disease while yet there is time." The audience sat stunned, exhausted, and then it stormed into applause. Edwin R. Embree, who was present, said: "The man's power was uncanny. It was not the sermon or the logic;

it was the magic of his voice and personality. He used speech as a great musician would use a symphony to move the multitude."

Johnson's speeches are usually made from notes; therefore, few are available in manuscript form. His extemporaneous style of speaking is terse and vigorous, since he deplores reading his speeches, as do many educators who rely too much upon written manuscripts. Dr. Dwight W. Holmes, former president of Morgan State College at Baltimore, Maryland, gave this description of the orator's public speaking:

I consider Dr. Johnson as deserving a place among the half dozen speakers our times have produced. He is highly an intellectual man, widely read, with a remarkable memory for details—notably in quoting statistics. These he is able to marshal clearly and logically. He then delivers his material with a combination of clearness, cogency and forcefulness which not only holds the attention of his hearers, but is also convincing. Doctor Johnson is gifted with remarkable vocal qualities and has mastered a platform manner that holds his audience from the beginning to the end of his address.[16]

Almost everyone who has heard Doctor Johnson has been impressed by the intense stillness of his hearers. In this atmosphere, he stands, as John McClorey stated, before "the grand organ of living multitude upon which he has been playing; upon which he will play again."[17]

During 1926, the American Friends Service Committee held, in Washington, D.C., a two-day conference on Interracial Relations, which southern and northern Friends attended. Johnson, the new president of Howard University, spoke one evening. Mrs. Anne Bibble Stirling, who had heard the leading Negroes of America,[18] gave close attention to Johnson, who was new to her. As he spoke, the audience yielded to the charm of his deep voice. He traced the difficulty between black and white people to its economic source. Eyes met in pleasant surprise, because he was saying things a new way. Mrs. Stirling said, "Presently tears came to my eyes, were dashed away to clear my eyes on this protean speaker and yet kept

coming; I strove to keep from visibly shaking. . . . Presently
that rich voice—sometimes booming in thunderous denunciation, sometimes persuading in softest sympathy—ceased, and
vibrant silence covered us." In the waking hours of the night,
Mrs. Stirling tried to analyze "what seemed like wizardry" and
"whence came the power of the man who played upon the
heartstrings of the audience as if it were a harp with never a
jarring chord."[19] Robert M. Bartlett, in commenting on the
delivery of the orator, remarked that Johnson was the only
college president in America who packed his own chapel every
time he spoke during his seventeen years as administrator.[20]

When Johnson was attending school at Harvard University,
three students traditionally delivered commencement addresses; and Johnson was one of the three men to appear on
the 1922 commencement program, along with Benjamin Jones
and Clyde G. Phelps. Mordecai Johnson, representing the
Divinity School, spoke on the subject "The Faith of the
American Negro" and was awarded the M.S.T. degree. In his
peroration, Johnson made this appeal: "When the Negro cries
with pain from his deep hurt and lays his petition for elemental justice before the nation, he is calling upon the American
people to kindle anew about the crucible of race relations the
fires of American faith." From then on, commented Brawley,
"Johnson was a marked man and the address has been termed
the most notable speech given by a Negro orator since the
address of Booker T. Washington in Atlanta in 1895."[21] The
following program contained Johnson's subject:

Orators Hoc Ordine Sunt

Dissertatio Latina

Benjamin Franklin Jones *dum omnes qui adsunt salutat de orbis
terrarum restituenda*

Clyde Guilielmus Phelps—*Disquisitio*—*"America's Russian Policy"*

Mordecai Wyatt Johnson, A.B., B.D., *Candidatus Theologae,*
"The Faith of the American Negro"

Without doubt, Mordecai Johnson is a social reform orator. "For all his excellence as a speaker," said Dr. Holmes, "I consider him at his best when dealing with social subjects, especially the problems of minorities throughout the world. He holds his audiences spellbound and impresses them with the strength of his position whether or not they agree with him."[22] On February 13, 1937, Johnson spoke at the All-Southern Negro Youth Conference at Richmond, Virginia, and called attention to the necessity of a New South and "good life" for all citizens. The orator said, "The old slaveholders drove the best section of white workers off the land into the mountains and impoverished the lowlands by hundreds of years of slavery. But a new kind of South is rising. There is enough machinery to supply everybody with plenty." In the Duke Auditorium of North Carolina College at Durham in January, 1946, he told students that our possession of the atomic bomb has determined the nature of the next war. The orator pictured it to be a war without announcement, a war without any formal declaration. "There will be a meeting of the great powers who will disagree, and the next noise we hear will be the screeching of elevators going up and down from heaven to hell." Predicting that atom control is unlikely, Johnson said, "We are living under the illusion that we have the power to determine what to do with it."

As a theologian, Dr. Johnson preaches without giving any inkling of denominational bias. It was while teaching at Morehouse College that he had a vision while searching for the meaning of life. In order to serve the poor, he felt he could best render service by entering the ministry. He became a well-trained theologian, a religious liberal in doctrine, basing his conclusions on logic. He refuses to be bound by religious lore and tradition. Johnson feels that criticism is good for the Christian church. Once he told a dignified church congregation in Ohio that the Christian church gave too weak a challenge to young people. Johnson urged young folk to leave the church unless it "dared to take the lead in human reconstruction." He admonished the Christian church to move out radically in social matters, unless it wants some other organization or movement to take its place. When the speaker concluded his address, young people and even bishops stood and cheered the oration.

Dr. Johnson's sermons emphasize (1) the brotherhood of man, (2) the need for unity as contrasted with sectarianism in the Christian movement, and (3) social reform to bring the Kingdom of God to the world. Attacking the hypocrisy of the church, the speaker warns his hearers that the time is past when Christians can take a long spoon and hand the gospel to the black man out the back door. He is original in phraseology, seldom quotes verbatim, and never recites verses from hymns as many ministers do. Johnson gets great satisfaction from his sermons, which his congregations follow closely and understand perfectly.

SOME PROTEST GAINS

In looking back over the Early Protest Period, it seems that the harder Negroes tried, the more unsuccessful they were in convincing white people that they deserved more than second-class citizenship and the general derogation to which they were subjected. Lynchings increased in number and barbarity, riots spread tragically in the early years of the century, and segregation was the order of the day everywhere in the southern United States. Small wonder that W. E. B. Du Bois declared that "the problem of the twentieth century is the problem of the color line," or that Booker T. Washington asserted that race prejudice was eating away at the vitals of the South, or that James Weldon Johnson cried out, "This land is ours by right of birth."

The period was dominated by organizations and their movements, by oratory to sear the public conscience, and by collective social action. What then did the Negro leaders and orators accomplish? From 1910 to the end of this period, the nation had not reached the democratic ideal. And yet the progress of the Negro following the rise of protest oratory in 1915 was a veritable transformation. For instance, in 1900 wholesome racicial relations, were at a very low ebb. However, by the 1930's a New South began to emerge in the area of human relations, but it was lamentable that many of these changes did not take place without coercion, such as was true of the reforms resulting from the NAACP lawsuits. The South was slowly developing more respect for Negroes as persons. It began to tolerate more Negro voting and condoned the removal of the insulting curtains in railroad dining cars. Another milestone in the area of human relations was the entry of the Negro into organized professional baseball. This was achieved without any sort of coercion whatsoever, although the Negro press and orators had for years urged the employment of qualified black ballplayers.

The Negro with artistic aspirations had faced many obstacles in entering the field of motion-picture acting. Hollywood, up to this time, had long portrayed him in the stereotype dance and domestic servant roles. During this period, however, Negroes were cast in more dignified parts in the movies. For instance, this was true in such photoplays as *Lost Boundaries, Home of the Brave,* and *Pinky.* Although many forces were responsible for progress in racial relations, it was traceable in part to the effectiveness with which Negro orators used their skill in speaking. Their messages of economic independence, of first-class citizenship, so clearly and compellingly presented, had at least served as a powerful agent in enhancing the hopes and aspirations of Negro citizens.

Footnotes, Chapter 6

1. Robert H. Brisbane, Jr., "The Rise of Protest Movements Among Negroes Since 1900" (Ph.D. dissertation).
2. Oliver C. Cox, "The Crisis in Leadership Among Negroes,"

Journal of Negro Education 19 (Fall, 1950), pp. 459–465.

3. *The New York Times,* October 23, 1950.
4. Edwin R. Embree, *13 Against the Odds,* p. 153.
5. *Tuskegee Messenger,* March and April, 1936.
6. *The Sign,* 29 (October, 1949): p. 9. This is a Catholic magazine.
7. *Current Biography,* March, 1941, pp. 65–66.
8. Embree, *13 Against the Odds,* p. 261.
9. Eslanda Goode, *Paul Robeson.*
10. *Pittsburgh Courier,* July 2, 1949.
11. *The Sign,* 29 (October, 1949): 9.
12. *Capital Times* (Madison, Wisconsin), September 3, 1949.
13. The author was teaching English and history at Mary Potter School in Oxford, North Carolina, and traveled thirty miles to hear Dr. Johnson. He has heard him speak six times.
14. Embree, *13 Against the Odds,* p. 180.
15. Ibid., p. 175.
16. Letter from Dr. Holmes to the author, July 23, 1945.
17. John McClorey, *The Making of a Pulpit Orator,* pp. 182–183.
18. Booker T. Washington, John Hope, George Cannon, W. E. B. Du Bois, and Leslie P. Hill.
19. Ralph W. Bullock, *In Spite of Handicaps,* pp. 11–13.
20. A. Craig Baird, *American Speeches,* 1944–1945; see also *The Pulpit,* June, 1944.
21. Benjamin Brawley, *Negro Builders and Heroes.*
22. See footnote 13.

7 / The NAACP's Big Three

The National Association for the Advancement of Colored People (NAACP), from its beginning in 1910, developed a program designed to increase industrial opportunity for the Negro, to secure more police protection for southern blacks, to abolish lynching, and to crusade against the lawlessness of the Ku Klux Klan. It has been most successful, however, in the civil rights movement by taking cases to courts of law. From 1938 to 1960, the NAACP attacked by court action the legality of the dual system of public schools. Its greatest victory was the 1954 Supreme Court decision, which outlawed segregation in public schools. Though the NAACP has generally avoided the sit-ins, Freedom Rides, and demonstrations, it has continued to use the courts as a sort of civil rights laboratory. In May, 1965, the organization focused its attention on the antipoverty program and expanded its area of operation to include registration and voting clinics. Because its action has been conservative, it has been criticized by impatient leaders.

The NAACP has been directed mainly by three strong executive secretaries: James Weldon Johnson, Walter White, and Roy Wilkins, whom the author has labeled "The Civil Rights Triumvirate." Unlike the Reverend Martin Luther King, Jr., whose most effective argument for civil rights was moral logic, NAACP leaders have lacked his magnetism and showmanship. While King led his civil rights followers into the streets like a general, the Civil Rights Triumvirate preferred to sally forth into the courts of the land. When the masses of Negroes wanted dynamic leadership in the early 1960s, they found it was lacking in the NAACP. Consequently, for a while, the Association fell from grace so far as the new Negro was concerned.

JAMES WELDON JOHNSON ("MAN OF LETTERS")

Probably the strongest voice that was heard during the New Freedom Period of Woodrow Wilson was that of James Weldon Johnson, who began his career as an orator at that time. Johnson was born in Jacksonville, Florida, in 1871 and attended Atlanta University. His first job was teaching in his hometown, but later he studied law and passed the bar examination in Florida. In 1901, Johnson and his brother Rosamond went to New York, where they produced a musical comedy. While in New York, the orator studied literature and drama at Columbia University.

From 1906 to 1913, James Weldon Johnson was United States consul in Venezuela and Nicaragua. When he returned to this country, he became field secretary of the NAACP. In the 1920s he served as general secretary of this organization. "As secretary," said Carter G. Woodson, "Johnson became widely known as an honest and fearless leader qualified to present intelligently the cause of the Negro or court."[1] In 1930, James Weldon Johnson was appointed professor of creative literature at Fisk University, Nashville, Tennessee. Part of the time, he was visiting professor at New York University. He died in an automobile accident in 1938.

James Weldon Johnson will probably be remembered more for his creative writing than for his speaking ability. As early as 1917, he published his *Fifty Years and Other Poems*. In the title poem of this work, the poet made it clear that Negroes were determined to remain in America and enjoy the fruits of their labors. Dr. John Hope Franklin said that Johnson "thus became something of an advanced advocate of the Harlem Renaissance and remained an integral part of it."[2] Johnson published a *Book of American Poetry,* which included the chief works of outstanding Negro poets. He published *God's Trombones,* seven sermons in verse (1927); the *Autobiography of the Ex-Coloured Man* (published anonymously in 1912 and re-issued under his name in 1927); *Black Manhattan* (1930); and *Along This Way* (1933). In literature and art, he urged the development of Negro writers who would tear down the old Negro stereotypes and replace them with newer and truer ones, and who could produce works that would reach and affect many American citizens who would probably never exchange more than a hundred words with a Negro during a lifetime.

As nearly as possible, James Weldon Johnson's racial progress program was a combination of the NAACP's militant approach and the opportunist philosophy of the southern conservatives. The orator never claimed he had a program, but he laid down certain lines along which a plan might be worked out. It was his belief that no one man or group of men could formulate a complete program of racial advancement. He felt that the Negro could gain victory over prejudice if he learned to draw the utmost from his potential resources—the church, the press, fraternal societies, and education. Politics, he believed, could aid the Negro only if it were divorced from sentimentalism and approached realistically and practically. Johnson[3] suggested that the Negro drop the role imposed upon him by a condescending tradition and play a part of his own choosing. Exodus of the Negro, as Garvey had proposed, was dismissed by Johnson as impossible, since Negroes had no real interest in migrating to Africa. The Negro needs to use his organizations for major purposes if he would make advancement toward full citizenship, thought Johnson.

When Johnson[4] entered college at Atlanta University, he recognized his ineptitude as a public speaker. He was impressed by the manner in which other students of his age rose without fear or hesitation and discussed current propositions. He said, "I was determined to make as much of an orator of myself as possible." Therefore, Johnson joined the Ware Lyceum, Preps Debating Society, and other organizations. The first year the young man participated in a debate in the Ware Lyceum he was terror-stricken with stage fright. During his sophomore year, he won first prize in an oratorical contest. The next year he tied another student orator for first place. Commenting upon his university speaking career, Johnson stated: "Before I left Atlanta I had learned what every orator must know: that the deep secret of eloquence is rhythm— rhythm set to motion by the speaker, that sets up a responsive rhythm in his audience. For the purpose of sheer persuasion, it is far more important than logic."

As field secretary of the NAACP, James Weldon Johnson made many trips across the country, speaking and organizing branches of the Association. At the end of 1919, there were 310 branches, with 130 of them located in the South. Negroes were awake and willing to join the NAACP, because the war and northern migration had shaken them loose from their "traditional moorings of standpatism and timidity." People in many cities were ready to participate in any social action movement that would assure them of the full rights of a citizen, while in other places the enthusiasm was lacking. The speaker observed, however, that Negro morale was on the upgrade. In the South, the audiences were mainly black people; but, in the North, Johnson spoke to many white groups.

The experiences of the orator on these trips were varied— thrilling, pathetic, and humorous. For instance, Johnson related that in one midwestern industrial city, he spoke to a group of Negro people in a church jammed to suffocation.

When he walked up to the pulpit, there was no applause—a demonstration that Johnson had been accustomed to—and the people regarded him with a worshipful silence as though he were a Messiah. The listeners hung on his words with childlike confidence and faith. Johnson stated that he could have wept because of his own lack of power to deliver them.

In his autobiography, Walter White[5] told of a visit made by Johnson to Atlanta for the purpose of addressing a mass meeting held in a moving picture theater in the Old Odd Fellows Building that was packed with eager-faced Negroes and even a few white people. It was difficult for the platform party to wedge through the crowd to enter the auditorium. White described Johnson's speech this way:

Mr. Johnson, calm, slender, and immaculate, stood on the narrow strip of stage between the footlights and a painted drop. There was none of that sonorous, flamboyant oratory of that era in the meeting—only quiet, irrefutable presentation of facts and the need to wipe out race prejudice before it thereby engendered and destroyed both victims and perpetrators.

A puzzled white listener, after the meeting, stopped Walter White and said, "This is a new doctrine. Imagine a Negro being as interested and concerned about white people who keep him down as he is about his own race."

Johnson, in describing the Atlanta meeting, spoke of the policeman stationed in the theater. "In other days," remarked the orator, "this would have placed a hand of chilling restraint on the proceedings, but now it had no such effect. Each person who took part spoke frankly and courageously about the business that had brought the people together." Walter White called a subsequent meeting to organize the Atlanta branch of the NAACP.

Two years after the Atlanta meeting, James Weldon Johnson told a vast audience in Carnegie Hall that "the race problem in the United States had resolved itself into a question of saving black men's bodies and white men's souls."[6] Other speakers on the program were Charles Evans Hughes and Anna Howard Shaw. Johnson's ambitious message registered surprise and bewilderment on the faces of the platform visitors. The NAACP orator felt that on this occasion he made the most effective address of his entire career. Every one of his nerves was quickened by the intensity of the feeling that comes across the footlights to a speaker when he realizes that by voice and gesture he is able to sway the crowd.

The orator described to his audience the marching of "The Buffaloes," New York's black regiment, as they drilled up Madison Square and Fifth Avenue to receive a stand of colors that was presented by the Union League Club. The soldiers came to a halt in front of the Club while a large chorus sang "The Star-Spangled Banner." When the song ended, the governor of New York came down from the balcony and presented the colors. And as the governor did so, he shouted, "Bring it back, boys!" At this point in the speech, Johnson said:

And the answer swelled up in my heart: Never you fear, Mr. Governor, they will bring it back as they have always done whenever it has been committed to their hands, without once letting it trail in the dust, without putting a stain of dishonor upon it. Then it is for you, gentlemen of the Union League Club, for you, the people of America, to remove those stains upon it; as these men carry it into battle, the stains of Disfranchisement, of Jim-Crowism, of Mob violence, and of Lynching. . . .

Before the speaker could finish his utterances, "the emotional tension of the listeners snapped with an explosion of cheers and applause." When the audience regained composure, the orator continued: "The record of black men on the field of France gives us the greater right to point to that flag and say to the Nation: 'Those stains are still upon it; they dim its stars and soil its stripes; wash them out! Wash them out!' " Johnson stood in silence and waited for the tumult in the audience and in himself to subside. Sometime later when Johnson read this passage over in cold print, he said that the words struck him as a piece of flamboyant oratory. "If it were not for my memory," he remarked, "I should doubt that they ever possessed the power to do what they did."

WALTER WHITE "(LITTLE DAVID")

One of the outstanding leaders of public address was Walter White, the second executive secretary of the NAACP. But somehow, the Executive Secretary never caught the public fancy as did Booker T. Washington. No Negro has unless it was Frederick Douglass, antislavery orator, or Martin Luther King, Jr. Casting a reflective glance backward, Roy Wilkins, also on the NAACP's staff, wrote that instead of one leader, Negroes are developing leaders in every section of the nation. White, therefore, was one whose leadership stood out in the field of social reform.

White had dreams of social reforms that he believed could be effected in our democratic republic. His work with the NAACP enabled him to direct his enthusiasm toward the realization of those dreams. He believed that Negroes should include in their strategy the education of the people to question and investigate existing conditions among minority peoples. In this way, he felt that Negroes would eventually surmount all obstacles of tradition and lethargy. As a lecturer, war correspondent, and NAACP official, White traveled more than 420,000 miles. For example, in 1921, he attended the Pan-African Congress in France. Six years later, he went to study in Europe on a writing fellowship. During World War II, he served as war correspondent in Europe, North Africa, Italy, and the Middle East. In 1944, Walter White traveled 30,000 miles during a four-month tour of the Pacific theaters of war.

13 Against the Odds (1945) by Edwin R. Embree and *Rising Above Color* (1946) by Philip H. Lotz are two well-known biographical studies that include the life of Walter White. He told his life's story in *A Man Called White* (1948), stating that he was born in Atlanta, Georgia, on July 1, 1893. While attending elementary school in Atlanta, he received some training in voice and speech. When the youth was thirteen, his family was spared in a terrible race riot, but White always remembered vividly the scenes of barbarity. What he saw made him hate violence of every sort with implacable and ineradicable loathing. After graduation from Atlanta University, White did postgraduate study in economics and sociology at the College of the City of New York. As a writer, he achieved distinction with two novels, *Fire in the Flint,* and *A Rising Wind,* which was an account of his 1944 European tour. Walter White died in 1955.

While working with an Atlanta life insurance company, Walter White had his first chance to work in behalf of Negro citizens. The opportunity came when petty politicians were campaigning on a platform of false economics. They proposed to reduce school expenditures by discontinuing public education for Negroes with the sixth grade. The politicians argued that "too much schooling is bad for Negroes, who don't pay taxes anyway." Young White took a leading part in the fight against this unfair proposal. He assisted a committee to draft the following case for presentation to the school board:

Negroes do pay taxes—on more than one and a half million dollars' worth of property in Atlanta—and their labor helps create much of the wealth which others *own.*

Regardless of taxes, the American principle of public education is equality of opportunity for all children, rich and poor alike.

The security and growth of any community—Atlanta or any others—depend upon the decency and competence of all its citizens, including that large group who happen to have brown skins.[7]

With the assistance of the NAACP, Negroes won the fight to keep their schools open. Later, when a bond issue was presented to the citizens of Atlanta, Negroes renewed their campaign, and the school board was forced to agree to use part of the funds for building and improving Negro schools.

Walter White became assistant secretary of the NAACP in 1918, when the organization was approximately nine years old. The Association needed a man who could investigate lynchings and other disorders while mingling freely with whites. Walter White could "pass" and filled the qualifications admirably. He was a southerner who was familiar with the ways of white people in the South. Not only this, but he was courageous, alert, and eager. Following his investigations of lynchings, he appeared before many audiences reporting his findings. When James Weldon Johnson resigned his post as executive secretary, White assumed the duties of the position. For thirty-one years, he fought to win full rights and opportunities for everybody, equal schools for all citizens, equal salaries for all teachers, and equal facilities in all public services.

The new NAACP secretary was popular as a lyceum speaker at colleges, and his duties with the Association required him to make hundreds of speeches in communities where branches were located. The speaker gave his audience the impression of a widely traveled, well-read, busy man of the world. As a social reformer, the secretary was dead set against compromise and was willing to lose a whole battle rather than accept a partial victory. His uncompromising stand on issues of civil rights led his opponents to label his program a stumbling block to progress "which to be lasting must be slow and gradual." This led White to say to his audiences that a country cannot exist half democratic. In 1949, White made a ten-day tour through the Midwest, speaking on civil rights wherever he addressed NAACP branch chapters and other groups in Illinois, Iowa, Missouri, Kansas, and Ohio.

When the NAACP was conducting its program for FEPC legislation, White spoke in its behalf in many places. For example, in an address at Eden Park in San Francisco in July, 1945, the orator remarked:

The vicious, below-the-belt attack on the FEPC by a reactionary Senate and House coalition is the most ominous portent of the possible future course of America which can be imagined. Eastland and Bilbo would be powerless did they not have quiet behind-the-scene assistance of Republicans and Democrats who want to kill the FEPC without permitting it to come to a vote. They do not want to face their constituents when reelection comes. We must see to it that there is a recorded vote and that those who fail shall not return to Congress.

Walter White spoke on a variety of subjects, and, once, when he addressed teachers in South Carolina in April, 1946, he told 3,000 people that the "crisis which faces the world today must be solved soon. There must be one world or none." Then, in Columbia, Tennessee, White scored British and American diplomacy. He added that "indifference, backwardness and the prejudice, not ideologies, are running people into the arms of Russia. No matter how many bombs are dropped or how many guns are fired, that burning desire for freedom by all people of the earth, regardless of color, cannot be stopped."[8]

Though not an emotional speaker, Walter White was aggressive in his presentation. This led some white people and newspapers to brand him as a furious agitator, too vindictive to accomplish worthwhile results for his race. A *Pittsburgh Courier* columnist, in an unfriendly article, wrote that "White could be of more service to his followers if he could understand statesmanship. But, unfortunately, it seems that White is saturated with vainglory."[9]

What about Walter White's qualifications as a public speaker? In his autobiography, the NAACP secretary described one of his first speaking efforts when he was on a program with James Weldon Johnson, who had come to Atlanta to organize a branch of the NAACP. White said:

It happened that at the Atlanta meeting I sat nearest to the platform, next to the gentle Dr. Hope. Suddenly I was called upon, to my dismay, to say a few words. Caught off guard, I nervously asked Dr. Hope what I should say. "Tell them about the NAACP," he advised with a perfectly straight face.

I launched into an impassioned and, I fear, a rabble-rousing speech. "We have got to show these white people that we aren't going to stand being pushed around any longer. As Patrick Henry said, so must we, 'Give me liberty, or give me death!' "

The audience loved it. But when I looked at the school principal, his face was ashen with terror, as he saw his job go glimmering when news of the meeting got back to the superintendent and school board.[10]

In May, 1947, the author heard Walter White give a lecture at Hampton Institute, Virginia, on the topic: "Can America Survive Racial Prejudice?" Though not eloquent, the speaker's ideas were well organized and supported with facts. He gave reasons why he believed democracy could not survive racial prejudice, but he employed none of that vocal variety that gifted orators use to evoke emotional response from their hearers. Ludlow W. Werner, then editor of the *New York Age,* said, "Walter White's style of delivery is effective. He acts like a lawyer presenting facts dispassionately in summation before a jury."[11]

The NAACP secretary was continually doing something, and this was an asset to his winning and unifying his audience to support his program. Winston Churchill, Franklin D. Roosevelt, Harry S. Truman, and John F. Kennedy were elected to leadership because each one promised to do something. Roosevelt promised a New Deal, Churchill promised victory, Truman promised a Square Deal, Eisenhower promised that he would go to Korea, and Kennedy indicated he would get this country moving again. White promised that he would agitate for total democracy for Negroes, because "democracy cannot exist half free." Negroes believed what White said from the platform, because of his reputation with the NAACP, his personality, and his identification with his audiences in seeking first-class citizenship. On the other hand, White had little to do with an audience called the "action crowd," who held the torch of "black power." He was aware that such auditorium mobs turned off their intellects and reason, and thus he practiced audience control by poise and factual presentation. He knew that emotionalism caused nonviolent devotees to lose their restraint in the face of provocation. Even before an aroused audience like the members of an NAACP branch, White considered his task to introduce the nature of the civil-rights issue at the moment, to arouse interest, to establish his right to speak on the subject, to furnish a background of the problems confronting Negroes, and to convince his hearers that serious problems confronted them; and by factual information, he enabled his listeners to let their actions be governed by logical reasoning rather than in effective emotionality. As a result of this approach, the orator had a stronger appeal with his "absent audience" who took time to read editorials on his speeches, radio summaries of his addresses, and releases of his addresses by the NAACP.

It is very difficult, though not impossible, to measure the influence of Walter White as NAACP secretary during his term. Many are his merits as a public figure in the field of human relations. His chief service to the civil-rights movement and cause was in stimulating people to think straight about an emotional subject or issue, about the evil of racial bias, and about the methods of solving this complex problem. In brief, his influence was mainly effective in the role of a fact-finder and agitator in the protest movement. Edwin R. Embree, friend in the cause of racial advancement, has probably made the best appraisal of Walter White in the following summary: "He has been fighting giants all his life. He is as full of zest as Little David, the shepherd boy. He is as fierce an enemy of the Philistines in our society as the great King David of Israel. And every campaign is to him as personal as the Biblical duel between David and Goliath."[12]

ROY WILKINS ("OLD PRO")

The present chief of the National Association for the Advancement of Colored People is Roy Wilkins, who has been called "Old Pro" because of his skill in heading probably the most efficient Negro civil-rights organization in the nation. Under his leadership, the NAACP refrained from becoming involved in alliances with certain undesirable groups—most notably the Communist party and the John Birch Society. More than this, he refused absolutely to get the Association involved with the program of "black power" so vigorously advocated by SNCC and CORE. Comprehensive accounts of Wilkins and his role in keeping the NAACP free from any red taints are adequately discussed in Wilson Record's *Race and Radicalism* (1964) and Louis E. Lomax's *The Negro Revolt* (1962). Yet, in spite of the sound record achieved by the NAACP under the leadership of Roy Wilkins, the organization has to deal with dissension within the body politic. From the outside, adult critics, who have been extremely impressed with the demonstrations of CORE and SNCC, have called the NAACP "too conservative for its own good."

Criticism has not disturbed the NAACP chief too much, since a person or organization that is doing something is always a target for criticism. The severest enemies of the organization will attest to the fact that it is one of the most efficient of its kind. It has nearly 500,000 members in 15 branches in 50 states. Its income has averaged $1.25 million annually since 1960 ($3,260,000 in 1968), and the majority of this amount is raised from membership fees and other contributions. The NAACP's program includes an efficient lobby in Washington, a research department to gather facts to support its program, machinery for getting Negro protest before high governmental officials and the strong white power structure, and provisions for legal aid to any Negro who has a worthy cause needing assistance. The Association's work in getting Negroes to register and vote brought tremendous gains, and they were accomplished, according to Wilkins, "not by speechmaking, sloganeering, or demonstrations but by hard work at the precinct level."

Roy Wilkins, who was born in St. Louis, Missouri, was reared in St. Paul, Minnesota, where he finished the public schools and was later graduated with a degree in journalism from the University of Minnesota at Minneapolis. As a career officer in the NAACP, Wilkins started at the bottom of the ladder and moved gradually to the topmost rung. He joined the staff in 1931 as assistant executive secretary, was editor of *Crisis* magazine from 1934 to 1949, and was its administrator.

In the wake of sit-ins, Roy Wilkins soon recognized the handicapping restrictions of the internal politics of the organization. Few branch officers[13] have shown a willingness to criticize the national NAACP policies in public, except, perhaps, for men like Raymond Brown, once president of the Jersey City branch of the Association. Once, during a television broadcast, Brown bluntly told Louis Lomax, who interviewed him, that the NAACP is "asleep at the switch. Hell! they don't know where the switch is!" In general, however, the national officials and branch leaders, whose qualities supplement each other, have achieved what neither of them could have done alone. Criticism has been sharp, yet Roy Wilkins has never faltered. Calmly, cheerfully, he has gone forward, lifting the spirits of his followers, and striking hypocrisy wherever he finds it. Always, when his critics attack him, they find him calm and ready.

What kind of speaker is the chief of the NAACP? James L. Hicks, editor of New York's *Amsterdam News,* told the author on October 13, 1963, that he had covered Roy Wilkins from the moment he took command of the NAACP in Atlanta at midcentury to the present. Hicks said:

Having grown up more or less in the NAACP movement, Roy Wilkins speaks on the platform with the warmness and respect of a young man in a family who went away, made good and based on his intimate knowledge of the family has dropped in to tell the other members of the family, including papa and mama, just what procedure to follow in their efforts to be successful. As such, Roy does not lecture his audiences, but communes with them in an almost homespun, chatty way.

Since he has travelled most of the routes that many of his fellow NAACP members will have to take, he almost invariably raises his right forefinger to the side of his head and says something like this: "Now when you get to Jackson, Mississippi, you may run into ————." He then proceeds to intimately link what he is saying to a segment of his audience so that there is authority in his every word.

His speeches are not scholarly presentations such as those of Ralph Bunche. I covered him recently when he spoke at the funeral of three bomb victims in Birmingham and I was surprised to find that he is not very much at home when he is seeking to comfort an audience in a moment of sorrow. He got off into a discussion of the Bible about which he is well informed and he ended up preaching more than did Rev. Martin Luther King who followed him. The net results were nil.

He is at best when he is talking for what he is—a hardbitten newspaper man, a labor leader or organizational man, trained in fighting and in the habit of being required to say things in four-letter words that people understand.

The editor of the *California Eagle*, Loren Miller, said, in 1963, that Wilkins "depends upon factual presentations of his materials and rarely rises to oratorical flourishes or resounding phrases. The impact of what he says often appears only after study and audience reflection." No matter where he speaks, Wilkins always has facts to present. When concluding his annual report at the fifty-third annual membership meeting at the national headquarters in New York City on January 2, 1962, Wilkins remarked, "I pledge you that we shall enlarge our operations, sharpen our assault, and broaden our attack in 1962."

Attending the funeral of three bomb victims in a church at Birmingham in September, 1963, were Martin Luther King, Jr., and Roy Wilkins, who shared a place on the speaker's platform. Wilkins told a tense, but quiet crowd of 4,000 listeners that "these deaths should inspire Birmingham Negroes to press forward in the crusade for rights and redemption." Although, as indicated above, newsman James L. Hicks of the *Amsterdam News* was somewhat disappointed in Wilkins's ability to comfort an audience in mourning, it seems that a *St. Petersburg* (Florida) *Times* reporter was differently impressed, for he remarked, "As Wilkins' final words rang out, the mother of one of the girls collapsed and was helped out of the church."[14]

The author, who has heard Roy Wilkins speak on numerous occasions, noted how the NAACP chief created effective response by his supporting materials, consisting of facts and examples. Wilkins discards the peroration so that he may spend his last few minutes in an abstract of his arguments for the purpose of making a final impression through the method of final summary. The orator can no more cheat his audience out of facts about their rights anymore than he could cheat them out of their money. At times his facts tend to irritate some of his listeners, as when he employs diatribes against oppression and discrimination. He has a perfect naturalness, a strong individuality, and dignity. He charges upon his foes, using logic like a horse, runs them down, tramples them in the dust, and finally scatters them. Wilkins knows full well the pitfalls of emotionalism and its tendency to make an audience impractical, such as has happened in the cry of "black power."

As a public speaker, Wilkins lacks the dramatic flair of Martin Luther King, Jr., and the persuasiveness of former CORE leader James Farmer. Wilkins admitted once in an interview with Louis E. Lomax that he was not a dramatic speaker or personality. "I can do all right on the platform but I'm not the spellbinder some of the other fellows are." The rank and file of Negroes would like to have Roy Wilkins take them up on the mount of transfiguration where they may catch a gleam of the falling star of segregation and discrimination. Although he is not silver-tongued, Wilkins performs best in the role of "Old Pro"—the modern symbol of a twentieth-century organizational man. The NAACP chief persuades his listeners with facts, but he cannot explain how he does it. He is a rhetorician who uses a system of logic of the highest order. His speeches are serious in tone and thereby demand a kind of mental alertness that prevents the hearers from being lulled to sleep, because he lays bare the innermost feelings of his inspired soul.

When home critics charged the NAACP with a "letdown" in vigor, by succumbing to economic pressure, Wilkins rallied to its defense by saying that the intellectuality of the NAACP prevents it from capitalizing on mass appeal designed to arouse emotions and nothing else. Recognizing Wilkins's ability to hold his own with critics, Dr. Channing Tobias, the late NAACP board chairman, remarked once that Wilkins is "a great rebutter." This remark is a well-deserved accolade. Since the rebutter is most effective with facts, Loren Miller, an attorney connected with the *California Eagle,* made an apt remark when he said, "Wilkins is an effective, but not spectacular or stirring speaker. As he depends upon factual presentation of his materials, he rarely rises to oratorical flourishes."

In conclusion, the best tribute that one can pay the NAACP chief is that he has a mind for putting creative leadership at the helm of the Association. That the NAACP has one of the most effective lobbyists (Clarence Mitchell) in the nation is indeed a credit to the organizational ability of a man like Wilkins. Lobbying, according to Senator J. William Fulbright, Arkansas Democrat, "is held by the court to be an important expression of the right to petition, the healthy essence of the democratic process." In addition, Wilkins has increased the Association's sources of research and distribution of information.

Footnotes, Chapter 7

1. Carter G. Woodson, *Negro Orators and Their Orations,* p. 663.
2. John Hope Franklin, *From Slavery to Freedom,* p. 493.
3. James Weldon Johnson, *Negro Americans, What Now?.*
4. James Weldon Johnson, *Along This Way,* p. 79.
5. Walter White, *A Man Called White,* pp. 32–34.
6. Johnson, *Along This Way,* p. 316.
7. Edwin R. Embree, *13 Against the Odds,* p. 82.
8. *Pittsburgh Courier,* April 13, 1946, p. 1.
9. Joseph D. Bibb, *Pittsburgh Courier,* October 21, 1950.
10. White, *A Man Called White,* p. 34.
11. Personal letter to the author from Ludlow W. Werner.
12. Embree, *13 Against the Odds,* p. 71.
13. Louis E. Lomax, *The Negro Revolt,* pp. 152–153.
14. "Alabama Bomb Victims Buried," *St. Petersburg Times* (Florida), September 19, 1963, p. 6-A.

8 / Public Addresses of Negro Women

Compared with Negro men, Negro women are considerably better educated, and their religious organizations, sororities, and fraternal clubs and societies have developed effective leadership on the local, state, and national level. Simeon Booker, a journalist, has said, "A tremendous pool of brains, insight and knowledge has been distributed among groups of women."[1] Heading sororities, church organizations, and federations of women's clubs are women with college, master's, doctoral, law, and medical degrees, and many of them are effective public speakers. However, most Negro women leave national crusading to male front-runners. If any organization of women could employ a staff of civil-rights workers and orators, we surely could expect it from the 800,000-member National Council of Negro Women whose community programs are very notable. In addition, the Association of Colored Women has national programs centered on social affairs, humanitarianism, and fund-raising for numerous undertakings. The Alpha Kappa Alpha Sorority has a progressive leader in Mrs. Julia B. Purnell, Grand Basileus, and the Daughter Elks have Mrs. Nettie B. Smith as Grand Daughter Ruler.

Black women have been, and are, ardent advocates for the uplift of "the man farthest down," and they have given their share of topflight female orators to this nation. They are worthy of the tribute paid to women speakers in the American dream projected by Doris Yoakim: "They brought simplicity of expression, sincerity of purpose, and enhancement of goals over speaker. They helped mightily in toppling oratory off its rhetorical stilts and in grinding it toward a more natural straight-forward and conversational manner of communication."[2]

There are scores of fine female orators among the Negro population, and some of the more prominent ones are Nannie Burroughs, Charlotte Hawkins Brown, Mary McLeod Bethune, Lillian Wheeler Smith, Belle Hendon, Daisy Lampkins, Mary Church Terrell, Dorothy Ferebee, Marjorie Parker, Julia B. Purnell, Lucy Miller Mitchell, Florence Lovell Dyett, Aurelia Mallory, Sadie Alexander, Gloria Richardson, and Ruby Hurley. Thousands of listeners have been stirred by their sincerity, impatience for a fundamental change in racial status, and desire to enrich the souls of men with art, music, and song.

PLATFORM PERSONALITIES

Among the many women who have achieved prestige as orators is Belle Hendon of Chicago. She has moved listeners with her pleasing voice and polished manner of delivery. Her auditors have been impressed as she poured forth passages of exquisite tenderness mingled with strong denunciation of racial injustices. Lillian Wheeler Smith, poet and writer of Detroit, is another first-rate woman orator who has filled lecture engagements all over the United States. Announcing one of her lectures, a Detroit journal said: "Some of the local clergymen are preparing to surprise their congregations during the holidays by presenting to them the lecturer and poetess, Lillian

Wheeler Smith, who is in Detroit preparatory to starting on her transcontinental lecture tour. According to her manager, the tour will take the artist to the Pacific Coast."[3] The lecturer, a teacher of dramatics and elocution, founded the Parliament, a Detroit club. Of her work on behalf of the Negroes in Detroit, Mrs. Carolina Johnson, secretary of the Parliament, said:

The Parliament, a nonpartisan, political, and cultural club, presents Lillian Smith as one who earned the reputation of a fine orator. She has poise and personality, and through her efforts the people of Detroit can thank Mrs. Smith for breaking down several doors which were closed to us because no one had previously presented our plea so eloquently. We challenge any Negro on the platform, who might presume that he can excell Lillian Wheeler Smith in oratorical ability.[4]

Her oratory has been greatly enhanced by an extended knowledge of Negro history. As an ambassador of goodwill, her eloquence has been the medium for telling Americans about the notable contributions of Negroes to American civilization.

The woman orator is not always a scholar or a member of the elite. She is often a worker who mounts the platform and eloquently pleads the cause of her fellow laborers. For instance, at the 1932 Communist nominating convention, one delegate, Laura Crosby, a Chicago stockyard worker, stirred her audience thus:

Comrades and fellow workers, I present Chicago, a great big beautiful city of starvation. Here in Chicago, when the workers come out in demonstration, we are lined up against the wall at the point of machine guns, and that isn't low and dirty enough to do to the working class. The dicks took baseball bats and whips to use against our comrades.

First of all, I want to speak to the Negro people especially because we have been the most oppressed nationality in the world. We get the lowest pay, the worst jobs. Never before in history can any of us look and see where the Negro had the privilege to run for vice-president. . . .

Fellow workers, you understand we are not only fighting for that little lousy amount of $15 a week. We are fighting for equal rights and social equality for all Negro people. Fellow workers, the only party that organizes the Negro workers with white workers, the Communist party has got the world of workers stirred up and don't forget it.[5]

SADIE MOSSELL ALEXANDER

When the complete history of the oratory of Negro women is written, Sadie Mossell Alexander, a Philadelphia lawyer, will be included as one whose mission is social reform, human justice, and liberty for all. In connection with her law practice, she is often pressed into service of the black man's cause, and also assumes an important role in public affairs. Sadie Alexander, without formal training in public speaking, has demonstrated unusual talent and power as an orator. She maintains that a good speaker must, first of all, have "a source of knowledge and next be able to tell it in language simple enough to be understood by every person in the audience." Although her appeals are primarily to the intellect and reason, the orator can move the emotions of her hearers. Her straightforward words go right to the heart of an evil. When she speaks, the woman is forgotten and only the nobleness of her message is important.

In commenting upon the platform delivery of Sadie Alexander, Eustace Gay, editor of the *Philadelphia Tribune,* wrote: "Sadie Alexander has a good command of language and a splendid choice of words. Her voice and carriage are both forceful and convincing."[6] One of the orator's best speeches was delivered in 1944 when she responded to an address made by Mrs. Eleanor Roosevelt. Alexander said: "Mrs. Roosevelt, you have by practice, and not by precept, demonstrated to our church, our race, our nation, and to the whole world, that you respect the rights and privileges guaranteed every man, not only by the Constitution of these United States, and endowed by God, the Creator of every good and perfect gift." The sentiments expressed in this speech[7] brought thundering applause from the church delegates of the General Conference of the African Methodist Episcopal Church in 1944.

MARY CHURCH TERRELL

Mary Church Terrell, like dozens of other Negro women leaders, overcame certain odds to become a leading orator. She was especially sensitive to discrimination and racial slights. Mary Terrell was the daughter of R. R. Church, a respected citizen of Memphis, Tennessee, who devoted his life to securing a square deal for Negro citizens of Memphis. She was educated at Oberlin College in Ohio, graduating with the M.A. degree in 1888. Later, she studied in France and Germany where she became proficient in the languages of those two countries. Her career has been varied: a teacher in the District of Columbia schools and Wilberforce University, and a member of the Washington Board of Education. Then, for a while, the orator lectured in the employ of the Woman's Suffrage Association. While teaching in D.C. schools, she met her husband, who later became a Federal Court judge in the nation's capital.

Besides lecturing for the Woman's Suffrage Association, Mary Church Terrell did a great deal of political speaking. She spoke in behalf of Ruth Hanna McCormick in the campaign of 1929. After observing her political speaking, Carrie Chapman Catt once said that Mrs. Terrell "presented a pleasing presence and possesses what the world called a *platform presence.*"[8] As an orator, Mrs. Terrell has rendered the cause of woman suffrage a great service. Perhaps it was because of this work that she was listed in Oberlin College's "100 famous alumni." Mrs. Terrell said that she found speaking easier than writing. However, one of her short stories was published in the *Washington Post;* and she contributed articles to numerous magazines. In 1940 she published her autobiography, *A Colored Woman in a White World.*

Mary Church Terrell made extensive lecture tours and spoke on the progress of Negro women and kindred subjects. She said that she enjoyed public speaking, especially filling lecture engagements in the South. On one occasion, she was invited to speak at the International Congress of Women in Berlin, Germany. She gave her address in German and received a great ovation. Then, at another session, she made a second speech in French. One correspondent said: "This achievement on the part of a colored woman, added to the eloquent diction, a fine appearance, carried the audience by storm and she had to respond three times to the encores before they were satisfied. It was more than a personal triumph, it was a triumph for her race."[9]

NANNIE HELEN BURROUGHS

The motivating life interest of Nannie Helen Burroughs was the educational uplift of Negro youth. This was why she founded the National Training School for Girls in Washington, D.C. Her profound interest in every progressive and cultural movement of her race led Sadie Daniels, a biographer, to say, "She is active in various movements for the betterment and economic progress of Negroes."[10]

Nannie Burroughs was born in Orange, Virginia, on May 2, 1883. Her parents were free people of color whose ancestors were owners of farms, or found a livelihood in mechanics. Her biographer said, "She sprang, then, from that fortunate class of freedmen whose energy and ability enabled them to start being economically independent soon after the Civil War."[11] When she was a child, her parents moved to Washington, D.C., where she completed public school training in domestic arts. Sometime later, in Philadelphia, Miss Burroughs obtained employment as bookkeeper and associate editor of the *Christian Banner,* after which she worked at the headquarters of the National Baptist Convention in Louisville, Kentucky.

The orator's interest in public speaking dated back to her high school days when she was a member of the Harriet Beecher Stowe Literary Society. The members of this club had the opportunity for oratorical expression. The press has not published any speeches of Miss Burroughs, because she spoke only from notes. She remarked, "I speak from sketchy notes or extemporaneously when I think I'm full enough to surcharge the listeners. I am in earnest, and I have no axe to grind. I do not speak when I'm lukewarm on a subject. I do not speak to show off." The orator often delivered speeches to raise funds for missionary work. On one occasion, she addressed the National Baptist Convention at Richmond, Virginia, in 1910, using the subject "Hindered from Helping." The speech was based upon the Bible verse: "Ye entered not in yourselves and they that were entering ye hindered." Following this address, the Convention elected her secretary of the Women's Auxiliary, then a feeble organization, and she breathed life into it.

What kind of a speaker was Nannie Burroughs? Commenting upon her style of delivery, W. N. Hartshorn said, "She has a remarkable facility of speech and she impressed her personality upon those associated with her."[12] Once Miss Burroughs was invited to participate in an interracial forum, sponsored by the Association for the Study of Negro Life and History meeting in Philadelphia. To those Negroes who were ashamed that the race had been born in slavery, she said: "Let me tell you that with all the vices and crimes of slavery, we got more out of it than those who had us."[13] The orator's soundest advice to Negroes appeared in *Negro Digest* for July, 1950, and it is found in these words: "Get used to being colored. Have faith in yourselves and in your race. Negroes who buy Cadillacs to bolster their ego are whistling in the dark. They are confused and don't want to be left out of things. The Negro must stop apologizing for not being white. He must qualify for the position that he wants."

CHARLOTTE HAWKINS BROWN

As an orator, Charlotte Hawkins Brown, like Ralph Waldo Emerson, should be classified in the field of general culture. She has worked consistently to uplift the Negro culturally, and, before she died, her school in Sedalia, North Carolina, was the only finishing school for Negro youth in the United States. Dr. Brown believed that "after all, the success of the American Negro depended upon his contacts with other races who, through the years, have had greater advantages of learning the proper approach to life and its problems." The orator preached that the Negro should acquire the social graces. She stated this most clearly in a radio speech broadcast over CBS on the "Wings Over Jordan" program on March 10, 1940. Thus spoke the orator:

The little courtesies, the gentle voice, correct grooming; a knowledge of when to sit, when to stand; how to open the door and close it; good manners in public places, such as railway stations, moving picture houses, and other places where we are constantly under observation—the acquisition of these graces will go a long way in securing recognition of ability needed to cope with human society, and will remove some of the commonest objections to our presence in large numbers.[14]

Because of her temperament and training, Charlotte Hawkins Brown could meet her audiences on a common ground. The secret of her platform presence and personal magnetism was that she was thoroughly at home in the community or among strangers.

"The story of this woman's life is nothing new," said *Brown American*.[15] She believed that "after all, the success of the

American Negro depends upon his contacts with others of all races." Therefore, her life followed "the pattern of the pioneer in every human undertaking: not much money; an idea; desertion by those who might have helped; perseverance and, at long last, the slow, painful dawn of understanding on the part of those who first stood apart."

Again, like Emerson, Charlotte Hawkins Brown never doubted that a part of her calling in life was to practice eloquence. She delivered from 100 to 150 speeches annually. "I have always been able to express myself in public," said Dr. Brown. "I have had some formal training in high and normal school speechmaking." A passion for freedom of thought and action was the inspiration of her success in public speaking. To convince an audience, she believed that a speaker must feel and know the things of which he speaks. She felt also that one must, above all, be sincere and support his cause with factual testimony. Charlotte Brown's chief persuasive power had its source in her graceful and charming manner, for she earned the title, "First Lady of Culture." She always had a word of commendation for the people of the community in which she spoke—using choice diction, yet simple enough for the masses to understand. At times, her rhetoric was high-flown and contained symbolic and poetic phrases. In ceremonial addresses, she exalted her tone but her speech remained conversational, flowed easily, and was enjoyable to the audience.

Benjamin N. Brawley said of her: "While raising money for Palmer Hall, the principal was making an impression on the state and the country. She bustled with energy, was effective in public address, and somehow inspired confidence with her audience."[16] In 1936, the orator was the first Negro to lecture at Berea College in Kentucky. J. S. Ledbetter, a traveling Buick salesman, mailed an article about her speech to the *Missionary Review of the World,* and it was published in the June, 1936, issue of the magazine. The article said in part:

In a scholarly manner, with a cultivated voice and gestures of unusual significance, a little black woman, Charlotte Hawkins Brown, protégée of Alice Freeman Palmer, founder and promoter of a unique school for her people in the Piedmont section of North Carolina, in an eloquent address and impassioned plea, challenged 1,600 or more students of Berea College in an address entitled: "What the Negro Youth Expects of the White Youth in Their Tomorrow." In her climax, the orator issued the following challenge to white college students:

There is no gift within the range of American people that cannot be yours as American white boys and girls. The industries, the wealth, the government are already bequeathed to you. Tomorrow the reins will be put into your hands. From the position of President, Senator, and Congressman, to the small but even more important offices of county sheriff, and the city councilman, you will have the administration of the American nation. The youth of my race, a minority group tied to you, in spite of whatever may be said, 250 years of unrequited toil of your forebears, are wondering if in your effort to achieve a greater civilization, you will ride roughshod over them, or in Christian institutions like this, built around a religion intelligently conceived and passionately believed, you will develop that sense of fairness and justice, that expression of neighborly-mindedness for the development of a finer and better America in which to live.

MARY MCLEOD BETHUNE

One of the most daring personalities that ever lived in this nation was Mary McLeod Bethune, former president and founder of Bethune-Cookman College in Daytona Beach, Florida. Her voice and platform decorum were known to thousands of people, because for more than forty-five years she spoke in hundreds of hamlets and nearly every important city in the United States. One of her greatest pleasures was advancing the causes of the Negro or lauding the achievements of black women who gradually were becoming an organized group with prestige. She was born in Mayesville, South Carolina, of slave parents, the fifteenth of seventeen children. In spite of the condition of poverty in which she was born, Mary McLeod Bethune was determined to get an education, and therefore attended Scotia Seminary in Concord, North Carolina. She dared to cross the boundaries of hatred and to rise above misunderstanding and prejudice. With the meager sum of one dollar and a half, she founded an institution for the training of Negro youth in the Deep South. Today Bethune-Cookman College is worth more than $5 million, and its alumni include thousands of trained, industrious, and loyal citizens.

For ten years, Mrs. Bethune was director of the Office of Negro Affairs in the National Youth Administration. She traveled over the country pleading for the inclusion of the Negro in American life. For her outstanding work in the field of racial relations, she was given the Spingarn Medal and the Thomas Jefferson Award. Her contributions to American life led Ida Tarbell, in 1932, to include the orator among the fifty greatest women in American history. In 1937, the *Literary Digest* reported that "she is worthy of being successor to Booker T. Washington."[17] During World War I, the American Red Cross sent Mrs. Bethune on a lecture tour through the District of Columbia, Maryland, Virginia, and West Virginia to boost Negro morale in fighting for the United States. In the fall of 1945 and under the auspices of the Southern Conference for Human Welfare, she made a speaking tour that carried her through ten southern cities, including Birmingham, Alabama; Durham, Greensboro, High Point, and Winston-Salem in North Carolina; and Savannah, Georgia. The membership of the Southern Conference for Human Welfare increased by 15,000, and more than 50,000 people in mixed audiences heard her speak.

Mary Bethune's speaking ability was first noticed while she was a student at Scotia Seminary. One biographer said, "She had a quick, logical mind, and debating and public speaking were her strong points."[18] When she was building Bethune-

Cookman College, the educator traveled widely and lectured to raise funds to carry on her educational work. It was at this time that Benjamin Brawley remarked:

Meanwhile the president of the institution was becoming a national figure. With a glowing personality, a pleasing voice, and a sense of humor, she has been most popular on the public platform. It has fallen her lot to appear before many distinguished audiences and on many occasions, one of the most important being the great patriotic meeting in Belasco Theatre in Washington in December, 1917.[19]

Commenting on the educator's platform delivery, Toki Schalk Johnson, women's editor of the *Pittsburgh Courier,* said in November, 1948: "Mrs. Bethune is the spiritual, visionary, idealistic type of speaker who can sway her audiences through emotional appeal. She cannot be beat there for her appeal to all groups, first, as an intelligent Negro woman, and second, through the appeal of her spiritual being which hits the right note with her public." On another occasion, Channing H. Tobias, himself a great pulpit orator, added:

The personality of Mary McLeod Bethune was too dynamic to be confined to a single college campus and soon she became an orator who was in demand on many occasions by her own race and the white group. Now she is regarded as one of the most attractive speakers in America regardless of race. I have heard her at Carnegie Hall along with Rabbi Wise and other distinguished speakers, and [on] another occasion with Carrie Chapman Catt and always she has impressed her audiences not only [with] the force of her eloquence but [with] the sincerity of her message and spirit.

Harkening back to his college days at Virginia State College, J. Farley Ragland, once journalist for *Journal and Guide,* waxed eloquent in his column "Southside Highlights" on August 4, 1945, by giving his first impression of Mary McLeod Bethune during a chapel speech. The journalist said:

It was noon during the chapel hour at a big city southern college, hundreds of happy boys and girls sat expectantly in the spacious audience hall. A celebrity was visiting the campus and was to speak that morning. The president of the college seemed vividly inspired as he eloquently introduced the esteemed visitor. A stately brown lady, with a most gracious smile, dramatically arose and faced the audience.

She began to talk in a charming manner and cultured voice that was electrifying. She held the students spell-bound and enraptured with stirring words of wisdom, truth, and beauty. She told of her early efforts, and of her hopes and dreams.

Thunderous applause greeted her as she impressively ended her short but powerful speech. That was my first meeting with Mrs. Mary McLeod Bethune.

Each speaker, like every great musician and singer, must develop his own individual style, platform and vocal techniques that he superimposes upon his knowledge of speaking theory. Mary Bethune could not be confused with any other orator of her times. Having had the privilege of listening to the educator a dozen times, the author observed that she utilized whatever would increase her spiritual persuasion. Rackham Holt, one of her biographers, stated that "before lecturing, to keep her throat clear and free of coughing, she read from Mary Baker Eddy's *Science and Health.*"[20] Many times she did not know in advance the nature of her audience or what she would say first. Being a deeply spiritual woman, she prayed silently before taking the platform to speak. She prayed, "I will be thy mouth and teach thee what thou shalt say." The educator was an inspired speaker and had the gift to interpret God to her fellowman. The right words came to her in some mysterious manner. She said that she "did not know how or whence." The author, as a listener in the audience, observed that Mrs. Bethune received considerable inspiration from her listeners in much the same manner as does an athlete from the cheers of his spectators. The educator said that she was lazy about preparing speech manuscripts. Notes were sometimes impediments that interfered with visual directness with her audience. The interplay between the orator and her audience brought tremendous response from the listeners.

Whatever may have been Mrs. Bethune's shortcomings as a college administrator, she was without doubt a powerful orator who held her own with any female contemporary. Holt said, "She had the uncanny knack of retaining and using words and phrases aptly and in creating object lessons by turning personal experiences into richly adorned parables."[21] On the other hand, the author has heard the criticism that the educator was egotistic and referred to herself and her personal experiences in violation of good taste.

It appears that confidence in God and in herself gave Dr. Bethune the personal strength to rise above the crowds. By this faith, she remarked many times: "I am Mary McLeod Bethune, I am black, I am a Negro, and I am going somewhere!" This was the essence of her pride in the black race, similar to that felt by Marcus Garvey. We do know that she used her speaking gifts to plead the black man's cause to the end that he might experience the good life, that he might be free from fear and want, and that he might receive justice at the hands of the courts. Her eloquence was one of the greatest forces toward facilitating the progress of the Negro and the man farthest down.

WOMEN SPEAKERS IN RETROSPECT

Women speakers have made sincere efforts to relate the insights of the Christian faith and community to the modern woman's quest for self-confidence and understanding, as well as women's fulfillment in the vocational world. Women are no longer engaged in the hard battle for woman suffrage, for they have won, and their emancipation has brought obvious advantages. Female orators apparently neither harbor feelings of an uneasy coexistence for their sex, nor do they feel they are examples of the two extremes of the nineteenth century: namely, the *showcase* and the *drudge*. In delivering their speeches, women have shown a keen perception of the nation's problems. They have demonstrated a brutal honesty as to how they can take in stride the pressures and values of the modern world. Thus, when addressing female audiences, the women orators endeavor to make the gentler sex aware that they must accept the fact that they are a part of the universal aspects of human existence—that cannot be "prettied over." Women's day programs have become forums where orators continued to tell women to be themselves, cultivate an appreciation for the arts and homemaking, and stoop down to assist in lifting up the poor, the indigent, and the "man farthest down."

Footnotes, Chapter 8

1. Simeon Booker, *Black Man's America.*
2. Doris Yoakim, "Women's Introduction to the American Platfrom," in *History of American Public Address* ed. N. Brigance, pp. 188–189.
3. From newspaper clipping carrying no identification except "Detroit."
4. Letter from Mrs. Carolina Johnson, February 14, 1947.
5. *Daily Worker,* June 3, 1932.
6. Letter from Mr. Gay to the author, June 12, 1947.
7. From written manuscript sent to the author by Mrs. Alexander. It was returned to the owner.
8. *Current Biography,* June, 1942, p. 81.
9. Benjamin Brawley, *Negro Builders and Heroes,* p. 361.
10. Sadie Daniels, *Women Builders.*
11. William N. Hartshorn, *Era of Progress,* p. 276.
12. Ibid.
13. *Opportunity Magazine* 2 (May, 1924): 155.

14. *Brown American,* Fall and Winter, 1944–1945, p. 9.
15. Ibid.
16. Brawley, *Negro Builders and Heroes,* p. 286.
17. *Literary Digest,* March 6, 1937, p. 8.
18. Ben Richardson, *Great American Negroes,* p. 140.
19. Brawley, *Negro Builders and Heroes,* p. 286.
20. Rackham Holt, *Mary McLeod Bethune.*
21. Ibid., p. 162.

9 / Labor Leaders

"One of the most important indications of the changing relationships of the Negro in American life," said E. Franklin Frazier, "has been the emergence of leaders of Negro labor."[1] For some reason, the work of early labor leaders was overshadowed by the prestige of intellectual and political leaders. While primarily an educator, Booker T. Washington was also responsible for developing in freedmen a sense of the dignity of labor. However, Washington had no plans for organizing Negro workers into craft unions, nor did he give much encouragement to Negro workers to join existing unions.

Most educational leaders have viewed only the racial aspect of the labor situation. In the words of Sterling D. Spero, "They consider the plight of Negro workers racial rather than a working class problem."[2] Yet, W. E. B. Du Bois noted that the problems of Negro workers were identical to those of all workers. The NAACP has been inactive in the labor movement, though it fought for the entrance of Negro plumbers, electricians, and railway workers in unions. Meanwhile, the traditional policy of denying Negroes membership in unions was largely responsible for the absence of strong labor leadership in earlier days among black people. After 1925, the development of strong industrial unions paved the way for subsequent Negro leadership in trade unions.

Negro labor leaders have essentially the same mission as that of other leaders, and their speeches must be persuasive in order to attract union audiences. Usually, they express a point of view in keeping with the policies of their parent unions. Fundamentally, there is little to choose between the positions taken by AFL and CIO speakers. Negroes who have been elected to positions of union leadership have had superior platform speaking ability. Several Negro figures stand out prominently as leaders in the labor movement in the United States. They include: the late Frank R. Crosswaith, Hilton E. Hannah, A. Philip Randolph, and Willard S. Townsend. Some historians would add George L.-P. Weaver, an Assistant Secretary of Labor, because he represents the integration of Negro workers into the labor movement.

FRANK R. CROSSWAITH

The late Frank R. Crosswaith, famous leader of the Negro Labor Committee—a federation of black unions—was an ardent worker in behalf of the working class. He came to the United States from the Virgin Islands as a teen-ager and found work as an elevator operator. Dissatisfied with his meager education, he attended and graduated from the Rand School of Social Sciences. As a member of the Socialist party, Crosswaith ran unsuccessfully for several public offices. In the role of a union organizer and orator, he achieved real success. For instance, he was responsible for the creation of the powerful International Ladies Garment Workers Union (ILGWU) and helped in the organization of the Brotherhood of Sleeping Car Porters and Maids, unions for mechanics, barbers, theater employees, and laundry workers. From 1942–1947, the labor leader was a member of the New York Housing Authority. He died in June, 1965, at seventy-two years of age.

As an orator, Crosswaith was often compared with Eugene V. Debs. They both spoke persuasively and uncompromisingly for the rights of the workers they represented. Crosswaith once toured the nation as a lecturer and spoke at many colleges. Unlike Debs, Crosswaith was anti-Communist and one of the few Negro citizens active in unions during the turbulent twenties. In his platform delivery, Crosswaith never sawed the air as some speakers did. He never acted for stage effect, but spoke with lively and dynamic articulation. He was cool, considerate, reflective in timing, self-possessed, and reliant. As he moved along in his speech, his voice became clearer and freer, and there was less uneasiness in his body movements. The membership growth during his union campaigns indicated that he spoke with effectiveness, always moving the emotions and judgments of men. His vocal range was wide—from an attention-getting pitch and volume to a more harmonious and pleasant tone. Finally, Crosswaith was the ideal of vitality, and every inch of him expressed alertness and motion. He had two important requisites of a good public speaker—a melodious voice and clear, sharply defined enunciation.

HILTON E. HANNAH

The lowly Nazarene urged men to make the most of their talents and not to hide their light under a bushel. This is exactly what Hilton E. Hannah did to become a labor union official in AFL-CIO's Amalgamated Meat Cutters and Butcher Workmen of North America.[3] While a worker at the Oscar Mayer Company plant in Madison, Wisconsin, and member of Local 538, Hannah became an active member whose hard work in the Madison union led to his election to several offices. It was during 1945 and 1951, when the author worked at the Madison plant of the Oscar Mayer Company, that he met and observed the activities of Hilton Hannah in the local union. More than a decade later, newspapers publicized Hannah's meteoric advancement to a position of union leadership on the national level.

Hilton Hannah has been a member of Local 538 since 1944, the year when he worked on the "kill floor" of the Oscar Mayer Company and, at the same time, did research on collective bargaining at the grass roots for his master's thesis at University of Wisconsin. Later, Hannah was an instructor in economic and labor problems in the school for workers from 1937 until he changed jobs. He has been on the staff of the International Union since March, 1946, first as organizer, International Educational Representative, and feature writer. After his first visit to Latin America in 1953, he was appointed special assistant to the International secretary-treasurer in October, 1957. Historically and traditionally in the AMCBW, the secretary-treasurer has usually been the principal executive officer of a local union or the International.

Hilton Hannah's speaking presently is limited to special occasions, such as the Emancipation Day Centennial at McCormick Place in Chicago on August 15, 1963. On the centennial occasion, Hannah said: "The emancipated Negro has discovered that the Emancipation Proclamation like a marriage certificate or a trade union contract is no automatic ticket to the land of perpetual bliss or the state of unending harmony and peace. The Negro has discovered that the Emancipation Proclamation, like life itself, is not what you desire it, but what you make it."

In many of his speeches, the labor chief compares the plight of the American Negro with the problems of labor some years ago. "When will labor ever be satisfied? The answer is simple: Labor will be satisfied when the captains of industry cease to reach, forever, higher profits, fabulous bonuses, yachts, summer estates, and all the other fancy frills that go with them or are thrown in for good measure," remarked Hannah. "So it is with the Negro in his fight for education, equality, dignity, opportunity, and responsibility."

Like all beginning speakers, Hannah became early a diligent student of platform address. He often practiced at home, recited to his family, rehearsed gestures before a mirror in order to polish his delivery and perfect his technique. From labor research, he became well informed about the problems of labor; from literature, he learned meter and how to build a speech to a climax; and by constant effort, he acquired poise and self-confidence. Early in his career, he suffered stage fright before listeners whose faces seemed like those of hostile witnesses at a court hearing. This type of audience seemed to stifle spontaneous speech, thereby injuring his pride. However, he learned from these experiences and built self-confidence. When he was engaged by the former Redpath Chautauqua, clamorous applause from audiences persuaded the management to bring him back each year to travel several of the lecturing circuits. As a labor organizer, Hannah utilized the glittering peroration to persuade workers to join his union by persuading them of his own real faith in the labor movement. Faith in the righteousness of the labor cause was, and is, the main source of his strength. People have followed his call to membership more from faith in the orator than in the cause.

A. PHILIP RANDOLPH

Elmer A. Carter, former editor of *Opportunity* magazine, remarked once that "if one were to compile a list of outstanding labor leaders in America on the basis of ability and achievement, he would have to include A. Philip Randolph, president of the Brotherhood of Sleeping Car Porters, among the first ten, and if one wanted to be absolutely impartial, among the first five. In leading the fight for the porters to obtain better wages and improved working conditions, Randolph bore the brunt of the battle. He never faltered, never succumbed to the lure of easy money, was never dismayed by the enormity of the odds which he and his followers faced."[1] Randolph earned for himself the name "most dangerous Negro in America" when he went about making speeches in protests against the war in 1918. The Department of Justice arrested him in Cleveland, Ohio, but he was soon released. During World War I, Randolph objected to America's entrance into the war. "I was fundamentally and morally opposed to war," he stated. "I am a pacificist so far as national wars are concerned. I criticized in the *Messenger* and in public speeches the hypocrisy of the slogan 'making the world safe for democracy' when Negroes were lynched, Jim-Crowed, disfranchised and segregated in America."

A. Philip Randolph was born in Florida and received his early training at Cookman Institute, now Bethune-Cookman College. After completing high school, he went to New York where he attended City College and took special courses in philosophy and psychology at the People's Institute. Prior to World War I, Randolph organized in New York the first Elevator and Starters Union, AFL, and assisted in the organization of the Negro Motion Pictures Operators of New York, the Negro Garment Workers of New York, and the Philadelphia Longshoremen. For thirteen years, until 1928, he was publisher and editor of the *Messenger,* a journal of Negro life that stressed economics as the basis of the solution of the Negro's problems in the United States. The Spingarn Medal was awarded Randolph in 1942 for his outstanding achievement on behalf of Negroes. In 1944, he received the Clendenin Award for achievement in behalf of organized labor.

More than forty-five years ago, Pullman porters worked from 300 to 400 hours monthly at an average wage of $67.50, out of which they purchased uniforms, shoe polish, and meals. The work month totaled 11,000 miles. Without job security, porters were victimized or favored, according to the whims of their supervisors. Randolph first led porters in revolt against these conditions in 1925. Porters demanded the right to collective bargaining through their organization, more pay, better working conditions, and shorter hours. The Brotherhood was refused recognition, the organization was labeled radical, and Randolph was called a professional agitator. Not only did opposition come from the Pullman Company, but the Brotherhood was criticized by Negro leaders and newspapers. The Brotherhood, however, received favorable endorsement from the AFL, NAACP, and the National Urban League. After twelve years of persistent effort, the Brotherhood won full recognition from the Pullman Company, which decreased the porter's working time from 400 hours to 240 hours a month and guaranteed a wage of $235. An editorial in the *Interracial Review*[5] said that this goal was reached without strikes, violence, or political pressure. Randolph said at the Brotherhood's twenty-fifth annual convention that "we have fought to dispel the fallacies of communism in the labor movement."

Because the national defense program and armed services were negligent in providing equal opportunities in employment to Negroes, Randolph organized a march on Washington movement designed to rally 50,000 Negroes in Washington on July 1, 1941, in a protest demonstration. Assisting him were Walter White, Congressman Adam Clayton Powell, and Frank Crosswaith. The demonstration was called off when President Roosevelt issued Executive Order 8802, which provided for equitable employment of all workers in defense industries without discrimination on a racial basis. The second mass movement organized by Randolph, with Grant Reynolds as the leading assistant, was the League for Non-Violent Civil Disobedience against military segregation. Negroes were advised not to serve in a segregated army, even if it meant going to prison. The movement was dissolved when President Truman issued an executive order on July 26, 1948, calling for termination of segregation in the armed forces. Randolph said that now Negroes could place the League in storage.

Randolph's civil disobedience program exposed different opinions among Negro leaders and the press. P. L. Prattis of the *Pittsburgh Courier* wrote that the movement constituted a "bluff tactic" to throw the enemy off balance, and he subscribed to it 100 per cent.[6] Horace R. Cayton, a columnist, declared that regardless of whether you liked Randolph, he had "unadulterated courage."[7] Several newspapers carried open letters from readers regarding civil disobedience, and Chester Hines of New York City wrote, "I am entirely in accord with the mass civil disobedience movement among Negroes if segregation is not abolished in the armed forces as proposed by A. Philip Randolph and Grant Reynolds."[8] A St. Louis resident stated, "I am sure that all clear-thinking Negroes are with him [Randolph] 100 per cent. Right now is the time to act. We are tired of that battlefront and election day citizenship, which means nothing."[9]

Enemies of the movement also had their say and were outspoken in their criticism. Benjamin Davis, New York City councilman, said that "civil disobedience ideas, like most of Mr. Randolph's so-called remedies, doesn't [sic] create unity against Jim Crow. It only creates confusion and spreads defeatism and disillusionment. The only way to fight Jim Crow is to oppose universal military training and the draft."[10] Earl Brown of the *New York Amsterdam-Star News* voiced the opinion that if "Negroes refused to shoulder a rifle for their country, they would be guilty of treason under the law."[11] Ben Davis, writing in the *Chicago Defender,* said that the inward aggressive personality of the total Negro was the greatest stumbling block to mass movements."[12]

Somehow A. Philip Randolph zoomed into popularity after 1933, and crowds sought to get a glimpse of him when he appeared in public places. Bontemps, in his *100 Years of Freedom,* attributed this prestige to his activities as a mass movement leader and miracle worker, his leadership of the Brotherhood, and also the Jericho-like victory achieved by the first march on Washington without taking a step. Randolph's crowning achievement was perhaps his efforts in assisting to organize the 1963 march on Washington during the Kennedy administration. *Jet* reporter John H. Britton said that Randolph won "with a full house though using only a part of his artillery.

It was his strongest hand, so he showed it. A massive force of Negroes gave this gambling statesman his twenty-year-old dream when they joined him for a giant March-on-Washington for jobs and freedom in 1963."[13]

A. Philip Randolph made his first speaking appearance shortly after he secured a tutor to teach him to read Shakespeare in sonorous Oxford English. He gave readings before church clubs and literary societies. Sometimes he stood on boxes, or any kind of platform, at busy Harlem corners and talked of the Negro's problem, the doctrine of socialism, and the shortcomings of capitalism. His passionate words and pleasant voice brought people flocking around him. Randolph adopted, at that time, the Received Standard of British English, using the long Italian *a* in such words as "glasses."

Like Henry Highland Garnet, antislavery orator, Randolph, during his early career, appealed to his audiences through religion. He knew that many of the porters came from homes that were deeply religious. Therefore, he relied on the Bible and made typical utterances like urging the church to support labor because Jesus was a carpenter. Sentences learned during his childhood were used to great advantage in his earlier speeches. "Let not your hearts be troubled, neither let them be afraid." To encourage the weak, Randolph exclaimed: "Stand upon thy feet and the God of Truth and Justice and Victory will speak unto thee."

In commenting upon Randolph's method of speaking, Editor Ludlow Werner said that Randolph is "a suave, persuasive speaker, who resorts to historical references and philosophy to back up his arguments. His Harvard accent and manner of speaking makes [sic] listening easy."[14] Dr. Reinhold Niebuhr of Union Theological Seminary made this comment: "I think Mr. Randolph is one of the most interesting lecturers I know. Gracious in manner, well informed and able to marshal his material. He speaks convincingly on economic problems of the modern Negro in particular."[15] Stanley High spoke of the labor leader as "eloquent on the platform, but unsmiling" and paid him the tribute "gifted with exceptional ability as a public speaker, possessed of high courage and unwavering purpose, unimpeachably honest, Randolph once he is started, never turns back."[16]

Once A. Philip Randolph was scheduled to speak at Mount Nebo Baptist Church in Memphis, Tennessee, in November, 1943. City officials, under the control of E. H. Crump, political boss of Memphis and Shelby County, sent for twelve Negro leaders and told them that Randolph would not be permitted to speak at the announced meeting. Although the meeting was canceled, Randolph returned on a later date and spoke at the First Baptist Church of Memphis. In his opening remarks, he said:

I have returned to Memphis because I consider it my constitutional right, my democratic privilege, and my moral duty. I am here because of the need for the people to hear me speak in order to be saved. I do not consider that I possess any unusual, extraordinary, or cosmic wisdom that anybody else lacks. I am just an humble official of a trade union which is doing its best to improve the standard of wages and working conditions of its members, and help to advance the general cause of the Negro people, and of all workers, regardless of race, color, or political affiliations.

Randolph has been able to catch and express the prevailing spirit of the working class. Early in his career, he found out that labor must eternally struggle against the employer. He has convinced Negroes that unions must develop economic power in order to demand the good things of life that workers want.

WILLARD SAXBY TOWNSEND

A random selection of smart labor union leaders, who seldom make headlines but who have earned the reputation of doing a good job for their members, would include the name of Willard S. Townsend, portly and mahogany-hued, with graying hair and brown eyes.[17] He was once international president of the United Transport Service Employees Union, and the type of union leader that "management is most likely to meet at the bargaining table, before a labor board, or in the picket lines." Townsend earned the reputation of being a good labor field officer, because he did the work himself.

Under the labor chief's leadership, the redcaps moved up from no fixed wages to six dollars per day. In addition, they received substantial increases in retirement benefits. And what is more, they won respect. Townsend said that his union activities stemmed from the desire to better the working conditions of redcaps and to end their nonsalaried status. His goal was reached through a United States Supreme Court decision giving redcaps status, and through the passage of federal legislation on June 1, 1940, on behalf of porters—making their services available in railroad terminals at a flat rate of ten cents per bag or parcel carried to and from trains. Against railroads, the favorite weapon of Townsend[18] has been the law.

During 1943, Townsend was selected as one of the eighteen Americans on the Honor Roll of Race Relations, a national poll conducted annually by the Schomburg Collection of Negro Literature of the New York Public Library. One investigator, in the *Phylon,* paid Townsend this tribute:

He is a "labor politician" in the best sense of the word, meaning that he knows human nature, understands the necessity of keeping his membership close to him, and is master of the "soft answer that turneth away wrath" when wrath is something to be avoided. On the other hand, he can be belligerent, sharp-tongued and emphatic when the need arises. Some of his statements on political and social issues have been remarkable for their failure to beat around the bush.[19]

Typical of the man's influence was his verbal challenge to the Eleventh Constitutional Convention of the CIO to set its house

LABOR LEADERS / *125*

in order. He told a large labor audience in Cleveland, Ohio, that "the union must make the fight against inroads made by the Communists in Negro communities by blending all efforts toward eradication of the ugly and vicious practice of discrimination against our brother workers."[20] Townsend's rise to the head of a union was remarkable. He was born in Cincinnati, Ohio, on December 4, 1895, educated in the public schools of Cincinnati and the Royal College of Science, Toronto, Canada, from 1922 to 1925. For his meteoric rise from obscurity to the national headlines, Wilberforce University conferred upon him the honorary degree of Doctor of Laws in 1943.

About one-half of Townsend's speeches related directly to matters of the United Transport Service Employees Union with the remainder on such subjects as civil rights, international labor issues, housing, vocational training, and labor legislation. The orator often spoke about the human desire for economic status and man's innate need to achieve spiritual and human kinship with his fellowmen. On the question of organizing labor in the South, the labor leader was calmly realistic. Once when addressing the press, Townsend said:

There has been the tendency to consider the decision of the CIO to organize the South in a rather unrealistic manner. It has been hailed as the millennium—the program that will immediately solve the collective ills of the Negro in the South. It must be remembered that our first task is to organize the unorganized, secure decent contracts, improve working conditions, and lay the foundation for economic justice and democracy. The remaining benefits will naturally follow but not overnight. Remember how long it took before our impact was felt in the North. The South is a tender, but tougher nut to crack, primarily because for a century it has been the economic stepchild of America.[21]

It was not emotionalism that characterized the oratory of Townsend, but rather the impact of the force of his ideas that seemed to explode upon the listener's ears. He not only gave an idea for every word that even the rank and file could easily understand, but he captured the imagination of the audience by his orderly arrangement of these ideas. The speaker's ideas were as real to Negro labor as bread and stones. His vocal delivery followed a logical unfolding of ideas toward a climax followed by a slower-paced delivery that was included in his peroration. Who could be so foolish as to resist the explosiveness of his pleas? Few redcaps did.

It cannot be said with absolute accuracy how much influence Townsend wielded during his career as a union organizer. He was repeatedly elected president of the union of porters. This was indicative, no doubt, of the confidence he inspired among the union members. His speeches gave information and facts, which he marshaled with accuracy from his prodigious memory. The labor leader stimulated the intellect of men for the purpose of making them think. Deeply moved by the plight of Negro labor, the orator laid aside all levity and tended to sermonize, since he was in dead earnest about what he said. If we are to judge him on the basis of his accomplishments, he did help the porters to achieve a salaried status, liberal retirement benefits, and substantial insurance coverage.

Footnotes, Chapter 9

1. E. Franklin Frazier, *The Negro in the United States*, p. 553.
2. Sterling D. Spero, *The Black Worker*, p. 462.
3. In a letter from Hilton E. Hannah to the author, October 13, 1964. It contained an account of Hannah's rise from the local union, No. 538, Madison, Wisconsin, to the international level. This information was included in the discussion of his leadership and oratory. The writer met Mr. Hannah when he was a graduate student at the University of Wisconsin and worked at night at Oscar Mayer and Company, Madison, and he, too, was a member of the Amalgamated Meat Cutters and Butcher Workmen of North America, Local 538.

4. *Opportunity Magazine* 15 (October, 1937): 299. A discussion of A. Philip Randolph by Elmer A. Carter.
5. *Interracial Review* 23 (September, 1950): 131.
6. *Pittsburgh Courier,* April 17, 1948.
7. Horace Cayton, *Pittsburgh Courier,* April 17, 1948.
8. Ibid.
9. Ibid.
10. *Chicago Defender,* April 24, 1948.
11. Ibid.
12. Ibid.
13. "A. Philip Randolph: Man Behind the March on Nation's Capital," *Jet,* September 5, 1963, p. 14.
14. Letter from Ludlow Werner to the author.
15. Faye Philip Everett, *The Colored Situation.*
16. Stanley High, "Black Omens," *Saturday Evening Post,* June 4, 1938, p. 38.
17. "Ten Who Deliver," *Fortune Magazine,* November, 1946.
18. *Current Biography,* January, 1948, pp. 61–62.
19. Lester B. Granger, "Phylon Profile, II: Willard S. Townsend," *Phylon* 5 (4th Quarter, 1944): 333.
20. *Pittsburgh Courier,* November 12, 1949, p. 1.
21. Ibid.

10 / They Speak Out

GEORGE A. SINGLETON

Since 1940, George A. Singleton has been a forceful spokesman for brotherhood in a world struggling for international
goodwill and peace. In this role, he has earned the reputation
of being one of the outstanding orators in the nation. His
utterances have seared the public conscience to a realization of
the need for a new democracy. Singleton says, "I wish I were
qualified to say what makes a great and successful speaker. In
my feeble efforts, I am unorthodox, iconoclastic, and I violate
the rules of the schools. The subject possesses me. It is in my
bones, and in some Jeremianic fashion burns its way out." In a
sense, most black orators are Jeremianic, since they must
bewail their racial plight.

George A. Singleton, former president of Paul Quinn College, Waco, Texas, was born in Conway, South Carolina. He
was graduated first in his class from the Whitmore Graded
School. When he was ready to enter high school, he went to
Columbia, South Carolina, to attend Allen University, where
he remained until he finished college. Singleton next entered

Boston University to do graduate study and was awarded the
M.A. and B.D. degrees. Then he became dean of Morris
Brown College in Atlanta. When the war broke out in 1918,
Singleton became an army chaplain.

When advancing the Negro's cause before integrated audiences, Singleton does not employ the Booker T. Washington
"stoop to conquer" technique. Rather, he takes the position
that the most effective way to protest is to attack rather than
defend. The author heard the Reverend Singleton deliver "A
New World A-Coming" at the Wesley Chapel Methodist
Church in Austin, Texas, in the fall of 1945. In this oration,
the speaker declared that the American capitalistic system of
old is gone forever; and he paraphrased the words of Heracli-
tus, the Greek philosopher, by saying that we are passing
through a stage of expanding horizons. The Reverend Singleton rose in full flight with these words:

A new world is a-coming. A new economic order is on the way.
The old profit motive under a ruthless capitalistic system is
doomed. The people are on the march toward a more equitable
distribution of returns from their labor. Never again will they sit
supinely by, without protest, and see the masters of finance drain
off millions of dollars while they barely exist. The time will come
when every man will receive a just wage for his labor.

Discrimination and segregation because of race will pass. Unborn
generations will regard us of today as objects of curiosity as we
once looked upon the society of the Romans who enslaved the
fair-skinned, blue-eyed Saxons.

Men with sweaty brows, aching hearts, tear-dimmed eyes, and
bloody fingers will build this new world in the midst of time. It is
the ultimate goal of humanity; it is the will of God.

As he uttered this portion of his oration, Singleton's vocal
resonance quickened the spirit. His voice was a blend of the
peal of an organ and a tenor flute. The variety and power of
his voice moved listeners persuasively. His manner carried

conviction. Every gesture graced and reinforced his ideas, for they were effective movements, as he himself puts it, helping his subject to "burn its way out."

The Reverend Singleton's philosophical background and theological training would have made him particularly popular on the Chautauqua circuit, and by popular acclaim he would have been invited back year after year. He hopes that man's character will undergo a moral change, or transfiguration, resulting from the humanitarian action in which he is involved. The orator's words are not dependent upon abstruse symbolism and convoluted forms, and therefore accessible only to listeners learned in the mystique of rhetorical interpretation. Any listener who is willing to think about the obvious symbols, and who isn't frustrated because their significance cannot be pinned down exactly, will profit from his encounter with the words of this orator. If the faith of Singleton is not expressed in comforting, conventional ways, it is because he is sensitive to confusion and compelled to speak honestly.

CHARLES SATCHELL MORRIS II

There have been orators who have remained longer before the eyes of the public, but few men have been more masterful in platform art than Charles Satchell Morris II. In the role of a speaker, he has been an inspiration to college students enrolled in his public speaking classes. Although he began public speaking when he was twelve years old, Morris first attracted wide public attention when he delivered the Emancipation address in 1914 at the courthouse in Hertford, North Carolina, before a large audience of both races. His father, who had a conflict in engagements for that occasion, went to Philadelphia after sending his son to Hertford. The *Norfolk Journal and Guide* published the speech, and overnight young Morris earned the title "the boy orator," a sobriquet that still clings to him. Some individuals said that the lad was a chip off the old block, for Charles Morris, Sr., was himself a brilliant orator, and few men of his generation could excel him in presenting the causes of prohibition and foreign missions.

In April, 1916, when he was sixteen, Morris entered his first speaking contest, representing Wilson Memorial Academy in an oratorical contest held at Vernon, New York. The lad, the only Negro contestant, won first prize, twenty dollars in gold, over representatives of the leading high schools in that area. The next month, he was awarded second prize in the state contest held at Hamilton College. The daily newspapers referred to him as "a native born Cuban." "This allegation," says Morris, "I denied in stirring language indeed for a boy of sixteen." Immediately young Morris began speaking in many cities, supporting the candidacy of Charles Evans Hughes for the Presidency. In succeeding campaigns, the orator spoke for Democrats and at other times for Republicans.

Charles Satchell Morris II was born at Newton, Massachusetts, on June 11, 1899, the first of five children of the Reverend Charles Satchell Morris, Sr., and Sadie Ugenia (Waterman) Morris. After graduating from high school, Morris attended Wheaton College, where he was one of the two Negro students enrolled. He volunteered his services in the United States Army and was assigned to the SATC (Student Army Training Corps) at the college, an outfit of 200 men. At Wheaton College in Illinois, Morris spoke on many occasions. Later he was graduated from Columbia University with the M.A. degree in English. Morris was ordained as a minister in Los Angeles on July 30, 1942. Soon he was chosen pastor of the historic 105-year-old Bethel Baptist Church at Jacksonville, Florida. Becoming weary of the prejudice and general apathy of the South, the Reverend Morris resigned in August, 1945, and returned to Los Angeles. He has traveled over twenty states delivering commencement addresses and sermons to various congregations and school audiences. One of these speeches entitled "Booker T. Washington in the American Picture" was delivered at the Second Baptist Church in Los

Angeles on April 5, 1940. Eloquence should champion worthy causes rather than one's personal interests, and the orator consistently adhered to this ideal throughout his career. His words have called for interracial understanding and amity, universal education, abolition of the poll tax as a prerequisite for voting. He has urged Negroes to join the AFL and CIO and make common cause with workers everywhere, so that the consciousness of being a laborer would transcend the consciousness of being a Negro.

Charles S. Morris II might be a successful lecturer and teacher, but it is known that he also preaches effectively the message that men must practice the philosophy of Jesus Christ or else civilization is doomed. Despite the poetic coloration that he gives his sermons, he seldom fails to preach that America can never spread the gospel of Christ in its purity, its passion, and its power in foreign lands until it learns to treat with justice and equity the 20 million black people in these United States. On several occasions, the orator called Jesus "the world's greatest democrat and most revolutionary radical." For a close-up of one of his sermons, a single newspaper report must suffice. Morris said, "Religion has emancipated womanhood, raised the status of the working man, for Jesus himself was a carpenter, and brought about whatever there was of love and charity in a bleeding world."[1] If philosophers want to reconstruct the religious thought of the twentieth century, they will find in the Reverend Morris a fertile course of reference.

The author recalls that during the spring of 1935, the Reverend Morris visited Timothy Darling Presbyterian Church at Oxford, North Carolina, of which the late Dr. G. W. Shaw was pastor. As visiting minister, the Reverend Morris used the subject "What Makes a Great Church?" That afternoon and evening the orator spoke at the Baptist Church. He walked forward behind the pulpit and began speaking in a quiet conversational tone of voice. Without ever raising his voice, he produced the greatest effect. Like Wendell Phillips, he was a gentleman conversing. The audience was charmed with his words and wanted him to speak on after he had taken his seat. The congregation witnessed a sample of what the orator had done hundreds of times in Virginia, North Carolina, Tennessee, California, and Florida. He was indeed one of the most effective speakers using the English language. No description of the teacher, who once taught at Tennessee A and I State University, would be complete that did not mention his ability to describe. His skill in painting verbal pictures was consummate.

CHARLES H. WESLEY

Like several orators in this history, Charles H. Wesley is an educator, orator, and preacher. He was pastor and presiding elder in the African Methodist Episcopal Church from 1918 to 1938. Twenty-odd years of preaching molded him into a master speaker. He is also a historian and a social reformer, and his utterances are characteristic of the new Negro described by Adam Clayton Powell, Jr., in his book, *Marching Blacks* (1946). In appreciation of his superb platform speaking, audiences have labeled Wesley "the Ambassador of Interracial Goodwill." People will remember him most vividly for his striking oration, "Propaganda and the Negro."

Charles H. Wesley, son of Charles Snowden and Matilda (Harris) Wesley, was born in Louisville, Kentucky, on December 2, 1891. After his twenty-fifth birthday, he was graduated with the A.B. degree from Fisk University. He was a university scholar at Yale from 1911 to 1913. In 1928, he was graduated from Harvard University with the Ph.D. degree in history and studied there on an Austin scholarship. He studied in Paris, France, and was a Guggenheim Fellow in London, England. Professor Wesley served at Howard University from 1911 to 1941, when he was successively teacher, chairman of the Department of History, and dean of the Graduate School.

He has written more than 125 articles for periodicals and fourteen books, among which are: *Negro Labor in the United States, History of the Alpha Phi Alpha Fraternity, Richard Allen: Apostle of Freedom,* and *The Collapse of the Confederacy.* Wesley retired from the presidency of Central State College in Ohio in June, 1965, and presently is engaged in research with the Association for the Study of Negro Life and History with headquarters in the nation's capital.

In the area of research, Dr. Wesley holds that the Negro's role in building the United States of America has been often ignored or treated in a stereotyped fashion. The struggle for integration, he contends, has focused attention upon the need for true knowledge about the Negro's historical past. During the 1966 Negro History Week celebration, Dr. Wesley delivered a speech at Florida A and M University at Tallahassee. He reminded Negro teachers of their responsibility in enriching the public school curriculum beyond state requirements in order to inform Negro children concerning their historical past—*who* they are and *what* they can become. Furthermore, the historian asserted that this contribution will give Negro youths the proof they need about their past and their heritage that only the truth can give them. Then he highlighted his subject, "Negro History and the Concept of Racial Inferiority" with historical evidence depicting efforts utilized to keep Negroes in a subordinated and bottom-of-the-ladder position. The orator added that "Negro history is in a sense an antidote to the concept of inferiority of Negroes in the United States. There is a need for Negroes to believe in themselves as members of an ethnic group which has made worthwhile contributions to the ongoing of society and civilization." The audience was led to understand that this is a basic, unmet need of Negro Americans.

In this Negro History Week address, the orator outlined four steps that might be followed in utilizing Negro history as a touchstone of pride for black people. They are: (1) knowing the history of the Negro people and getting rid of stereotypes that represent "bad history and poor taste," (2) working for the elimination of objectionable culture traits of the Negro people, (3) setting higher standards of conduct, courtesy, morality, and ethics for Negroes, and working together to realize them, (4) publicizing all creditable facts about Negroes and their accomplishments. Wesley, in his conclusion, proclaimed that Negro history unlocks the door of the past and fills in the missing pages of a glorious Negro heritage.

As he summarized, descriptively, the forgotten Negro giants of the past, hearts throbbed in response to the melody and rhythm of the speaker's words. A deep chord was struck in the hearers, and it was expressed in vigorous applause. Somehow their spirits were quickened with the idea Negroes must remove the stereotyped images that tend to stifle their motivation. The peroration was effective through the technique of compliment.

To give some idea of the orator's vocal style, let us hark back to November, 1935, when Dr. Wesley delivered an address before the Montreal Rotary Club. *The Freelance,* in its reporting, remarked: "Doctor Wesley, a man of culture and learning, not only impressed his audience with the logic and sincerity of his remarks but also with the force of impelling personality." After one speech in Cincinnati in the 1930's, *The Union* printed this remark under the headline "Wesley Electrifies Cincinnatians": "Developing the thought that any understanding of racial relations must have sound factual basis, Charles Wesley held Cincinnatians in suspense throughout a masterful address on the subject, 'Education for Freedom in a Democracy.'" Commenting upon a speech delivered at North Carolina College in Durham, *The Morning Herald* of Durham said: "Dr. Wesley is a fluent speaker, a deep thinker, and a clear reasoner. His voice carries well and it possesses splendid modulations." At another time, Dr. Wesley appeared on the platform at the Ecumenical Conference of the Methodist

Churches in Atlanta. The Afro-American newspapers of Baltimore stated: "The address was received with deafening applause which was frequently interrupted with demonstrations. English delegates were most enthusiastic and gave him a prolonged ovation as he concluded. Everywhere hands were outstretched to greet him as he came down from the rostrum while the applause died out only to be repeated. It was the noisiest demonstration of the week."

There is substantial value in the work accomplished by Dr. Wesley in the ministry and theology. Since the truth of God is eternal, the orator's sermons do not grow old. Even now, when he preaches an occasional sermon, the language, the mode of expression, and the illustrations are never obsolete. These are kept apropos for the Space Age and attuned to the nature of modern problems facing the Negro. In speaking to audiences, he says that "truths which will enable black people to meet successfully the changing conditions in which they live" are found in Negro history, literature, and culture. Sensitive to the moral issues of our times, Wesley won't brook the idea of a watered-down Christian message; and his congregations react with deep appreciation. They want to hear the truth, even when it hurts, and they do not appreciate a lot of "playacting" on the platform or in the pulpit. The present-day congregation or audience is not notably complacent, and therefore Dr. Wesley brings them an enthusiastic message. The orator takes thought and reason, spreads an emotional "meringue" over them, to make the address more palatable, and encourages his listeners to put real enthusiasm into their religion and the "Father's business." People need to get "worked up" over the great Biblical truths and national issues, and Wesley helps them to seek the Second Emancipation they sorely need.

Charles H. Wesley considers it his mission to stimulate people to think and question everything they hear or read, so that they might be led to constructive action. He has used oratory and eloquence in the righteous cause of human improvement and the happiness of all people. Throughout his life, he has felt personally charged with the irresistible and inspiring duty of helping raise from the mire of discrimination and segregation 22 million black citizens of the United States.

GEORGE W. LEE, ("TAN-SKINNED SPELLBINDER")

One of the most remarkable men to attend a Mississippi voter registration meeting to kick off the campaign in Mound Bayou in 1955 was the Reverend George W. Lee. He had come to hear Congressman Charles C. Diggs of Chicago deliver the main address. Simeon Booker, a newsman who covered the meeting, described the minister as "a tan-skinned spellbinder" and added that the Reverend Lee won attention with the "bareback" punch line, "Pray not for your mama and papa." Lee urged the 13,000 auditors who assembled from the Delta section of Mississippi: "They have gone to heaven. Pray that you can make it through *this hell*." When the Reverend Lee finished his short speech at the meeting, Simeon Booker called him a religious powerhouse.[2]

The Reverend Lee never limited his eloquence to heavenly purposes, "fire and brimstone," or the pearly gates and the New Jerusalem. He got himself generally disliked by local white people because he had the nerve to register and vote, and he did not remove his name from the list when strongly advised to by Caucasians.

Lee pastored four churches within easy commuting distance from his home near Belzoni, Mississippi. The minister also operated a grocery store and owned a printing plant. Preacher Lee taught his congregations about the here and now and sermonized about the potential power of Negroes if only they would use the ballot or would elect one of their number from Mississippi to the halls of the United States Congress in Washington. He knew this was possible, since, in the Black Belt, Negroes outnumbered whites in the population. "Do you believe you can elect a Negro?" Simeon Booker asked the

Reverend Lee. "Someday," said the minister. "Maybe my grandchildren will. But Negroes in Mississippi, and white folk in Mississippi, need something big to shoot at, or they don't get excited."

The Reverend Lee would have been a big-time politician were he a white man, because he knew how to employ back-slapping with the Delta farmers while he left with each one a printed sample of his fiery message. Newsman Booker observed that the minister could be eloquent with his "down-home dialogue and his sense of timing." Definitely, he was a Christian who wanted to help his fellowmen. He seemed able to do wonders with the cotton farmers in the immediate community and area. Many of these Negro land tillers who were not conversant with national affairs received instruction from Dr. Lee.

Following the meeting in Mound Bayou, Booker took a plane en route to Chicago to write his news story of the meeting. The story was never written. Reverend Lee was shot to death by an anonymous assassin as he drove home from a tailor shop with a suit he was going to wear the next day at his church. In commenting upon his death, Dr. T. H. M. Howard, who was residing in Mississippi at the time, remarked, "Reverend Lee was a warrior who refused to lay down his arms in the civil-rights battle." Those that attended his funeral conceded that Lee did not die in vain, for like the martyr John Brown, his soul goes marching on.

The speaking style of the Reverend Lee was much like that of John Brown, a preacher described by James Weldon Johnson in *Notes from an Old Camp Meeting*. The antebellum preacher John Brown was a "bareback" messenger who, in one of his sermons, caught attention by a startling statement— "Yo' arms too short to box wid God!" Whereas John Brown delivered messages typical of those included in *God's Trombones*, authored by James Weldon Johnson, the Reverend Lee wanted Negroes to enjoy the blessings of the here and now— the right to register and vote, the right to be employed at a decent and well-paying job, the right to live in a decent home, and the opportunity to get the best education possible. In telling Negroes about these things, the "tan-skinned spellbinder" had few equals in bringing his hearers to attention with the power of his intensely felt beliefs frequently expressed through homespun axioms and postulates.

Footnotes, Chapter 10

1. *California Eagle* (Los Angeles), September 7, 1945.
2. Simeon Booker, *Black Man's America,* pp. 161–165.

11 / Fraternal Oratory

In their struggle to become economically and socially self-sufficient, Negroes have established numerous fraternal organizations, for example, the Elks, Knights of Pythias, Masons, Odd Fellows, Knights of Tabor, Good Samaritans, Ancient Sons of Israel, Order of St. Luke, Daughters of Jerusalem, and many more. These organizations have provided their members with illness and death benefits, given aid to orphans and widows, and made available opportunities for social intercourse. Many of them, like Greek letter fraternities and sororities, have built clubhouses and homes to meet the recreational and social needs of their members. This is particularly true of the Improved Benevolent and Protective Order of Elks of the World, of which the late J. Finley Wilson, a powerful orator, was for many years Grand Exalted Ruler. The Elks, for example, own a $75,000 home in Tucson, Arizona, and a $50,000 club in Phoenix, Arizona.

The officials of fraternal orders give hundreds of public addresses each year for the purpose of increasing membership and setting up lodges. Usually, each lodge has a grand lecturer whose duty it is to give instruction to lodge members whenever the need arises. Such a man was J. Finley Wilson who worked his way up to the position of Grand Exalted Ruler. Because the oratorical efforts of twentieth-century Negro fraternal leaders have been overshadowed by the speaking of J. Finley Wilson, this chapter will be limited to his speechmaking.

The Elks was founded in Ohio in 1898. Its early history is the story of two orders: one led by B. F. Howard, and a second by J. E. Atkins, When the two factions merged in 1910, J. Frank Wheaton was elected Grand Exalted Ruler. The Elks' history[1] was similar to that of other Negro organizations that were founded because racial prejudice prevented black people from joining white organizations. For instance, the white BPOE denied Negroes membership, and therefore they formed their separate organization the IBPOE (Independent Benevolent Protective Order of Elks) and simply added "of the World." The present Grand Exalted Ruler, Grant Reynolds, is working to keep the Elks a progressive organization in tune with the demands of the time. The Elks campaigned for a Freedom Fund goal of $45,000 in 1965, which was used for civil rights purposes. Reynolds is not an orator like J. Frank Wheaton or J. Finley Wilson, but he is effective as an Elks leader.

The leading fraternal orator of his time was J. Finley Wilson of Washington, D.C. For more than twenty-five years, he was the head of the largest Negro fraternal order in the world. "Those who challenged his authority were humbled and crushed down in ignominious defeat," said Joseph D. Bibb. "He was the ruling Czar of a great order."[2] As political bosses, Negro fraternal leaders have controlled delegations to national political conventions and have been consulted on patronage and important appointments in the party. In this way, Wilson received his training in political strategy. Although dictatorial in his leadership, he was progressive and modern.

During his twenty-six years as head of the Elks, the organization increased in membership from 25,000 to 500,000. The organization purchased $25 million worth of real estate and invested $30 million in war bonds. Finley Wilson inaugurated many constructive projects, including ten annual scholarships of $1,000 each to worthy and needy students. To carry out a program of education, a Commissioner of Education was appointed and given an annual salary. W. C. Hueston held this position while Finley was in office. A program of health was also established and a Commissioner of Health elected. Wilson said, "We have in our program civil liberties, economics, 'Antlered Guard' and 'Junior Herd,' and public relations. We make an annual contribution of thousands of dollars each year to abolish the poll tax through the Anti-Poll-Tax League and to abolish lynching through the Anti-Lynching League, and to all agencies working to wipe out disfranchisement and other human ills."

J. Finley Wilson was born in Nashville, Tennessee, on August 28, 1881. His parents were the Reverend James L. and Nancy (Wiley) Wilson. As a boy, he attended the public schools of Nashville and later attended Fisk University. Wilson has been office boy in Kansas, railroad employee in Colorado, and bellhop in New York City. In 1898 and 1899, he worked in the Klondike. Wilson worked a year in Arizona as a miner and was a cowboy in Wyoming with Buffalo Bill. From Wyoming, he went to Chicago and then to New York City where he worked with Thomas Fortune on the *New York Age* and then with Roscoe Simmons on the *National Review.* Later, Wilson moved to Baltimore where he started a newspaper, the *Baltimore Times.* Then he published the *Advocate-Verdict* in Harrisburg, Pennsylvania, with Robert J. Nelson as editor. Finally, Wilson established *The Sun* in Washington, D.C. This paper developed into the *Washington Eagle,* a fraternal monthly. He was affiliated with the Masons (thirty-second degree), Odd Fellows, Knights of Pythias, and Order of St. Luke.

The fraternal leader received his training in politics through experience. "In his own fashion," said Joseph Bibb, "he kept alive a peculiar pattern of lodge politics that has played such an important part in the history of colored Americans." Most aspirants to high office in the federal government recognized the power of the Exalted Ruler, who supposedly carried his membership in his vest pocket. He spoke for all Elks in a strident voice, with compelling logic and convincing emphasis.

Without doubt, J. Finley Wilson was an orator par excellence. Once, in the spring of 1933, the author was among a crowd of listeners who jammed a church in Anniston, Alabama. They had come to witness the Alabama State Finals of the Elks Oratorical Contest of which there is detailed discussion in the book of *Rules and Regulations*.[3] The contest was open to Alabama high school students who were interested in speaking upon some phase of the Constitution and to win, if they could, a scholarship to the college of their choice. One young orator on this occasion won first place with an oration entitled, "Frederick Douglass and the Constitution."

J. Finley Wilson was present and arose to pay tribute to the several student speakers. The contest had lasted two hours, and the audience was becoming restless. Before many minutes had passed, however, the Exalted Ruler had cast a spell over his listeners, and, to use the trite phrase, "they hung onto his every word." He displayed all the tricks of oratory, and the occasion, as it were, set him on fire. First, there was conversation mixed with dramatic pauses for effect. Frequent modulations of his voice were followed by rapid-fire sentences. All the while, the orator was warming up to his subject. When he reached the climax, his Elks fez fell off his head onto the floor. And when he stooped down to pick it up, pandemonium broke loose in the audience. When the clamor subsided, the orator concluded his message in a loud and thunderous voice which brought forth prolonged applause. Wilson then took his seat, and it was some time before the presiding officer could restore order amid shouts of "Go on!" and "Give us more!" This exhibition stunned the author, who had come to serve as one of the judges in the contest.

The fraternal orator was the embodiment of all he believed about successful public speaking. "My opinion of a good speaker is that he should be familiar with his subject," remarked Wilson. "He should have poise, good diction, and put himself into the subject without overdoing it." Wilson's pet subjects were human rights, equal opportunities, and even-handed justice to the end that the Negro might vote as freely in New Orleans as in New York. He drew lavishly upon modern examples and incidents in order to give concreteness to his utterances. Wilson was not content to tell; he had to show and act. Like Demosthenes, he believed in action and more action. His voice seemed to grow stronger with use and was more vibrant and booming at the end of his speeches. Frequently, he used historical references to stimulate racial pride. For instance, his speeches ran something like this:

Wherever and whenever the American Negro has had a fair deal and equal opportunity, he has demonstrated great worth, ability, and often superiority. Witness: our Marian Anderson, 'voice of a century'; Joe Louis, world's greatest fighter; Henry Armstrong, one and only triple champion in boxing; Jessie Owens, fastest human; Booker T. Washington, apostle of racial goodwill; and Frederick Douglass, the slave who became orator, diplomat, and statesman. . . .

One of the long-time friends and able assistants of the Grand Exalted Ruler, according to the *Negro History Bulletin* for May, 1952, was Edward Lawson, Sr., a newspaper man and English scholar. Lawson was often Wilson's speech ghostwriter, but he always decorated the addresses with Wilson's own ideas and niceties of style and oratory that only a master can command. When the addresses were delivered, they were those of J. Finley Wilson and nobody else. The ideas belong to Wilson and the borrowed words came out exactly as written, but reflecting the humor and wit of the speaker. The fact that many of his speeches were written for him, as is now true of Presidents, did not detract from the greatness of Wilson as an orator. After years of writing for Wilson, Edward Lawson knew the type of speech to write for a given occasion. At the height of his career, Wilson was in great demand as a speaker. He often sent word to Lawson from New York, saying that he needed a speech for an engagement in Alabama the following night. Lawson would come to the railroad station in Washington with the speech to hand to Wilson as he passed through the city. Wilson usually read the speech through once and it would become as much a part of him as if he had written every word.

How did J. Finley Wilson rank as a leader among Negroes in the United States? The Exalted Ruler held a philosophy of life that enabled him to achieve personal happiness through fellowship and service. To this end, he organized the best talent in the Elks lodge to do each job, and he saw to it that his helpers were justly rewarded. For this kind of treatment, competent workers idolized Wilson until the end of his life, and each one was always ready at his beck and call. Added to this, Wilson was a showman, a powerful orator, "who understood the art of *mixing; he* was indeed a prolific personality." At each convention, Joseph D. Bibb said, "He staged parades, put on shows and extravaganzas. He put drama into his leadership. . . . And this was why he sat undisturbed upon his throne so many years."[4] Paying tribute to Wilson for his twenty-six years of leadership, the *Norfolk Journal and Guide,* in an editorial on September 21, 1946, said:

In the light of this record alone, whatever the comment may be, critical or laudatory, regarding his regime as the titular head of the Elks Order whose membership approximates a half-million persons, he has unmistakably evidenced capacity for leadership.

Significantly, while his is an elective office, held at the will of the majority of the members, during the last two decades, he organized a movement that has arisen among the vast and still expanding Elks membership of sufficient force and vitality to constitute an effective move to displace him.

Such an uninterrupted and protracted leadership of an organization, the scope of which embraces the whole United States, parts of Canada, and the Canal Zone, whose members represent diverse creeds and classes, depends for its survival upon the individuality and ability, no less than personal popularity of the leaders.

The Grand Exalted Ruler organized more lodges than most of his predecessors combined. Unless it was Marcus Garvey, no man has attracted and captivated such large groups of followers in a membership as did the head of the Elks.

It cannot be said with absolute accuracy how much influence J. Finley Wilson wielded during his long fraternal career. It was known that he had to overcome many obstacles in building this organization. there were financial difficulties, violations of rules, need for increased membership, and the imperatives for education and health programs. The economic depression during Hoover's administration brought added problems. In spite of these disturbing events, Wilson worked on and preached the spirit of Elkdom. His organization expanded, and its members were scattered over the United States, Canada, and Canal Zone. The effect of the orator's speeches upon listeners cannot be generalized easily. It is known that audiences liked his speaking. Often, he stirred their emotions and stimulated their thinking and often their action. He aroused pride in the black race, and he made the audience feel the enjoyment of oratory as an art. Finally, he aroused in Negroes a desire to be somebody and to exercise the privilege of voting.

Footnotes, Chapter 11

1. "Who's Who Among the Big Elks," *Color* 3 (January, 1947): 8–13.
2. Joseph D. Bibb, *Pittsburgh Courier,* May 6, 1950.
3. Order of Elks, "National Oratorical Contest, Rules and Regulations."
4. Bibb, *Pittsburgh Courier,* May 6, 1950.

12 / Hats in the Ring

Five years after the Civil War, Negroes made bids for state and federal political offices, which they filled from 1869 to 1901, when George H. White's retirement from the United States House of Representatives marked the end of a political epoch for Negroes. Then for twenty-eight years after the retirement of Congressman White in 1901, no Negroes were elected to that body. The period became a sort of political interregnum. The notion therefore developed that the Negro was, humanly speaking, out of politics for good, or certainly for an indefinite period. Consequently, the American Old Guard was disturbed and surprised when Oscar S. DePriest, a Negro, took a seat in the United States Congress from the First District of Illinois in 1928.

CONGRESS AND ORATORY

The Atomic and Nuclear Age, 1945 to 1965, with its microphones and loudspeakers, seemed to have bridled the tongues of our lawmakers into a group of manuscript readers who have failed to command the respect once held by such front-runners as Daniel Webster and Henry Clay. Often one listens in vain for an echo of the oratory that once was heard in the legislative chambers of the nation. P. L. Prattis, writing in "Capital Confetti," *Pittsburgh Courier* for May 3, 1947, stated that one exception to this rule was the eloquence of Adam Clayton Powell, Jr., the New York Democrat, who has captivated his colleagues in the House where dull speakers are drowned out by a buzzing bedlam. Continuing his remarks, Prattis added:

The House is a chamber of horrors for the ungifted speaker. But there are members who can take the House in the hollow of their hands. One of these, you will be pleased to know, is Adam Clayton Powell. He is not able to do this because he has a loud voice. Halleck of Indiana has a loud voice also, but somehow fails to impregnate the atmosphere roundabouts as does Powell. Rankin can rant and scream, but he can't stop the buzzing in the chamber. Powell *can*. He is not only eloquent, he is portentious. He is shrewd, cunning, and daring. He is smart and unpredictable. He's a tough man. He is feared where he is not respected.

Mr. Powell's dominance of his minute, or five minutes, cannot be questioned. He ought to be leader of a team, but he isn't. You sense that he is somewhat of a rambunctious lone wolf. They listen to him, but there is doubt that they will follow him.

It was back in 1947 when Editor Prattis made the foregoing remarks; but, from 1955 to 1965, Powell had an associate vocal "wind-binder" in the person of Senator Everett Dirksen,[1] who held the Senate with his eloquence. With his tousled hair and a voice that throbbed "like a hi-fi set in need of adjustment, Dirksen is one of the easiest senators to recognize." Some call him "the wizard of ooze whose tonsils are marinated in honey." To get some idea of the kind of leader he was, one has only to recall Dirksen's push to revise the Supreme Court's one-man vote in legislative reapportionment ruling.

Regardless of what we may say or think about the quality of speaking in the United States Congress, it must be remembered that oratorical style is being largely influenced by our modern methods of communication—the radio, television, and loudspeaker system. Yet, there is no excuse for mediocre speaking in Congress. One remembers our beloved President Franklin Delano Roosevelt, who rose to oratorical heights because of his "fireside chats" broadcast over radio and television networks.

OSCAR STANTON DEPRIEST

Oscar S. DePriest, the first twentieth-century Negro in the United States Congress, was elected in 1928. For him, it was a long, hard journey. He advanced from a limited educational background in Alabama to the highest political position in the First Congressional District of Illinois. He had been a migrant from the South, a laborer, a businessman in Chicago, Republican precinct captain, a political propagandist, and a party organizer. According to Lem Graves, Jr., journalist, "Somebody had to break the political bottleneck which had stymied the Negro Community of the United States."[2] It took DePriest to achieve it. Enemies of DePriest have charged that he didn't win fairly the election in 1928, but regardless of this allegation, Lem Graves said, "But history will hardly question his technique. It will record that the national political drought which had been visited upon the largest minority was ended by a two-fisted, courageous and personable man from Chicago's First District."

Oscar DePriest was by no stretch of the imagination a silver-tongued orator in the usual sense. He was often crude, and sometimes uncouth in his delivery, the by-product of tough ward politics. His stand, however, was uncompromising, and this made him the idol of thousands. On one occasion, he defied a Ku Klux Klan threat and spoke in a Catholic Church in Mobile, Alabama. The Congressman never pretended to be an orator, and his enemies said that he was bombastic and talked as though his mouth was full of hot potatoes. This criticism did not disturb DePriest, because he knew that when he spoke people listened. In political meetings, he was gifted in arousing sentiment among Negro voters. He was inclined to support his main points with startling statements. Thus he said on one occasion: "I spoke in Nashville, Tennessee. Someone said I should talk on social equality of the races. But whites in the South are not appropriate audiences for talk on social equality. The federal census shows an increase by thousands in the births of mulattoes, mostly in the South. They have jim-crow theater laws and jim-crow streetcar laws, but what they need is jim-crow bedroom laws."

As a leader of his race, DePriest was instrumental in becoming the spiritual leader of 13 million Negroes. This role he assumed with a great deal of pleasure. Invitations to speak came from every section of the nation, and the Congressman accepted them. Under these circumstances, he had to neglect his legislative duties so that he might speak to arouse Negroes from political inactivity. Public speaking increased his prestige immensely, and he became a forthright defender of the rights of Negroes. This reputation made it easy for him to win reelection to the Seventy-second Congress. During the campaign, DePriest "bucked successively the nationwide swing to Roosevelt in 1932 and later angered Franklin Delano Roosevelt by insinuating that Roosevelt *lied* to Negroes. He asked the President to throw his influence behind his [DePriest's] civil rights bills."[3] The President coldly dismissed DePriest, but the Congressman's stand endeared him to American Negroes. As a member of the Indian Affairs Committee in the House of Representatives, Oscar DePriest introduced several bills and delivered fiery speeches on them in debate. He successfully supported an amendment that restored thousands of dollars to the appropriations for Howard University. DePriest did all in his power to force a Washington restaurant to serve his secretary, Morris Lee, but lost the battle.

ARTHUR W. MITCHELL

"One of the most unorthodox stories of Negro political history is that of the farmer, lawyer, and congressman, Arthur W. Mitchell," said Lem Graves, Jr.,[4] a newspaperman. In comparison with DePriest, his predecessor, Mitchell was a novice in Chicago politics. When DePriest went to the United States Congress in 1928, Mitchell, an attorney, was a newcomer to Chicago from Washington, D.C., where he had been affiliated with the Republican party. In 1932, he became a Democrat and actively participated in the national campaign. Therefore, in 1934, the novice Mitchell ran against DePriest, the incumbent Congressman.

When Mitchell sallied forth into the campaign in 1934, DePriest did not pay much attention to the smart young lawyer from out of town, who set himself up in the "giant-killing" business. But Mitchell didn't underestimate DePriest, the old pro, in the least, and therefore he conducted a person-to-person campaign among the people who would listen. Thus, in a political upset, Mitchell won the 1934 campaign by a vote of 27,963 to 24,820 votes polled by DePriest.

Although Mitchell called the voters' attention to the conspicuous absences of DePriest from the sessions of Congress, there was another factor that deprived DePriest of thousands of the votes he expected to poll. This factor was the psychological effect of the Hoover administration upon the people. Voters had become tired of the promise that "prosperity is just around the corner," and it so happened that Mitchell entered the campaign when the time was ripe for a change. Again, in 1940, Mitchell campaigned with the slogan, "Reelect Roosevelt and Mitchell, Friends of the People." Political advertisements heralded the incumbent as "the Ambassador of Goodwill between the Races." Dean Gordon B. Hancock, in a *Dayton Forum* editorial, acclaimed Mitchell as "the Major Prophet of the Negro race today."[5] Hancock stated that although Mitchell received criticism from certain know-it-alls, he stood by his guns and won. One of the Congressman's most striking and far-reaching achievements was his fight against Jim-Crow cars and racial discrimination in the South. He filed a petition with the Interstate Commerce Commission to force railroads to give Negroes equal accommodations with other races. His fight was also directed against racial discrmination in the Civil Service and sought to do away with their use of photographs.

According to Mitchell's *Crusaders,* the Congressman was a little above medium height, rather unusually handsome, with shoulders and chest giving evidence of exceptional strength. He dressed conservatively and in excellent taste. He was inclined to be reserved and to keep his own counsel, but this was not a weakness. On the contrary, he made a definite impression as a man of purpose and determination, who tried to do as much as he could in behalf of Negroes. The Congressman was a temperate individual and "eschewed tobacco, liquor, nightclubs and underworld dens."

The Congressman took his office seriously and chalked up one of the best records for legislative votes and presence on the floor of any Negro Congressman before or since. After completing four terms, Mitchell made his farewell address on December 14, 1942. He told his colleagues that he was retiring voluntarily, and remarked: "Tomorrow, I go to live in the great state of Virginia. . . . I will go down there to dedicate anew my life and every bit of energy I possess to working out a better understanding between the two races in the South."

The Congressman did not consider himself an orator, although he made many speeches upon invitation. He spoke on subjects dealing with the Negro and migration, the Democratic party, the New Deal, lynching, and how the Negro sought to overcome adverse circumstances. Once, in 1939, Mitchell spoke to the Colored Intercollegiate Association which met in Richmond, Virginia. Students and townsmen turned out in large numbers to get a close look at the Congressman. Mitchell did not spend as much time cursing the white man as he did showing Negroes their duty and responsibility. He made it clear that the future was largely a matter the Negro must settle for himself. Gordon Hancock, professor at Virginia Union University, said: "The speech was well received, for students applauded and called for more. Staid old professors sat in solemn meditation, while townsmen seemed bewildered at what was transpiring before their eyes. For two and half hours, the Congressman *laid it on* and students and faculty cried for more."[6] One of Mitchell's speeches was on the subject of "The Coming Democracy." He first delivered it before the Commonwealth Club of San Francisco on December 4, 1942. He called upon Negroes to defend America in her most crucial undertaking and reminded Congress and the government that Negroes expected the same treatment under our so-called democratic form of government that was accorded to all other citizens.

The Negro press, in reporting the activities of Mitchell, labeled him neither radical nor conservative. Editors apparently could not make up their minds about Congressman Mitchell. They hailed him one week and criticized him caustically the next. Some journalists considered his speeches of the appeasement type, with much included about friendship and good feelings between the races. However, they could never forget the Mitchell who personally stood off an Alabama lynch mob with a Winchester rifle.

WILLIAM DAWSON

Congressman William L. Dawson launched his political career in 1933 as an alderman of the second ward in Chicago, and held this office until 1939. During the campaign for the United States Congress, Dawson won the support of his buddies who fought with him in World War I. As a young attorney, he entered the congressional race as early as 1928 and made the Republicans more uncomfortable than any former Negro candidate. Dawson asserted that a Negro should represent the people of the First District, and added:

By birth, training, and experience, I am better fitted to represent the district at Washington than any candidate on the field. Mr. Madden, the present congressman, does not even live in the District. He is a white man. Therefore, for these two reasons, if no others, he can hardly voice the hopes, ideals, and sentiments of the majority of the District.

Although DePriest won the 1928 election, Dawson polled 29 percent of the Republican primary votes. It was not, however, until 1942 that he was elected to succeed Arthur Mitchell. Since then, he has served continually at the nation's capital and became chairman of the Committee on Expenditures, Executive Department. Today the Congressman holds an influential place among the leaders of the Negro race. By shrewdness and tact, his words carry weight in the councils of the party leaders.

As a speaker, Dawson is not spectacular, because he does not employ bombastic oratory or vigorous arm-waving. To win favor for the cause of the Negro, he allies himself with powerful political figures. It is Dawson's idea to break down prejudice by patience and diplomacy. Although not eloquent, the speeches that have been delivered by the Congressman have been firm in structure and harmonious in mood. He does not resort to bold assertions that arouse sentiments and excitement, but rather his delivery is logical and unemotional. Mr. Dawson drew perhaps the greatest praise of his career when the Negro press reported his attack on the Winstead Amendment, which favored segregation of races in the United States armed forces. For firing his big gun vocally on this occasion, the *Pittsburgh Courier* labeled the incident "His Finest Hour."[7] In addressing the House, Dawson cried out:

How long, how long, my confreres and gentlemen from the South, will you divide us Americans on account of color? God didn't curse me when he made me black, anymore than he cursed you by making you white. Give me the test that would apply to make any full-fledged American, and by the living God, if it means death itself, I will pay it—but give it to me.

In his noncongressional lecturing, Dawson stresses the idea that Negroes cannot win by pitting race against race. The following statement from his Wilberforce University commencement address illustrates this point of view:

There are thousands of patriotic, fair-minded white people in this country—North and South—who will stand at our side and fight for the things we are entitled to and deserve. This number will increase by leaps and bounds in proportion as we intelligently use the proper means at our disposal to meet the situation. Any Negro leader or institution whose action, words, and propaganda are calculated to breed racial hatred in the hearts of Negroes against any people because of race is a greater menace, a greater detriment to the group from within, than any outside person could ever be. We cannot win by arraying race against race. We cannot win by engendering and holding hatred against white people because they are white.[8]

ROSCOE CONKLING SIMMONS ("THE GOLDEN-VOICED ORATOR")

The reputation of Roscoe Conkling Simmons hinged upon his political activities and his "golden-tongued speeches." His strongest bid for political office was in 1930 when he ran unsuccessfully against the "old pro," Oscar S. DePriest for United States Congress from the First District of Illinois in the Republican primary. Simmons was no political neophyte; he had already been active in the Republican Presidential campaigns of 1920, 1924, and 1928. For Mr. Simmons this was a mammoth opportunity, and he readied his big vocal guns for the purpose of "ramrodding" his way to victory. DePriest certainly had reason to be concerned, for Simmons was the most formidable of the four candidates who entered the primary race. The First District was a prize to be desired, since it comprised the Loop and most of Chicago's great black belt.

The versatile Simmons was a man to watch, for he was capable of breaking through political lines of opposition for a touchdown campaign. His speaking attributes attracted large crowds who were impressed by his arguments. It should be noted here that Simmons was a past president of the Second Ward Republican Club under Dan Jackson, a committeeman who died on May 17, 1929. But Alderman Anderson, who was appointed committee chairman in the deceased Jackson's place, backed Oscar DePriest in the 1930 campaign. Nevertheless, Simmons launched a vigorous campaign on the grounds that Congressman DePriest had not submitted his candidacy to the people, and that it was the desire of Congressman Martin B. Madden that he (Simmons) should become the United States Congressman from the First District. Simmons, in his various platform speeches, promised he would "represent the spirit of this country, the patience, the intelligence and the progress of his people." Unfortunately, Simmons, who got little support from the GOP headquarters, was defeated by DePriest by a plurality of 12,000 votes.

Roscoe Simmons made his campaign vigorous by dynamic oratory. At one of the campaign meetings, Simmons said:

The word *congress* means a "meeting of minds." Now that is the kind of meeting where Roscoe Simmons belongs. No one has a right to keep him out of that body. I am you; when I go there, you go there. . . . If I had one word to give to the Negro in Chicago, it would be *patience*. I deal with white people in the charming language of undefeated *patience*. I was raised in the home of Booker T. Washington, whose motto for the colored people was "Labor and Humility."[9]

It was this type of speaking that led the *Chicago Daily News,* during the DePriest-Simmons campaign, to label Simmons a "mellifluous-tongued Negro orator and spellbinder." And yet, with hurt pride, Simmons lamented the failure of DePriest to get the voters' approval for his candidacy, inasmuch as De-Priest was selected by a committee of gentlemen on the instruction of certain GOP powers whom they could not afford to refuse. This situation developed because Governor Len Small did not call a special election to fill the vacancy caused by the death of Mr. Madden. Thereby the Governor violated a certain provision in the United States Constitution, which states that "whenever vacancies happen in the representation from any state, the executive authority thereof shall issue writs of election to fill them." And so Mr. DePriest, in being selected by a committee, appeared in the Congress without submitting his candidacy to the judgment of his party in keeping with the law.

Roscoe C. Simmons was endorsed by the Second Ward Republican Club for the office of Illinois state senator in 1932 to represent the Third District, of which the incumbent was Adellient H. Roberts. As a candidate for the Illinois State Senate, Simmons addressed 5,000 voters one Sunday afternoon in the old Eighth Regiment Armory in Chicago. Several thousands more heard him over loudspeaker amplifiers in the streets. According to P. L. Prattis, in "Capital Confetti," a column in the *Pittsburgh Courier* (May 3, 1947), Simmons bowed low over the microphone, taking the listeners into his confidence, and declared:

The Senate means debate! [He stepped back from the microphone, tapped himself upon the chest and got the audience to agree: "That's me!"]

The Senate means disputation! [The audience moved forward expectantly as the great orator again stepped back from the instrument, beat his chest once more and declared anew: "That's me!" He wasn't through though. He allowed time for these words to sink in, then bowed low over the microphone again.]

The Senate needs [He began, then paused, and] *eloquence!* [The words were uttered explosively. Quickly Mr. Simmons stepped around the microphone to the edge of the platform and screamed]

AND GOD KNOWS THAT'S ME!

Mr. Simmons was not elected.

Roscoe Simmons was a good public relations man for the Republicans in many ways, and especially in the role of orator. The election of 1936 led the GOP to assign him to the state convention credentials committee. In the campaign, Simmons declared at a luncheon that Harry S. Ditchburne as state attorney and Wayne Brooks as governor were essential to victory for the Republican national ticket in the November election. "My people," declared Simmons, "are deeply concerned over the threat of dictatorship [meaning Franklin D. Roosevelt] and the reality of centralized bureaucracy. Governor Alf Landon of Kansas and Col. Knerv of Chicago should be elected, but the strength of the national ticket depends on local effort."

Simmons spoke eloquently, and his oratory took him to high places in national Republican circles. In 1932, he seconded the nomination of Herbert Hoover for reelection as President at the Republican Convention in Chicago. Full-voiced, fluent, impressive in manner without being pretentious, Simmons possessed all the equipment for platform spellbinding. Such gifts may not be very profound, but their effect upon the convention listeners was very exhilarating. Simmons, with far-carrying tones, stirred thousands of convention attendants; and in a tribute to Hoover and Lincoln, the orator said, "History will dip her pen in the dews of truth and beneath the story of Lincoln's patience she will write the story of Hoover's endurance." When recalling Frederick Douglass, the forensic genius who had seen his emancipator fall in death, Simmons said: "As he lifted me, and those with me, from the living, merciless death of the fetters, I also, like Douglass, cry out, 'the Republican Party is the ship: all else is the sea.'" These words evoked prolonged applause.

In 1936, the oratory of Simmons was given credit for the defeat of Senator Tydings, Democrat of Maryland, who was seeking reelection. The orator was commissioned to tour Maryland and tell the Republican story. He began the Maryland tour on October 4, and worked under the management of Marse S. Calloway, a Baltimore real-estate man and Negro political leader. In the state, the orator spoke for Alf Landon. His speeches traced liberty from the Pilgrims to 1950, and in every address he terminated his speech with the words: "My countrymen, on one side are *Landon* and *Liberty;* on the other side are *Roosevelt and Ruin.* May God be with us!"

It was Roscoe Simmons's brilliant political oratory that brought him invitations to speak before nonpolitical audiences, and in this role he was not without charm. Named after one of America's greatest orators, Roscoe Conkling, Simmons modeled his vocal style after that of Robert G. Ingersoll, who is remembered for his classic funeral oration at his brother's grave. Typical of Simmons's speaking engagements was the invitation to address the Young Men's Jewish Charities on January 21, 1933, at the Covenant Club. He also spoke to the West End Catholic Women's Club in February, 1937, at a Lincoln's Day program.

Roscoe C. Simmons was born in Greenview, Mississippi, and rose from a humble environment to a position of prominence enjoyed by few Negroes during his times. He was nephew of the wife of Booker T. Washington, the educator at Tuskegee, Alabama. When young Simmons was thirteen, he was sent to Washington to Senator Marcus A. Hanna, a powerful millionaire industrialist who was famed as a "President-Maker." For a while, he lived with the family of Senator Medill McCormick of Illinois.

The orator's flair for writing gave him connections with two newspapers, the *Chicago Tribune* and *Chicago Defender.* In the *Chicago Daily News,* he wrote a column entitled "The

Untold Story," and was a staff member of the *Chicago Defender,* a Negro newspaper, for more than twenty years. When Simmons died on April 27, 1951, his funeral was held in St. Anselm's Church on Michigan Avenue in Chicago. Journalist Trezzvant W. Anderson paid him this tribute:

Death has stilled the tongue of one of the nation's greatest orators— Roscoe Conkling Simmons, friend and confidante of Presidents and Democrats alike, even though he was a Republican.

The world knew him as the silver-tongued orator who wove a spell of magic and brought pretty pictures into the very sight of the mind's eye to linger indelibly. The picture of Roscoe Simmons striding across the platform, with expressive hands waving and his voice, as it were, were a familiar sight in many parts of America, where he has spoken.

The experience gained with the Hanna and McCormick clans gave Simmons a political seasoning enjoyed by few Negroes as politicians.[10]

Because Roscoe Simmons was a strong politician to be reckoned with, Republicans could not afford to offend him even though they did not elect him to any public office. They knew that the man's oratory had an uncanny power in defeating political aspirants whom he wanted to destroy. Republicans first noticed the oratorical genius of Mr. Simmons when he campaigned for Theodore Roosevelt in 1910. After one burst of oratory on Roosevelt's behalf, the great orator, William Jennings Bryan, said, "Tonight's speech by young Roscoe Simmons has assured him a place among the great orators of the world."[11] Evidently Simmons wanted this to be his mission in life, for when Booker T. Washington asked him to take a teaching position at Tuskegee Institute, he turned down the offer forthwith, answering, "I have been called to teach, but the rostrum and the public hall will be my classroom."

The world of politicos felt the dedication of the man who rose into the limelight upon the wings of service and an enchanting voice. While there is no concrete evidence to support the conclusion, Simmons must have been bitter when various political elective prizes were denied him. But, in death, the deceased orator was honored by the Illinois House of Representatives when it adopted resolutions in the form of a eulogy at his death and expressed profound sorrow and heartfelt sympathy at the passing of a true and staunch Republican. Note was taken that the Honorable Roscoe C. Simmons "worked ceaselessly throughout his life for the betterment of his race and a closer understanding between his people and others."

The *Chicago Defender* came into its own in 1918 as a journalistic success. The full account of the history of this paper has been admirably told in *The Lonely Warrior* (1955) by the late Roi Ottley. Noting that Simmons was a public relations man par excellence, the *Chicago Defender* engaged his services for nearly twenty years. The newspaper sent Simmons, the spellbinding Republican orator, on a tour of the South as their newspaper representative at large for the purpose of stimulating circulation and sales. Roi Ottley referred to Simmons as "the *star* personality of the *Defender*," for he eventually became the highest paid employee in Negro journalism, earning more than $600 monthly plus expenses. For this reason, Simmons was continually plugged. To boost the sizes of his audiences, the newspaper described him as "America's Greatest Orator," and added, "With nothing behind him save the truth and his amazing genius, this man at 35 years, is the ambassador of 12,000,000, the wisest champion his Race has ever had, and his country's foremost orator." All of this high-powered billing had a purpose, and Robert Abbott, the publisher, was no fool: Simmons, a nephew of Booker T. Washington, in truth could attract audiences of several thousands anywhere he spoke; and he often made five or six promotional speeches a week, which enabled the *Defender* to cash in on his popularity. His critics called him "that Rascal Roscoe," but the publisher had an undeniable affection for him.

Thus ends the narrative of Roscoe Conkling Simmons, orator, journalist, politician, columnist, and public relations expert. It is known that people listened to his speeches attentively, and he felt his body and brain move into "free-wheeling" motion while from his lips poured brilliant phrases that were accompanied by magnificent gestures. Realizing that the spoken word is evanescent, Simmons repeated his main ideas several times in a dramatic manner. During life's little hour, the orator did not have the opportunity to demonstrate in CORE fashion, but he could lift up men's spirits and inspire confidence by the power of the spoken word.

PATRICK B. PRESCOTT

It would be inaccurate to classify Judge Patrick B. Prescott, Jr.,[12] as strictly a political orator, although it was in this phase of his platform activity that he received the most newspaper publicity. It was in the political arena that he was constantly in demand, and this was the type of speaking he enjoyed most. Personally, Prescott regarded his work at meetings of an "inspirational" nature far more highly. He was frequently invited to deliver commencement addresses in Chicago and the surrounding area, as well as at colleges in various parts of the country. Very often he was on programs at interracial conferences and at meetings sponsored by the NAACP, the Urban League, fraternal organizations, churches, and women's clubs.

During his last years, he was invited to address various Kiwanis clubs of the Illinois area and was accorded honorary membership in this organization. At the time of his death, he had a long list of unfulfilled engagements to address other Kiwanis clubs. Prescott was popular as an afterdinner speaker.

But he liked best those addresses that gave him an opportunity to discuss civic life, government, and public affairs. He was considered an authority on the history and development of the American Constitution. The orator averaged three to five nonpolitical speeches a week. According to various speaker's bureaus, there was no other speaker on their list for whom there were as many requests.

The Republican party found in Patrick B. Prescott a top-flight speaker who appeared on the platform in its behalf from 1928 to the time of his death. These speeches include keynote speaking at state conventions, mass meetings held in the Coliseum in Chicago, the First and Eighth Regiment armories, downtown theaters, the Chicago Stadium, and radio stations. His last political address was given when he seconded the nomination of Thomas E. Dewey in June, 1944.

Patrick B. Prescott, Jr., was born in New Orleans in 1890. As a lad, he attended the public schools of New Orleans. His high school and normal school study was done at Southern University, Baton Rouge, Louisiana. The doctor of jurisprudence degree was conferred upon him by the John Marshall Law School in Chicago. In 1908 Prescott came to Chicago to study mathematics at the University of Chicago, and architecture at Armour Institute of Technology. He gave up his study of architecture on the advice of the dean, because of the effect of the work upon his eyesight. Always interested in writing, Prescott produced a number of articles and stories between 1910 and 1920. Some of his stories appeared in the *Saturday Evening Post, Colliers,* and the Street and Smith fiction magazines. During this period, he studied law and was admitted to the bar of Illinois in 1924.

Prescott held many high and responsible positions. He was assistant corporation counsel of Chicago in 1927. In 1941 he was appointed associate judge of the Municipal Court of Chicago by Governor Greene. He was also chairman of the Speaker's Bureau of the Western Division, National Republican Campaign in 1940. From 1941 to 1945, Prescott was special appeal agent of the Selective Service in Chicago. He died of a heart attack in December, 1945.

The subject matter of Prescott's oratory was most remarkable for its versatility. His composition was fresh, nonrepetitive, and keenly analytical. The content of his speeches was optimistic in its tone and marked by broad vision and originality of ideas. Court reporters and stenotypists said he was difficult to keep up with because of his rapid-fire delivery. On the platform, he presented a vigorous presence; he was a decisive, dynamic, and possibly a bit too serious personality. Rarely effective as a humorist, he nonetheless had a successful light touch. His vocabulary was distinguished for its variety, freshness of expression, felicity, and appropriateness. He often told his wife that his proficiency was the result of years of self-discipline as a writer.

Judge Prescott rarely read from a prepared text. Whenever he used one, he did so because he was compelled to by regulations of broadcasting stations. Even then, he frequently pretended to read from a blank sheet of paper to be independent of a manuscript, and yet satisfy the radio technicians. He attributed his success in speaking to following the rules that a speaker's ideas must be well organized and fresh, and that delivery must be vigorous, with a voice that could be listened to without strain. He credited his effective style of speaking to the excellent training given him in the normal course at Southern University by an exceptionally gifted teacher.

William E. Stewart, columnist for the *Chicago Evening American,* once cited Prescott as one of the three outstanding orators of his time. Another writer, Clifton Utley, in his news comments on the doings of the 1944 Republican Convention, called Prescott's speech seconding the nomination of Thomas E. Dewey for President "unquestionably the most brilliant speech of the morning." In October, 1932, Prescott spoke to nearly 20,000 people at the Kankakee County Fair. The *Chicago Defender,* in reporting the speech, said:

Patrick B. Prescott, well-known attorney and public speaker, was one of the headliners last Tuesday evening at the Coliseum. . . . Prescott differs from most speakers of his race in that he deals with issues vital to all races and peoples and does not confine himself to those of race and religion. He spoke at the Kankakee County Fair to thousands of Chicagoans, at the Coliseum on George Washington's birthday, and has appeared on platforms all over the state of Illinois.[13]

At a Republican meeting in the Coliseum on October 26, 1932, Prescott's speaking led the *Chicago American* to comment: "Anna L. Smith, former Democratic committee-woman, and Patrick B. Prescott of the second ward, aroused the crowd to great enthusiasm by eulogies on Hoover, Len Small, and other candidates."

ARCHIBALD JAMES CAREY, JR.

The Reverend Archibald James Carey, Jr., is versatile in three fields: jurisprudence, theology, and oratory. He belongs to that group of orators who have taken the platform in the interest of a sorely oppressed people. In politics, Carey is known for his fighting spirit. He has spoken in many political campaigns, appearing in forty of Chicago's fifty wards, a dozen counties downstate, Cleveland, Toledo, Cincinnati, Detroit, Des Moines, Kansas City, Milwaukee, Minneapolis, St. Paul, Louisville, and Baltimore. Some of the speeches were made in political campaigns on the national level for Willkie and Dewey. Others were given in local campaigns made in support of Governor Dwight Green of Illinois, with whom Carey started in politics when Green made his first successful run for the mayorship of Chicago.

"Archibald James Carey is a political anomaly. He is a Republican—but sometimes the Republicans don't think so,"[14] said Horace Cayton. For example, Carey took issue with the Republicans on the Taft-Hartley bill. Although loyal to

Governor Green, he sometimes opposed the governor's principles. "The reason he is able to do this and still be supported by the reactionary Green machine is that he is articulating the hopes and ambitions of more than 400,000 Negroes who live in Chicago," declared Cayton. Carey speaks for public housing for all races and for many social reforms. On one occasion, he went to see Congressman DePriest, who gave him the brush-off. Because of this incident, Reverend Carey said that he was determined that "DePriest would have to send for him before he would ever go back."

Although he differs with the party leaders on many ideals, Carey has remained loyal to the Republican party. Horace Cayton said there are several reasons for this:

In the first place, his family has grown up in the tradition of the party. His grandfather was a Republican member of the Georgia state legislature, and President Garfield appointed him postmaster at Athens, Georgia. His father was secretary of the Republican Club of Atlanta at ten years of age because he was the only one in the club who could write. At that time, the G. O. P. was the party of progress, at least for the Negro.

Perhaps another reason why Carey remains in the Republican party is that it is easier to get along faster where he has connections. He is frank to admit that Republicans no longer represent the liberal tradition; he is courageous enough to back them on many issues and they cannot discipline him because he is winning over many Negroes to the Republican ticket.

Archibald James Carey, Jr., was born in 1908. His father was a bishop in the AME. Church. As a lad, young Carey attended Wendell Phillips High School. In 1924 he won a year's scholarship at Lewis Institute in Chicago. While attending the law school of the University of Chicago, Carey won the Edmund Burke Scholarship for excellency in debating. He participated in debates with Notre Dame, Wisconsin, Chicago, Northwestern, and other institutions over radio station WLS in Chicago. Carey's yen for service can be attributed to his parents, who convinced him that he had certain obligations to share the cultural advantages he had enjoyed. That is why he chose the ministry, and why he is busy in civic organizations of every description.

Just how did Carey get his start as an orator? His father was a minister who no doubt gave his son some tutoring in the art of public speaking. As early as 1924, Carey, then sixteen years old, exhibited enough eloquence to win a prize of $1,000 for a twelve-minute oration on "The Constitution," a prize that was given by the *Chicago Daily News,* which conducted an oratorical contest for high school students in Illinois, Iowa, upper Indiana, Wisconsin, and Michigan. The boy who won the second prize of $500 was Joseph Metcalfe, once a Hollywood reporter for the *Chicago Daily News.*

Archibald Carey's stage presence is dynamic, and his figure commanding. He has fiery red hair, a light complexion, and weighs almost 200 pounds. His amazing energy can be described thus: "One night he addressed nine meetings. The year before his election to the city council in 1947, he spoke at thirty-three towns. Once he spoke in Portland, Oregon, two days later in Los Angeles, and the following week in Richmond, Virginia." One Sunday he delivered the baccalaureate address at Tuskegee Institute and spoke in his own church in Chicago a few hours later. On the plane coming back, he prepared a brief for a case to be tried the following day in court.

The Reverend Carey thinks fast and has a rapid-fire delivery. Forceful and effective, he voices the sentiments of Negroes in Chicago. Horace Cayton[15] said that Carey knows the wishes of the common man, his problems, his hopes and aspirations. The orator himself has said, "I am dead serious about being useful to people, but I know that my value to the GOP lies in the fact that I take up the issues of the masses of Negroes and deprived whites, and this gives me an immunity from the control of the party bigwigs."

When speaking to an audience, Carey is earnest and adept

in expressing his ideas in a way that stirs the emotions of his hearers. He can convince his listeners, after he himself has been convinced, upon the great issues. His voice is not always loud, and this very fact sometimes adds emphasis. His words are not always flowery, but he likes his audience to admire his garnishment of ideas. He uses rhythm with great effect, and his change of pace is highly important to his platform delivery. In short, he is a great preacher of a new century. One can with considerable confidence call his speech on "Unenforceable Obligations" a classic oration. He is not too much concerned about homiletic form. It is the substance of his thoughts that holds the interest of his audience. His composition is the work of an original and trained thinker. Anything that is unique and distinctive in the thought of a Bible text readily attracts him, and he is certain to call the attention of the listeners to it.

Whether in the church or before a political rally, Carey achieves perfect adjustment of voice to the physical surroundings. His tones are smooth and round, unlabored, and yet penetrating. Judge Carey's oratorical powers cannot be appraised by hearing his sermons alone. One gets a true picture of his eloquence only when he advances a political issue or attacks an injustice against the Negro.

The ideas and concepts of the Reverend Carey attract attention. At a Charter Day address and convocation, Carey told an Atlanta University audience in October, 1945:

Great souls do great work, and the highest obligation we can perform as we move out into the world is to do the best we know in any situation. Every Negro who goes into a new opportunity, by his performance is going to open up or close down the door for other Negro Americans who come after him.[16]

During Negro History Week in 1946, the *Chicago Bee* sponsored a series of radio programs.[17] Carey appeared on one of them and delivered an address entitled "A Page of History." He desired to inspire his black listeners. Witness the following excerpt:

In spite of handicaps imposed by a previous condition of servitude and the resultant restraint of movement imposed by racial discrimination, the Afro-American has made strides which are no less than astounding. Take the matter of acquisition of property, for example. When Negroes were freed in 1865, they owned approximately 12,000 homes and 20,000 farms. Today they own some 700,000 homes and more than 200,000 farms.

Addressing the annual board meeting of the Chicago Urban League in 1940, Carey stressed a significant point in his speech "Unenforceable Obligations": "In the day in which Jesus lived, a Roman soldier could compel a male civilian to carry his pack for one mile. . . . Now Jesus knew the requirement was wrong in the first place. It was oppression, and he hated oppression. But he also knew that even more damaging to the human spirit than suffering from without was the withering experience of determining to do *only* what one had to do. And fearful of this erosion of human character, Jesus counseled, 'And whosoever shall compel thee to go one mile, go with him twain.' " Carey's speeches cover a wide range of topics, but he especially likes to stress for Negro youth the necessity of realizing that he is on trial for about 20 million other black citizens. In pursuit of this goal, he urges everyone "to put his best foot forward, share the benefits and blessings you have with others, and create an atmosphere of brotherhood."

ADAM CLAYTON POWELL, JR. ("THE SLOGAN MAKER")

From the time he was graduated from college to his election as Congressman from Harlem, Adam Clayton Powell, Jr., had worked actively in the civic affairs of New York City. He secured jobs for Harlem Negroes where they had not worked before, and he became a mass-movement leader and crusader. He also assumed the role of a slogan-maker. In 1938, he organized a boycott against the Consolidated Edison Company to force it to hire Negroes in capacities above menial status.

One night each week, thousands of Harlem homes burned candles instead of electricity. This, however, did not work, and Powell called a mass meeting and persuaded people to swarm the office of the company and pay their bills in pennies. After much vocal agitation and picketing, the company promised to give Negroes better jobs. Powell's next target was the telephone company for refusing to hire Negroes. He persuaded Negroes to tie up telephone exchanges in New York City at a designated hour. The movement was successful in helping Negroes to gain their objectives.

Adam Clayton Powell was six years old when his parents brought him to New York City in 1914. His father took over the ministry of the Abyssinian Baptist Church, "celebrated in those days for little more than age, old-time Negro aristocracy, and debts." After graduating from high school, young Powell entered Colgate University where he was graduated in 1930 with the A.B. degree. Two years later, he earned his M.A. at Columbia University. In July, 1934, Powell received the D.D. degree from Shaw University. Then he succeeded his father as pastor of the Abyssinian Baptist Church, probably the largest Protestant congregation in the world.

In the early days the Reverend Powell preached no "valley-and-dry-bones" sermons, but salted his messages with nicely chosen Negro idioms about everyday issues. He was then an outstanding orator and spellbinder of no small stature. In short, said Roi Ottley, "he is the new and different kind of leader of the Negro church—as modern as jive talk."[18] Ben Richardson, who had heard Powell preach his trial sermon on Good Friday night, 1929, made this statement:

Adam preached. His eyes flashed his deep and searing convictions. He was not content to ride the oft-repeated platitudes of other preachers, but he chiseled out new images from old stones of Biblical truths. He went to the source and quarried new stones that others might shape unheard truths for the coming days. The whole congregation was a deeply moved group, and especially for the young preacher.[19]

Most modern-day preachers steer clear of politics, and until 1941, Powell had not thought of a political career. He accidentally drifted into politics when John Ford, a ward politician, told him he might be elected to the city council if he entered the campaign. Powell took Ford's advice and was elected. When the new pastor announced to his church that he was running for the city council, first there was silence. Then, according to Roi Ottley, "as if blitzkrieged with religious fervor, the congregation suddenly turned the sacred meeting into a bedlam of hallelujahs and vociferous handclapping, lasting twenty minutes, leaving no doubt that he had the full backing of his membership."[20]

The passage of a new reapportionment bill in 1940 created in Harlem the Twenty-second District, which was composed mostly of Negroes. In 1944, the Reverend Powell threw his hat in the ring for this seat. He won the primaries of the Republican, Democratic, and American Labor parties, which exempted him from running in the general election. In his campaign speeches, Powell said that he had no program beyond that of securing the total integration of Negroes into the political and economic schemes of the United States. Shortly after his election as United States Congressman, the *Afro-American's* Michael Carter published "Meet Adam Powell," a summary of an interview with the new Congressman. Powell declared:

I don't expect to do much in Congress the first year. A freshman congressman doesn't have a lot of influence. However, I will not be a silent congressman; I shall be vocal. Representative Dawson and myself shall work together hand in glove. Together, aligned, of course, with such liberals as Representative Marcantonio, we shall form the core of a liberal bloc to protest and enlarge the rights of the people. The first thing I shall do when I get to Congress will be to start cracking down on the House restaurant.

Overjoyed at the election of the new Congressman, the people staged a testimonial banquet at which Powell spoke and reiterated his campaign pledges. He said that he would work for the establishment of a council of government, labor, and industry, which would include Negroes in all postwar planning. Meanwhile, before Powell took office, Joseph D. Bibb wrote an article in the *Pittsburgh Courier* that stated:

The new Congress will include two colored representatives for the first time since the days of Reconstruction. During such far-reaching movements, it is expected that the battles against poll tax, lynching, segregation and other evils that bedevil us will continue with new vigor. These two representatives will be greeted by an entrenched and reinvested Democratic Party. The much-vaunted liberalism and humanitarianism of the President will be put in the crucible and the eyes of 13,000,000 colored Americans will be focused on the activities of Dawson and Powell.[21]

After hearing reports of Powell's debate in the House, Gordon B. Hancock, columnist and educator, declared: "If Powell continues in his indicated course and uses the common sense he so far manifested, he is going to advance the fortunes of his race and nation."[22]

Congressman Powell has served in the House since 1945. While loudly applauding his achievements in the early days of his political career, Negroes are beginning to distrust him. They resent his "playing both ends against the middle." His opponents say that he performs his congressional duties "too much like a part-time sideline." This charge has grown out of the fact that Powell absents himself too often from the sessions. In spite of these criticisms, Powell has had no stiff opposition in his campaigns for reelection. These campaigns featured glamour, emotional ideological appeals, fire-and-brimstone speeches, and spectacular labels. Congressman Powell knows that, in New York, prestige and popularity count more in campaigns than well-organized wards and precincts.

Of late, Congressman Powell has been severely criticized for his flagrant absences from the sessions of Congress, treks around the world in high style in the company of female associates, dodging the payment of a libel suit he lost, and discarding two wives to take a third. The recent appearance of a modern biography[23] of the Congressman, entitled *A. C. Powell and the Politics of a Race* by Neil Hickey and Ed Edwin, gives a close-up of an alleged "thumb-to-nose" attitude of a man traveling first class, and titillates the imagination of thousands of his race who have led second-class lives. Powell fell from "grace" when a congressional committee started a probe of alleged mishandling of governmental funds. There was sufficient evidence to warrant a denial of his seat in 1966. Although elected again by his Harlem constituents in 1968, Powell faced considerable opposition in being sworn in office. He was seated finally but with the provision that a specified amount of money be withheld from his salary check each month until the government is reimbursed.

There is widespread belief that one listens in vain for an echo of the oratory that once dominated congressional chambers. However, the eloquence of Powell, before his political downfall, contradicts this notion, for he has captivated his House colleagues where dull speakers were drowned out by a buzzing vocal undercurrent. The man who almost paralleled him in the Senate was Everett McKinley Dirksen[24] who represented the epitome of a Senator. Arthur Edson, AP Writer, once remarked, "Dirksen is the easiest senator to recognize and also the easiest to lampoon. . . . In an arena where the stuffed shirt remains a precious garment, Dirksen dares to poke fun at himself. No one enjoys his masterful performances more than he does. This is why he is a born thespian on the national stage."

Perhaps as a Congressman, Powell's speeches are not expected to be as stirring as those of the Senate, but his fiery oratory defies this assumption. The oratory of the Senate is now less colorful, because it has no more Huey Longs and

Alben Barkleys and Everett Dirksens. We know that Powell is a good public speaker, even if he has absented himself much too often from the congressional proceedings. In February, 1946, a $50 million federal school-lunch bill was introduced in the House. Powell, in a two-hour speech, urged the insertion of an antidiscrimination amendment. Both the bill and amendment passed the House with a vote of 247 to 101. The story of this legislation is reported in detail in the *Pittsburgh Courier* of March 2, 1946.

Adam Clayton Powell, former chairman of the House Education and Labor Committee, proposed amendments on nearly all federal bills appropriating money for public schools in the South. For such activities, he receives more publicity than for anything he does outside of Congress. For instance, in September, 1963, Powell urged Negroes to boycott Santa Claus, claiming he is a commercial invention of white people. In a sermon at his Abyssinian Baptist Church, he asked members, "Have you ever seen a black Santa Claus?" The members replied as a chorus, "Preacher, you said it." During a news conference following the church service, Powell indicated he was making plans for a national rent strike in which tenants of run-down residences would refuse to pay rent unless repairs were made to the buildings.

It is difficult to savor eloquent oratory without the pulsating voice, just as it is to feel the surge of a jet airliner by reading a timetable. Thus, only those who have heard Powell can know that he is the very ideal of vitality and can stir the emotions enough to drive his listeners to action. "But it is left to others to formulate concrete programs,"[25] said Roi Ottley. In this connection, *Life* reported: "Actually, Negroes are more dazzled than lifted up by him and this makes him a hard man to beat."[26] The magazine added that Powell's specialties were "preaching, politics, and enunciating aims." It labeled him the rabble-rousing Champion of Negro rights, who is a flamboyant political curiosity indigenous to the city, who has all parties in his pocket because his hold over Negro voters is so great that politicians fear to fight him. It is known that the dynamic and explosive Powell is an orator who does not hesitate to grapple with fundamental issues that confront the country. Editor Ludlow W. Werner of the *New York Age* has remarked, "Congressman Powell is a master of mob psychology and an effective showman and speaker. He is inclined to be demagogic because he has found it to be his success pattern."

Congressman Powell once spoke at the Wesley Methodist Church of Austin, Texas, in March, 1946. This engagement was the first of a series of lectures that carried him to Waco, Fort Worth, Dallas, and Houston. The lectures were sponsored by Samuel Huston College (now Tillotson-Huston College) in Austin, Texas. When Powell arose to speak in Austin, the audience of 2,500 including the author, had waited two hours because his plane was late. Nevertheless, when the orator started speaking, he immediately captured the attention of his listeners. His arguments were original, his illustrations were striking and apt, his diction was powerful, and his enthusiasm was overwhelming. He was both actor and showman. His language stirred people immensely, and the hearers answered "Amen!" During the speech, the Congressman declared that he was glad to be called a radical because this country has gone forward only as the ferment of radicalism produced men and women of daring.

When the Congressman reached Houston the fifth night, he was at his best. In his introduction, he remarked, "I feel more like I am in Harlem than in the Fifth Ward of Houston." Using the subject, "Let My People Go!" the orator began with these words:

We have just brought to a close the Second World War in a generation for the saving of democracy. We have a V-E Day and a V-J Day, but we will not establish the peace until we have a V-A (Victory in America) Day. There is no going back to yesterday. On

August 6, 1945, the old world went up in smoke over Hiroshima; we are living in a new world, the atomic age, and there is no turning back.

Powell outlined four steps that Negroes must take to gain freedom, and these four steps are printed in his book *Marching Blacks* (1946) as follows: (1) disciplining his resentment, (2) sustaining his indignation, (3) developing militant leadership, and (4) utilizing only collective social action. Above the cheers of his listeners and with outstretched arms in a last gesture of appeal, Powell shouted the words of an old Negro spiritual: "Walk together, Children, Don't You Get Weary, There's a Great Day Coming After While." Cries of "More! more! more!" rang to the rafters for several minutes after the orator had taken his seat.

What Congressman Powell did on his Texas lecture tour is just a sample of what he has done dozens of times during his career. For instance, Powell created pandemonium in the audience when he delivered the Freedom Day address in Independence Hall in Philadelphia in 1947. He stated:

The crack in the bell will never be closed until the black and white common man become united. That crack of hatred, prejudice, and man's inhumanity to man. There is no metal in the world nor skill of an artisan which can weld this bell together so there will be no crack and its tone will be true—the summons to pure freedom. That crack will only be closed by the unity of blacks and whites."

This speech created an effect comparable to the one made by James Weldon Johnson in memorializing the dead of a black New York regiment. In referring to the stand of colors, the orator Johnson cried out, "Mr. Governor, they will bring it back!"

POLITICAL ORATORY ON TRIAL

It has been said that national political oratory is on trial because there are no longer any burning issues like those of yesteryear. Unmistakenly, the Negro has not confronted significant and burning domestic issues in this country. If Negro orators do not have the manner and technique, they have the motivation and zeal, commitment and dedication. No other political specimen can quite match a Negro in pleading for votes, for the vocabulary is vituperative and rich with the earthy words of the poor combined with street vernacular and "hipster jive" talk. They move into high gear immediately, and their vocal intonations hit the popular chords of the audience give-and-take pattern so effective in the Negro church. If the voting booths were available at that moment, the candidate would easily pass his opponents. "This is clear proof," said Professor Harold F. Gosnell in *Negro Politicians,* "that some of the Negro leaders were masters in the manipulation of slogans and symbols."

Considerable criticism has been published of the oratory in our state and national legislatures. The blame has been laid to the election of men with inferior talents, and this criticism does not direct itself to Negroes because few of them get elected to our legislative bodies. What is more, the only Negroes who get elected to Congress and the state legislatures are individuals who have already proved themselves successful in other careers prior to entrance into politics. Of the Negro congressmen on the national level, Adam Clayton Powell is perhaps the most eloquent.

Representative Augustus Hawkins from Los Angeles, California, on the basis of his Los Angeles record in the California state legislature, has been acclaimed by Simeon Booker as "tough, articulate, broadminded, balanced, and a statesman."[27] Yet Hawkins has not distinguished himself in oratory, contending that "one does not need to make a lot of noise to get things done." Next, Representative William L. Dawson, a long-time powerhouse from Chicago, has been more of a "doer" than a vocalizer." Detroit's wealthy businessman, Representative Charles C. Diggs, Jr., is a comparative newcomer in Washington. Naturally, it will take some time for him to attract significant attention to himself in the role of a debater.

Finally, in taking a close look at the quiet and reflective Congressman Robert N. C. Nix from Pennsylvania, one hears that he is a "lackadaisical lawmaker." Journalist Simeon Booker said, "Nix quietly attends to political chores, rarely speaking on the House floor or leading any civil-rights moves. Of the Negro legislators of the present he is the least known and probably has least to show for his tenure of office."[28]

The reader may be inclined to change his views about Representative Robert Nix,[29] who last year blasted southern solons for their double-talk and hypocrisy. The incident was instigated by a speech delivered on the House floor during the Los Angeles rioting by Alabama Democratic Representative James D. Martin, who condemned the rioters and insisted that they individually bear the blame for murder, looting, and pillaging, without being given the comfort of sociological excuses. In responding to the Alabama Representative, Nix, in his introduction, admitted that all decent citizens were aware that the rioters should suffer the consequences when found guilty. He reminded the southern white congressmen that Dr. Martin Luther King, Jr., and President Johnson both had taken strong positions from the beginning and fixed "blame on the rioters and encouraged all lawful means to put down the rioting." Moving into high gear, Representative Nix added:

Violence and terror against the Negro are part and parcel of the situation out of which the Los Angeles riots sprang. [Pointing at his Southern colleagues, Nix spouted] Let them be reminded, too, that such patterns of behavior, both organized and unorganized and by both public officials and private citizens, are a way of life among southern whites in their treatment of Negroes as a race. Thus there can be only an unfavorable comparison of that behavior when contrasted to the extraordinary highly exceptional occurrences in Los Angeles, Harlem, Philadelphia. . . .

Let them be reminded of the violence and terror perpetrated against Negroes by white persons in their own states.

Let them be reminded and lest they forget, remind them I will. . . .
Let them be reminded that they exemplify the epitome of hypocrisy

when they condemn the Los Angeles rioters with righteous indignation but fail to condemn white violence against Negroes and civil rights workers in their own states and constituencies. I am determined that they shall not forget. What were their responses to the Tuscaloosa and Oxford riots on the campuses of state universities? . . . Did they publicly demand that state authorities deal with [those] criminals as criminals, as the Member insists that California do with the Los Angeles rioters; or did they justify those riots as legitimate responses to a so-called *federal invasion?*

Mr. Speaker, what did they say when the Selma-to-Montgomery marchers were set upon and ruthlessly beaten and trampled by unconscionable men acting under color of law? How did they react to the cold-blooded murder of Medgar Evers, James Chaney, Michael Schwerner, Andrew Goodman, Reverend James Reeb, Jimmie Lee Jackson, Mrs. [Viola] Liuzzo, and Reverend Jonathan Daniels? Perhaps the obvious difference between the views and responses of President Johnson, Dr. King, on the one hand, and some of my colleagues on the other, is that the President and Dr. King are unalterably and unequivocally opposed to all violence, terror, murder, and intimidation; while those Members only condemn when perpetrated by persons other than their own white constituents or by the Klan.

Negro politicians are fully aware that violence hangs menacingly over the Negro revolution in many areas in the North, East, West, and South. It is the hatred and emotional passions of white demagogues that block more peaceful transition toward first-class citizenship. Whites throw monkey wrenches in the mechanism of progress, but they should walk upright in order to achieve racial peace and brotherhood. And a significantly large group of minority citizens want to know if this is asking too much of the leaders of democracy, wherever they may reside, and particularly in the South.

Footnotes, Chapter 12

1. *Fayetteville (North Carolina) Observer,* July 1, 1965.
2. Lem Graves, *Pittsburgh Courier,* July 23, 1949, p. 11.

3. Ibid.
4. Lem Graves, "Negroes in the Halls of Congress," *Pittsburgh Courier*, July 30, 1949.
5. Gordon Hancock, Editorial, *Dayton (Ohio) Forum*, February 21, 1941.
6. Ibid.
7. William L. Dawson's speech on segregation in the Armed Forces, *Congressional Record*, 82nd Congress, 1st Session; cf. "His Finest Hour," *Pittsburgh Courier*, April 28, 1951.
8. From "Race Is Not a Limitation," delivered by William L. Dawson at the commencement exercises of Wilberforce University, Ohio, June 14, 1945.
9. Harold F. Gosnell, *Negro Politicians*, p. 64.
10. Trezzvant W. Anderson, *Pittsburgh Courier*, April 5, 1951.
11. Roi Ottley, *The Lonely Warrior*.
12. Most of the materials relating to Patrick B. Prescott were submitted by his wife, Mrs. Anabel Prescott.
13. *Chicago Defender*, October, 1932. Inadvertently the clipping carried no date.
14. "Carey, the Republican," *New Republic* 119– (October 18, 1948): 10. A discussion by Horace Cayton.
15. Ibid.
16. *Pittsburgh Courier*, October 29, 1945, p. 11.
17. Mr. Carey doesn't remember the name of the radio station.
18. Roi Ottley, *New World A-Coming*.
19. Ben Richardson, *Great American Negroes*, p. 240.
20. Ottley, *New World A-Coming*, p. 233.
21. Joseph D. Bibb, *Pittsburgh Courier*, November 25, 1944.
22. *Journal and Guide* (Norfolk, Virginia), July 28, 1945.
23. Neil Hickey and Ed Edwin, *A. C. Powell and the Politics of a Race*.
24. Arthur Edson (AP writer), "Dirksen and Senate Made for Each Other," *St. Petersburg Times*, January 27, 1965, p. 3-D.
25. Ottley, *The Lonely Warrior*, p. 235.
26. *Life*, August 13, 1945, pp. 30–31.
27. Simeon Booker, *Black Man's America*, pp. 92–93.
28. Ibid., p. 223.
29. "Nix Blasts Southern Solons for Double-Talk Hypocrisy," *Jet*, September 16, 1965, pp. 8–9.

13 / Church and Pulpit Oratory

To understand the highly emotional nature of most Negroes as it is related to their religion, one must hark back to the days of slavery. Slavery placed Africans in a hostile environment that strained their emotions to the breaking point. Religion offered these bondmen a way out, for in worship the slaves could release their suppressed emotions and feelings without revealing their resentment to enslavement. At first, untrained slave preachers helped their congregations to work out a technique of survival in a land of bondage. After more than a century, most of the "old-time" preachers have disappeared from the American scene.

In many rural areas, even today, the church is the high spot of the Negro's existence. Religious worship is his main medium of physical, emotional, and mental recreation. After working hard during the week, domestic workers and laborers, who have had very little time for fun, go to church and rock their bodies in complete abandon to the powerful rhythm of the Negro spirituals, gospel songs, and piano music. As the minister utters the word of God, church attendants show their approval with "Amen!" and "Hallelujah!" Some members shout until they are exhausted, but they seem strangely rested afterward. E. T. Kreuger said, "It is not uncommon to see several people participating at the same time, and neither the audience nor participants are concerned over the fact. Songs break out at any time, and the preacher readily pauses to permit outbursts of religious melody."[1]

The preacher follows a somewhat set pattern of vocal delivery, resembling mournful chants in a prayer. He might begin in a low-pitched conversational tone, which later rises as he strides the platform. It often takes an hour before the sermon reaches the point of full fervor. The author has observed this religious feat at least a hundred times during his youth in South Carolina and has been impressed by the emotional response of congregations that were moved by shouts of incoherencies. The voice and action of the minister overshadowed subject matter.

The function of the Negro church following the Civil War was generally the education of the masses, because a host of members could not read to improve their minds. In the South, Negro congregations were cut off from many cultural contacts, such as attendance at operas and the best theaters. "Furthermore," said Benjamin E. Mays, "a goodly number of Negroes believed what their pastors told them. They still exercise a dominant influence in the lives of many."[2]

It appears, however, that the influence of the church is disintegrating, and that pastors are steadily losing ground. It is alleged that the collection of money in churches has overly burdened many aggressive ministers, thus keeping them from taking the lead in community affairs. Many years ago, editors and publishers were compelled to camp at the door of the parsonage in quest of support. Now it is just the reverse. Even in politics the control of the church has been weakened, and it resulted from the suspicion prevalent among voters that subsidies were being given to the religious bigwigs earlier in this century.

A small percentage of Negro churches have a highly intelligent membership, and their ministers are well educated and preach sermons that help members to grapple with their problems. Emotional oratory fails to sway these congregations who are seeking the truth that makes men free. This trend is manifesting itself increasingly, and gradually churches are decreasing emphasis upon emotional preaching, song-singing, and raising finances. Its leadership, meanwhile, has become bold, and the ministers are forming civil-rights armies that are unsurpassed in dedication and fervor. Like four-star generals, many pastors have rushed to the battlefront, wherever it may be. As a consequence, for example, thirty-eight Negro churches were destroyed by fire in 1964. Law-enforcement officials claim they have evidence that proves only eight of them were connected with civil-rights activities.

The white church has generally closed its doors in the face of Negro worshippers. The movement "to let the Master come in" was called "kneel-ins," but they failed miserably in their effectiveness. Conversely, recognition must be given to a few white pastors[3] for openly engaging in demonstrations, often at the cost of their lives or pulpits. Southern white churchmen increasingly have said that abstinence from direct involvement will make it possible for them to be agents of reconciliation after the worst of the battle is over. This attitude, however, does not commend itself to members who want to get involved in the Christian movement and follow in the footsteps of Jesus Christ. In addition, it should be noted that the white church[4] has generally steered clear of politics, the labor movement, and very noticeably from participation in the civil-rights struggle.

Regardless of whatever else may have been accomplished by the Negro church, it has made many of its preachers star salesmen. They are popular with their audiences because they can present ideas in a dramatic and zestful manner. In fact, they deserve to be called orators. The late W. E. B. Du Bois long ago recognized these qualities and described them as follows in his *Souls of Black Folk* (1903):

The preacher is the most unique personality developed by the Negro on the American soil. A leader, a politician, an orator, a "boss," an intriguer, and an idealist—all these he is, and ever, too, the center of a group of men, now twenty, now a thousand in number. The combination of certain adroitness with deep-seated earnestness, of tact with consummate ability, gave him pre-eminence, and helps him to maintain it.[5]

Professor Gosnell[6] said that in the struggles for political power and influence, the Negro church has been a forum in which ministers have assumed the role of campaign orators. Besides, these preachers know that emotionalism in church services has a cathartic and therapeutic value, making it possible for members to drain off mentally some of their increasing personal problems. But they also are aware that congregations must be given information that will help them cope with their daily problems and prevent their neighbors from taking advantage of them.

DR. HOWARD THURMAN ("THE THEOLOGIAN")

For more than thirty years, the Reverend Howard Thurman has agitated against fundamentalism in theology, espoused the doctrine of intuition, and flayed social abuses, racial discrimination, and religious hypocrisy. Although he is a front-rank minister, one searches in vain for information concerning the man and his style of speaking. It is known that he is a dynamic orator and one of our few Negro theologians.

The Reverend Thurman was born in Florida in 1899 and received his early education at Florida Baptist Academy in Jacksonville, Florida, which was later moved to St. Augustine and renamed Florida Normal Institute. While at Florida Baptist Academy, Thurman was a religious worker and debater of exceptional ability. In 1923, he was graduated from Morehouse College with the A.B. degree. He received the B.D. degree from Rochester Theological Seminary, where he earned the reputation of being a distinguished pulpit orator. Then he visited colleges in Burma, India, and Ceylon on a student "pilgrimage of friendship." He was pastor of a church in Oberlin, Ohio, for a time and later served as student counsellor at Morehouse College. After this, the Reverend Thurman was professor of Christian Theology at Howard University. Following his career at Howard University, Dr. Thurman became dean of Boston University's Marsh Chapel, and during 1964 was minister-at-large at the University. At a testimonial program honoring Thurman upon his retirement in June, 1965, the Honorable Joseph Palmer II, Director General of the United States Foreign Service, delivered the main address.

Although many religious fundamentalists criticize Thurman's views, they express enthusiasm for his preaching and personal appeal as an individual. If one were to examine his written sermons, he would discover that the minister commands a language of power. When preaching, he makes his case and gives the audience intellectual meat for our times. The sermons are food, not froth. He does not entertain the souls of men, but rather feeds them with solid speculations in the realm of theology. Dr. Thurman is a most gifted defender of the American ideal of brotherhood and humanitarianism in our nuclear age. Where numerous ministers are emotional and pedantic, Dr. Thurman possesses a profound learning supported by a genuine mystical experience and persuasive logic. The beauty of Thurman's method is that there is nothing left but his own position on faith and denouncement of religious hypocrisy in denominational institutions. What ever may be thought of his oratorical style, it enables him, most often, to preach the gospel of Christ, pure and unadulterated.

One critic described the Reverend Thurman as "most effective as a religious mystic, a dramatic preacher known for his undertones, pointing finger, and mystifying presence."[7] Thurman himself said: "It is my belief that in the presence of God, there is neither male nor female, white or black, Gentile or Jew, Protestant or Catholic, Hindu, Buddhist, or Moslem, but a human spirit stripped to the literal substance of itself before

God." Theologians laud his powers of vocal delivery in the area of "spiritual discipline." His oral composition embodies a style similar to prose set to music. Thurman preaches to the human race rather than to black and white races. He has no axe to grind and preaches to soothe the spirits of the dispossessed of humanity. With his sermon, "Good News for the Underprivileged," he has touched the hearts of many congregations.[8] The challenging question that he puts to his listeners is, "What is the message, the good news that Christianity wants to give to the poor, disinherited, and dispossessed?" In reply, he urges his hearers to absorb the violence directed against them by the exercise of love. He insists that religion gives the "underprivileged man no cover for personal hatred and isolation, but it sends him forth to meet the enemy upon the highway."

In listening to Dr. Thurman preach, the author was lifted spellbound to an apex of spiritual grandeur that often placed him under an enchantment completely separated from the reality of the national issues. When under the spell of the man's oratory, a listener can hardly imagine an equal. The oratorical technique of this theologian includes dramatic presentation in striking at the heart of an ethical and moral issue, undergirded by specific illustrations and imagery. One hardly expects him to lead a civil-rights army from his pulpit; yet his character and attainments have been good propaganda and public relations for civil rights.

During the first week in December, 1965, Dr. Thurman delivered a series of sermons at Livingstone College in Salisbury, North Carolina, and lectured on the campus of nearby Catawba College and before the Salisbury-Spencer Interracial Ministerial Fellowship. At the Sunday afternoon vespers and convocation, the speaker used the theme, "What Shall I Do with My Life?" with the message entitled "Giving Oneself to Something." Combining New England poetry with lines from the New Testament, he drew an analogy to illustrate that the difference between effective living through commitment and aimless existence due to lack of it is a matter of total surrender. "Life always seeks nourishment," he declared, "and in seeking nourishment life always understands where nourishment can be found. But conditions of growth and development have to be met, since growth and development follow normally and automatically."

At another session on Livingstone College's campus, Dr. Thurman preached in Varick Memorial Auditorium and emphasized, "If man is only concerned about material things— food, clothing and the like—his heart will rot." The orator cited the following three conditions requisite to personal commitment: Life has to be accepted, no exceptions will be made for special privileges, and one must live his life in this world in the midst of struggle.

The Reverend Thurman does not need to march in civil-rights demonstrations, since his burning messages expose the hypocritical Christian protestants for what they are. His descriptive language cuts like a two-edged sword in arousing the public conscience and indignation against racial identity, white supremacy, and denominational lethargy. In the peroration of his speeches and sermons, he transfixes the mind while he issues the joyous call to go forth and render to mankind a great service, and to walk the second undemanded mile in making the world a place in which men can live like brothers. In response, listeners cry aloud with a joyful noise. Given an occasion and a pulpit, the "theologian" can play upon the hearts and minds of "the sea of upturned faces" with all the artistry of the gifted and experienced orator. Approbation cannot be denied him.

BENJAMIN E. MAYS ("THE EDUCATOR")

Benjamin E. Mays, president of Morehouse College in Atlanta, is a journalist, orator, preacher, and social reformer. He believes in mixing religion with education, economics, and politics. To him the pulpit is a place for adjusting man's relationship to other men and to God. For more than forty years, Dr. Mays has used the platform to uplift and improve the condition of his fellowman. Standing as he does against racial discrimination, America's chief ill, Mays brought a lawsuit against the southern railway in 1941 for segregating him in a dining car, a practice outlawed by the Supreme Court in 1950. As a crusader, he has joined various progressive movements. While several of these organizations have been declared Red-tainted,[9] no one has questioned his loyalty and right to fight for the fulfillment of constitutionally guaranteed democracy.

Benjamin E. Mays was born in Epworth, South Carolina, on August 1, 1895. His parents sent him to high school at South Carolina A and M College in Orangeburg from which he was graduated as valedictorian in 1916. In 1920, he was graduated from Bates College where he was president of the Phil-Hellenic Club, member of the YMCA, and an honor student. Bates College elected him a Phi Beta Kappa in 1935. He earned the M.A. and Ph.D. degrees from the University of Chicago, and the D.D. degree was conferred upon him by Howard University. Mays became a pastor in Atlanta while he was teaching at Morehouse College from 1921 to 1924. He taught one year at South Carolina A and M College and later was executive secretary of the Tampa Urban League, after which he was national student secretary of the YMCA. From 1930 to 1932, he directed a study of Negro churches in the United States. In 1934, he became dean of the Howard University School of Religion. Benjamin Mays was elected president of Morehouse College in 1940. He has written several books, including *The Negro's Church* and *The Negro's God,* as well as contributing chapters to four other books.

The speaking career of Benjamin E. Mays began at Bates College, where he participated in debating and engaged in public discussion on the Bates Forum. During his sophomore year, Mays won the Sophomore Declamation Contest; during his senior year, he was class orator. In college, he took two courses in public speaking and pursued a homiletic course while studying theology.

Mays outlined two major prerequisites for a successful public speaker. He says that the speaker should be sure that his message has real content and should say only what he believes. This theory embodies the secret of the public speaking of Jesus Christ who spoke his doctrine as utmost truths. *The Mirror,* the Bates College Yearbook of 1920, often referred to Benjamin Mays's convictions. Of his speaking delivery in college, *The Mirror* said:

Did you hear that rich mellow voice, that Southern dialect? Who can it be with that enchanting voice, that clear deliberate enunciation to his oratory? That's Bennie Mays and say can't he speak! If you hear him once you will always remember him. Bennie came to us in the fall of 1917 and immediately made his name by running away with the Sophomore prize decs. Since then, he has been in many speaking contests and debates.

Sensitive to the fact that a speaker using a manuscript cannot adjust his remarks to every circumstance that may arise, Mays does not read his speeches. Evidently he realizes that a manuscript is a handicap to forceful gestures and dynamic eye-contact, or impressive movements on the platform. If this is his theory, then he is amply supported by Alan H. Monroe,[10] who was once head of the Speech Department of Purdue University, and who recommends ample body movement and visual directness as means of capturing and holding the attention of listeners.

As a college president, Mays encourages youths to prepare themselves for the competition of the future. Students are urged to have faith in the future, for the things they are now seeking will surely become a reality. He also speaks against the segregated system of education and proposed ways of perpetuating it. When the southern states proposed regional education for Negroes in the South, plans were drawn to finance Meharry in Nashville, Tennessee, and a veterinary school at Tuskegee Institute in Alabama; the cost was estimated conservatively at $660,000 biennially. Mays attacked the plan from the platform, questioned the motives of southern governors with reference to providing equal facilities for the professional education of Negroes. He said it was impossible for the South to provide enough monies to maintain separate but equal school systems for the two races.

Two hundred Negro patrons in Atlanta filed a suit in 1950 against the Atlanta School Board for discriminating in the provision of equal facilities for Negro and white pupils. Before the Hungry Club, Mays spoke vigorously in behalf of the parents:

If we believe in the democratic way of life as a means of perfecting change, we should be willing to trust the federal courts. This is the machinery which our founding fathers have set up as one of the ways to resolve differences and adjust grievances.

There is no need to be panicky; there is no need for rabble-rousing; this is no time for name-calling; and there is no need for fear. For when we get rough, the question will be: Can there be two separate but equal school systems? The question is not mixed schools—the question is, can there be equality in segregation?[11]

In addition to his stand against the dual system of education, Dr. Mays believes that Negro colleges should work toward first-class status in order to be able to serve students from various parts of the country whenever integration comes.

As a minister of the Christian church, the Reverend Mays calls upon humanity to accept the Lord of Creation as Father and to practice brotherly love. One of his most striking sermons is the one entitled "The Inescapable Christ." The sermon is based upon the Biblical question: "Pilate saith unto them, What shall I do with Jesus which is called Christ? They all say unto him, Let him be crucified." In a nutshell, the speaker gave his introduction in these words: "For nineteen centuries Jesus has been a disturbing element in society. And for nineteen centuries the world has been trying to get rid of Jesus. We don't like him! For nineteen centuries, the world has been trying to answer the question, What shall I do with the Christ?" Then in his peroration Dr. Mays concluded:

Let us hear the conclusion of the matter. We cannot get rid of Jesus. The only way to get rid of Jesus is to accept him in mind, heart, and in soul. Jesus represents God and God is absolute—not man, not race, not economics, not politics—but God. And whenever men in their arrogance and pride set themselves up as absolute, they will be beaten to the ground.[12]

Another popular sermon is "Democratizing and Christianizing America in the Generation." It sets forth the principle that the church should be the one spot in the nation where all men are free and equal. It should be the setting where all men can break down artificial barriers, where group, class, or race do not count. We are as democratic as we live and as Christian as we act.

On one occasion, in 1963, the famous evangelist, Billy Graham, stated that there was love between the races in the South. Immediately, Dr. Mays took objection and said, "Having been born a Negro in South Carolina, I am in better position to speak out on this point than Mr. Graham. It was in the South where I was slapped momentarily simply because I was a black rascal trying to look too good; it was in the South where I was almost lynched while riding in a Pullman car; and it was in the South where I had to step backward out of a dining car to keep from being *beat up* from the rear."[13]

Every Negro who reads the newspaper has pursued the column written by Dr. Mays in the *Pittsburgh Courier*. He has taken the role of an educator and minister naturally. Aside from his administrative duties as a college president, he delivers almost one speech every week. He prefers the role of a social reformer whose messages are tempered by the doctrines of the Man from Galilee.

CHANNING H. TOBIAS

Because he was averse to publicity, the Reverend Channing H. Tobias was rarely thought of as a leader by the rank and file of Negroes. But those who knew him said that he was one of the elder statesmen among Negroes in the United States. He earned the title "mystery man of race relations" because he appeared to do his work behind closed doors. He traveled thousands of miles annually, but few people knew his missions. Somehow he managed to escape the headlines and newspapers while meeting regularly with executives of industry and government. One editor remarked, "Channing Tobias gets constructive work done by operating quietly behind closed doors but manages to accomplish more for Negroes than any other single Negro leader in this country."[14] In the role of "elder statesman," said Fletcher Martin, "his activities are in no way emeritus. Tobias's workday is as vital as it has always been."[15] At the bargaining table, Tobias demonstrated logic, shrewdness, tact, and common sense. He summarized his technique in these words, "The secret of any success I might have had is independence. By this I mean independence in approaching public issues. I have repeatedly and deliberately turned down offers to accept public office."

United States Cabinet officials have offered Tobias several choice political appointments, including the ministership to Liberia. During 1942, he turned down an opportunity to run for the New York City Council on the Republican ticket. Tobias said, "I don't like to engage in the usual campaign hoopla." In the interest of Negroes he crossed party lines and supported candidates who stood for measures that would lead to true democracy. According to *Ebony* the Tobias method "is a crafty blend of diplomacy, persuasion and intelligent pressure at the right time and place. He has been immensely successful with it, and right now he is quietly engaged on a number of social projects without fanfare or publicity."[16]

Channing Tobias was born in Augusta, Georgia, on February 1, 1882. He attended the public schools of Augusta and later was graduated with the A.B. degree from Paine College. Drew Theological Seminary awarded him the B.D. degree in 1905. During 1908, he studied at the University of Pennsylvania. From 1905 to 1911, he was professor of Bible literature at Paine College, Augusta, Georgia. For twelve years, Tobias was student secretary of the International Committee of the Young Men's Christian Association. Later, he became senior secretary of the Colored Men's Department of the YMCA and held this position until he retired in 1946. At the time of his death, he was executive secretary of the Phelps-Stokes Fund, which had $1 million to improve Negro education. As a worker in community areas, Dr. Tobias was awarded honorary degrees by Gammon Theological Seminary in Atlanta, Morehouse College, Jewish Institute of Religion, the New School for Social Research, and New York University. For his work in religious service and race relations, Tobias received the Harmon Award, Spingarn Medal, *Chicago Defender* Citation, and Schomburg Race Relations Honor Roll Citation.

Pleading the Negro's cause, the orator believed in a calm and sane presentation. He usually spoke in a clear, conversational manner, and his rate of delivery was slow—giving his audience time to think with him as he proceeded. This was the opinion of the author who was in the audience when Dr. Tobias spoke at Hampton Institute, Virginia, in 1947. The voice of the speaker was soothing and swayed hearers with its rhythmic tones. There was no shouting, and yet the message reached every ear.

The Reverend Tobias was not a bitter man, even though he was once nearly lynched by a mob in Metter, Georgia, who mistook him for another Negro who allegedly shot a white man. He preached from the pulpit the principle of brotherly love. While he admired the late Mohandas Gandhi, he did not advocate Gandhi's method in the quest for justice in the United States. He told his listeners that Gandhi was striving to throw off the control of a foreign power, while in the United

States Negroes are seeking integration. The implication was that the Negro was fighting his cause in order to give meaning to the words of the United States Constitution which guaranteed equal rights to all citizens.

On many occasions, Tobias delivered commencement addresses, and typical of such speeches was one given at Texas Southern University in Houston on August 27, 1950. Highlights of the speech were:

The place we attain in the final analysis must necessarily depend upon how well we appraise the situation, how intelligently we master the circumstances, and how skillfully we plan and execute our battle strategy.

Let us make friends where we find them and rally to those friends who support our cause. Let us have pride in our race and demonstrate to all mankind that race is no limitation to any of God's children.

The Reverend Tobias brought to his audiences an intellectuality, courage, and richness from his many years in working to solve racial problems. Since the solutions of these problems were not always easy, Tobias was forced to improvise as he went along, from tact and shrewdness in the presentation of his cause to subtle coercion. But he did not resort to demonstrations of a nonviolent nature as did Dr. Martin Luther King, Jr. His manner of getting substantial work done at the conference table was that of untroubled calm, and he maintained his poise in conference and on the platform, even when discussing a heated issue.

JOSEPH H. JACKSON

Perhaps the most powerful Negro in the United States is Dr. Joseph H. Jackson, president of the National Baptist Convention, which has 5.25 million members. Factional opposition has threatened to unseat him several times, but, for some reason, the enemies cannot get their wrecking machines full steam ahead. Thus, the Baptist president[17] still holds the reins and with his "silky voice" continues to be a skillful organizer and administrator.

The annual conventions of the National Baptist delegates have not always been peaceful. For instance, the 1941 annual convention was the scene of disturbance among the delegates; it was precipitated by a political contest among the factions. The fracas was stopped by city policemen, who finally restored order. When everything seemed quiet, a floor fight erupted through an attempt of "independents" to get the convention to pledge a secret ballot. Without doubt, the unbecoming decorum of ministers and church laymen has created an unfavorable public image.

To understand why the Reverend Jackson has had to contend with disturbing elements at conventions, one must consider the circumstances connected with his election to the presidency. Preceding him was the Reverend David V. Jemison, formerly the strong leader of the National Baptist Convention. Jemison retired in 1953, and Dr. Jackson was one of the candidates for the office of president. After twelve hours of balloting, the Reverend Jackson emerged the winner. This was achieved by the support of the membership of Olivet Baptist Church in providing Jackson with campaign funds. This support enabled Dr. Jackson to defeat soundly his five opponents, and his enemies have never forgiven him for that victory. Therefore, in 1957, they "bucked" the president, cried out fraud, demonstrated, and "killed" microphones. Then, shortly after, before the 1958 convention, a federal court ruled the attempt to limit Jackson's tenure illegal and the Baptist president was reelected in a more peaceful meeting. Simeon Booker, in *Black America* (1964), stated, "As a God-fearing Baptist, Dr. Jackson is as potent for the Baptist members as was the late 'Sweet Daddy Grace' [of the House of Prayer]."[18]

Risking being called an "Uncle Tom," Doctor Jackson is

individual in his ideas concerning the role of the ministry in the civil rights-movement. Too conservative for most Negroes, the Baptist president aroused the ire of Negro newspapers when he stated his opposition to sit-ins and demonstrations. Instead, the minister emphasized good citizenship. In 1964, the Reverend Jackson attended the annual NAACP convention and tried to present a check for $15,000 in behalf of the National Baptist Convention for its civil-rights activities, but the delegates booed him from the platform without giving him a chance to speak. While he is opposed to demonstrations, Jackson does favor voter registration campaigns. He answers his critics thus, "It is not enough to sit at another man's lunch counter and close up his store; you must build yourself a store."

Dr. Jackson once spoke in Tulsa, Oklahoma, in 1964, and stated that he saw no reason for demonstrations, which can easily be turned into anarchy, and contended that the civil-rights struggle should operate within the framework of the United States Constitution. "Civil disobedience," Jackson said, "is a form of revenge, and no acts of revenge can bring out the best in any man." In a speech delivered at the East Baptist Convention of Mississippi, at Waynesboro, Mississippi, during the first week in November, 1965, Jackson said,

We must inform young students who are destroying their draft cards and who are protesting the action of the government in Vietnam that by these acts they create suspicion and doubt regarding the sincerity of our government and stab in the back their own brothers and sisters who are now facing shot and shell on the battlefields of Vietnam.[19]

In comparing the dangers of the White Citizens Council, the Ku Klux Klan, and the John Birch Society with the Communist party, Jackson said: "Of all the groups in the United States, there is only one that is so constructed that it cannot pledge allegiance to the nation's flag and life, and that is the Communistic [*sic*] party." The National Baptist president panned the House Un-American Activities in investigating the

Klan, calling it "a smoke screen to atone for its refusal to deal with more serious problems."

Dr. Jackson is an eloquent orator who has many occasions to speak in the course of his duties as NBC administrator. Having come up through the ranks as a pastor, he remains an outstanding firebrand of the verbal war with Satan. He started preaching at a time when Baptists conceived of God as an Omnipotent Being of anger and wrath, who meted out a strong-handed justice by letting sinners fall into the hands of the devil who stood ready to receive them as his own. Often his sermons emphasize that "man had better get right with God and do it now." In earlier days, the Reverend Jackson felt impelled to use language that could play upon men's minds and incite fear. The goal was achieved through the use of rhetoric that was intensely personal and emotional, technically erratic but of great power and beauty. Sinners could not resist the call, "Whosoever will, let him come."

Now, in the maturer stage of his career, Jackson has become a symbol of dignity in his platform manners. His appeal is to both the emotions and intellect of the audience, and he uses a style of delivery aimed at clarity rather than rhetorical bombast. He never lets his theology and teaching become tainted with the malignancy of intolerance for others. Perhaps his attitude toward racial demonstrations may be traced to his maturing point of view. The pulpiteer uses language that is marvelously simple, but yet vivid and impressive and kindly so that it does not offend the sensibilities of little children, who understand his words perfectly. The minister's voice is moderately "silky," highly resonant for his vocal range, and his platform variety keeps his audiences eager, alert, and attentive even when they disagree with his ideas.

GARDNER TAYLOR

Heralded as "the World-Renowned Prelate," the Reverend Gardner Taylor is a strong leader in Baptist circles and a world traveler, who, for some reason, has not captured the public spotlight as an orator; and yet he stands as a public speaker of the highest caliber. People who have heard him speak once will travel a hundred miles to hear him preach again, and this is what the author did on one occasion. The trip to Baton Rouge, Louisiana, in the summer of 1954, was well worth the trouble.

The Reverend Gardner Taylor has been accorded numerous honors as a speaker. When Providence Baptist Church in Chicago, established in January, 1863, wanted an orator during its hundredth anniversary celebration, it invited the Reverend Taylor.

A native of Baton Rouge, Louisiana, Dr. Taylor is the son of the late W. M. and Mrs. Selina Taylor. He was graduated from Oberlin College, which later conferred upon him one of its first citations as an outstanding graduate of the School of Theology. Honorary degrees have been awarded him by Benedict and Leland colleges. While in college, he met and married Laura Scott in 1940, when she was a graduate student and Phi Beta Kappa scholar. The Reverend Gardner has been vice-president of the General Council of the American Baptist Convention.

The Reverend Gardner's voice has been heard around the world. In 1947, he preached in Copenhagen, Denmark, during a session of the World Baptist Alliance and again, in 1950, at the Sunday morning worship services of the Alliance in the Municipal Auditorium in Cleveland, Ohio. Other distinctions have included addressing the Golden Jubilee of the World Baptist Alliance in Westminster Hall in London, England, in 1955. In 1959, he was the preacher on the National Radio Pulpit series, which was sponsored by the National Council of Churches and was heard by listeners turned in to 100 NBC stations across the nation and in Hawaii. When his Concord Baptist Church of Christ in Brooklyn, New York, was destroyed by fire, in 1952, the sum of $1,700,000 was raised under his strong leadership, and the church was rebuilt.

When Dr. Taylor spoke at the Baptist Church, of which the

Reverend T. Jemison, son of Dr. D. V. Jemison, was pastor, he stepped immediately to the lectern and delivered a powerful address, which more than justified the advance notices of his reputation as an eloquent orator. Upon the termination of the address, the audience gave him a loud and long ovation, which required, as theater people would say, four curtain calls, or platform acknowledgments of the listeners' approbation. During the address, which was delivered during the summer of 1954, the pulpiteer analyzed events leading up to the 1954 Supreme Court decision and scathed southern white leaders for their inaction, which forced the high judiciary to set the conscience of white people free. The vocal tempo and humor of the speaker enlivened his pace and added vigor and variety. He created dramatic effects by diminishing vocal fadeouts, appropriate body movements, and gestures.

If the rhetorician could have summarized the message at that time, it was a catalyst for the persecuted Negro soul, burdened for almost a hundred years after the Civil War. The author remembers how Dr. Taylor employed the "technique of freewheeling into vocal high gear on the double" as military men might say. When the orator had warmed up to his subject, his language was persuasive and sharp, the progressive flow of ideas was direct and incisive, and body postures and gestures definitely superior. Naturally, the mood rose to a high key, since he had strong moral support from his listeners who chanted regularly, "Amen!", "Now you are talking," and "Preach, Reverend, preach!" All too suddenly, the minister's voice faded into silence, and the hearers, enthusiastically let him know they wanted him to continue.

Stories concerning the leadership of Dr. Taylor reveal both the strength and weakness of this fiery orator. The experience of listening to the minister is like that of Elijah caught up from the Moab wilderness in a chariot of fire, while the mantle itself falls upon the congregation as a reminder that they should carry on the prophetic challenge extended by the speaker. The entire Negro minority can truthfully say that the work of the Reverend Taylor is a protest against the practice of discrimination and against every departure from the freedom and equality of a true democracy. "Back to the old path of God" is in reality the orator's philosophy for the salvation of man who will find that the Kingdom of God is in the hearts of men rather than on some far-off mountainside. This idea became the basis for denunciation of every violation of the moral law as embodied in the Ten Commandments. He can clear the path for reform by patient teaching; and, if he were living in ancient Israel, historians would have labeled him "The chariots of Israel and the horsemen thereof." He has been the bulwark against segregation and discrimination, but it is his uncompromising and aggressive loyalty to "God Our Father" that has served to place his name near the top of the list of the men of cloth.

EVANGELISM

Observers of religious evangelism have noted that the religious life of the United States wears many faces, from the monastery to the conventional church to the itinerant preacher. Many persons have changed their lives for the better after hearing the preaching of traveling evangelists and their plea, "Repent and be saved, for the time to save your life is now."

Originally, when we lacked modern transportation, these evangelists carried the gospel to people living in remote areas. And the heart of the evangelistic movement is its fiery preaching. The history of evangelism in the United States begins with the circuit preacher roaming the frontier on horseback, the tent meetings, and goes on to D. L. Moody, Billy Sunday, and now Billy Graham and Oral Roberts. Regardless of the preacher, American evangelism has always been a blend of humor and hellfire.

Billy Graham has an organization that takes on circus proportion in order to help God do his work. Evangelism in the United States is big business. Since Negro ministers lack the capital, they have shunned the evangelistic big time. They have been contented to confine their mission to those churches that hold week-long spring or fall revival services.

SUMMARY OF PULPIT ORATORY

From time immemorial, the public speaking of the minister and theologian has been most compelling. William Highland Garnet mesmerized antislavery audiences, Joseph Charles Price had a fantastic charm and charisma, William H. Borders stimulates thousands with his keen and lovable humor, and Howard Thurman has a powerful, personal magnetism that begets loyalty and commands respect. Although some have derided magnetic and brilliant pulpit speakers, scientists in the laboratories of our great universities are presently investigating hypnotic appeals as natural phenomena.

The reader may well ask: What is this thing that puts an audience in the grasp of a dynamic preacher? Why do listeners find their own thoughts suspended, hearing only the words of the speaker, his thoughts and appeal? By what means are the hearers mesmerized, hypnotized, and held spellbound? With the majority of trained Negro preachers, this hold is very strong indeed.

Footnotes, Chapter 13

1. E. T. Kreuger, "Negro Religious Expression," *American Journal of Sociology* 38 (July, 1932): 22–25.
2. Benjamin E. Mays, *The Negro Church,* p. 58.
3. Robert Spike, "Our Churches Sin Against the Negro," *Look,* May 18, 1965, p. 36.
4. "Religious News Magazine," *St. Petersburg* (Florida) *Times,* October 16, 1965.

5. W. E. B. Du Bois, *The Souls of Black Folk,* pp. 190–191.
6. Harold F. Gosnell, *Negro Politicians.*
7. Howard Thurman, *The Creative Encounter,* p. 140.
8. Complete text of sermon found in *The Negro Caravan,* ed. Sterling Brown, Arthur Davis, and Ulysses Lee, pp. 686–692.
9. William Fowlkes, *Pittsburgh Courier,* Magazine Section, October 21, 1960.
10. Alan H. Monroe, *Principles and Types of Speech.*
11. *Pittsburgh Courier,* October 14, 1950, p. 12.
12. This address was first delivered at Howard University, June 8, 1945.
13. Benjamin E. Mays, "My Views," *Pittsburgh Courier,* October 19, 1963.
14. "Mystery Man of Race Relations [Channing H. Tobias]," *Ebony,* February, 1951, p. 15.
15. Martin Fletcher, *Our Great Americans.*
16. "Mystery Man of Race Relations [Channing H. Tobias]."
17. Simeon Booker, *Black Man's America,* p. 118.
18. Ibid., p. 118.
19. *Chicago Defender,* October 30–November 5, 1965.

14/ The Vessels of God

In the United States, there are dozens of religious cults, including Mt. Sinai Holy Church, United House of Prayer for all People, Church of God (Black Jews), Father Divine Peace Mission, Moorish Science Temple of America, and Washington's Church of God under the leadership of Elder Solomon Michaux.

Negroes are attracted to cults for different reasons, but the compelling forces are the personalities of the cult leaders, relief from physical and mental illness, the quest for an all-powerful God, and racial consciousness. "There is one main attraction which stands out in all cults, making a kind of common bond among them," said Arthur Huff Fausett. "It is the desire to get closer to some supernatural being or power, be it God, the Holy Spirit, or Allah."[1]

Singing, dancing, shouting, and hand-clapping are characteristics in the worship of most Negro cults, but the most compelling force is music. Fausett declared:

Often there is only a piano to accompany the singing. An interesting thing about the player is that he usually picks up the melody according to the key of the singers, reversing the practice in the orthodox church, where the instrumentalist first gives the key and the singers follow. The first method makes for indefinitely greater spontaneity in the singing.

Oratory makes the cult leader and is the magic of his drawing power which often consists in uttering only a *magic word*. Without eloquence, the religious movement is a failure. There must be constant preaching to indoctrinate the members, and the cult leader must convince his followers that he knows the way to God.

ELDER SOLOMON MICHAUX

Elder Solomon "Lightfoot" Michaux, whose radio war on the devil won a large following, is called "the Happy Am I Preacher" of Washington's Church of God. "Just like President Roosevelt declared war on the depression," said Michaux, "I declare war on the devil. I'm the General of the International Forces of good against evil."[2] Listeners who tuned in on Michaux's program during the early part of this century knew they would hear one of the best programs on the air. It resembled a Negro camp meeting that depended upon the perfect timing of music, preaching, and audience response.

Michaux always started the meeting with the theme song, "Happy Am I." Shouts, wails, and audience "Amens!" combined with tom-toms to add rhythm to the song. The evangelist always mixed his preaching with songs. If he detected a lag in the services, he called out something like this: "I am no long-faced preacher, and I want my precious ones to be happy in this country. If a man isn't happy in this country, it's because he don't know how." When radio station WJSV in Washington was bought by CBS, all stations canceled their programs except Elder Michaux's revivals, which featured his 156-voice choir. Later CBS placed the program on a coast-to-coast hookup and gave it a better spot on Saturdays at 6:30 P.M. These programs held the spotlight for some time until they were discontinued.

On many occasions, Elder Michaux conducted services in Griffith Stadium to an overflow crowd of as many as 40,000 people. At these meetings, the notables of Washington mingled with cooks, domestics, and laborers to hear the stirring services. Once the minister took his church to the Golden Gate Ballroom in New York City to conduct "a second front fight against the Kingdom of Satan."

Elder Solomon Michaux was born in Virginia. The history of his movement began in 1917 when he gave up fish peddling in Hopewell, Virginia, to preach for the Gospel Spreading Association. The revivals he conducted drew thousands of Negroes to hear him preach. He featured baptisms in the James River and washed away sins in its murky waters. In 1929, he went to Washington, D.C., and established the Church of God. The movement was very successful, and he added to its popularity by organizing a splendid choir. To keep his meetings from dragging, he planted confederates in the congregation to feed him lines.

Michaux preached against liquor, rowdy women, slot machines, and big talk. The members usually got plenty of excitement in those earlier days, and this led Michaux to say: "That was a great meeting we had this morning, Pilgrims," and then the audience really cut loose. "You can always tell when the Holy Ghost and fire come down. I got burnt myself this morning." The minister warned his followers not to be overoptimistic: "Some of you Pilgrims think when you are buried you'll wake up as white folk on Resurrection Day. Let me straighten you out on that right now. If you plant an Irish potato, you don't get no sweet potato vine. When God plants a colored boy, he ain't countin' on diggin' up a white fellow."

Critics of Elder Michaux, especially the intelligentsia, admit that he was a good showman. They object, however, to his using the pulpit rather than the stage to give his shows. And, most of all, they scorn his injection of a "jive" atmosphere into the church of God.

FATHER DIVINE

Father M. J. Divine started his peace movement in Harlem in 1932. Since that time and until his death, the Divine Mission grew into a membership of several hundred thousand people of the black, white, and yellow races. When the movement started, Negroes were hard hit by an economic depression and many were deprived of the necessities of life. Father Divine appealed to the public by proposing simply to substitute abundance for scarcity. Professor Edward Palmer said:

Divine preached no imaginary heaven to come after death. He was definitely more practical, for he told of heaven here on earth accessible to all who believed in him and followed his teachings. Entrance into his heaven ends the fear of uncertainty of life after death, since heaven's inhabitants, as long as they followed the Divine commandments, are immortal. Nor is this all. In heaven there are no worries, no wants, no pain, no racial discrimination. There is, instead, peace, prosperity, joy, health, and every good thing.[3]

Father Divine employed the familiar techniques of propaganda. His members took part in demonstrations, pilgrimages, peace missions, mass celebrations of new extensions, and parades with banners and pennants announcing the Advent of the New Day. His organization was built upon a hierarchy of archangels, angels, attorneys, advisers, secretaries, and stenographers. His magic phrase from the pulpit was, "Peace, brother—it is wonderful." Father Divine declared, "I am *joy, peace, life,* and *love* and everything else that is good."[4] The

God image was kept constantly before the people's eyes and ears through songs, sermons, and signs.

As an orator, Father Divine's eloquence was crude, but to his followers the sermons were filled with words that released a hidden power. His language re-created their personalities, his words inspired them with a new zeal, and his endless repetitions imprinted his ideas upon their subconscious minds so that their behavior became consistent with his admonishments. His voice was in the high-pitched range, often too soft for emphasis, sometimes monotonous on account of repetitions. And yet, in spite of this, his messages filtered through their minds and made a lasting impression. Critics stated that Father Divine's language contained an excess of verbiage, but if the content were edited, trimmed, and pruned, the rudimentary wisdom of his messages became clear. No matter how the critics felt about him and his speaking, his audiences responded like an invisible electric current in response to his chanting voice whose lilt resembled that of a priest singing a mass.

The last appearance of Father Divine was in April, 1963, on the seventeenth anniversary of his marriage to Edna Rose Ritchings, a native of Montreal, Canada. She was known as "Sweet Angel" when he chose her as bride from many secretaries. It is known that during the early years of his movement, he was beset by legal troubles and once was put in jail. Those who knew him remember his restaurants, which served meals for fifteen cents during the depression years. His rooming house provided lodging for two dollars a week. Divine died in the fall of 1965 of hardening of the arteries, just as his physician, Dr. Joseph A. Wagner of Bryn Mawr, Pennsylvania, arrived.

The historian, ignoring the question of Godship, cannot minimize the importance of a man who did good unto his fellow men. Father Divine not only saw the hungry and shelterless, the poor and the needy, but he did something about it. The enemies of Father Divine charged him with wine-bibbing, eating and drinking with sinners in sumptuous banquets. But, as it was said of the Man from Galilee, the Reverend Divine "went about doing good." What better tribute could a man want to commend him and his activities?

PROPHET JONES

Prophet James Francis Jones, a Detroit evangelist, who is now fallen from grace in the eyes of the public, was head of the Triumph of the Church and Kingdom of God in Christ, whose membership at one time numbered thousands scattered over the nation. He broadcast his services twice every Sunday to about four hundred thousand radio listeners. The Prophet refrained from strong drink and was considered a celibate and mystic. He did not read secular literature, because it would corrupt his own inspired thoughts. He asserted that God spoke to him when a small boy and told him to "distil" good thoughts in the minds of men.

Speaking in disconnected syllables in a loudly intoned voice, the Prophet thumped the Bible, gazed into the heavens, and shouted, "Thank you God for Christ. I thank you, sir." In response the audience said, "Amen!" As the musical background subsided, the evangelist prophesied. Frequently, after the collection, Prophet Jones said, "Let everyone in the house give God a hand!"[5] His services were held in an atmosphere where anything might happen from handclapping to tap dancing to jitterbugging.

CHARLES MANUEL GRACE ("SWEET DADDY" GRACE)

The late Bishop Charles Manuel Grace, referred to as "the grandiloquent preacher," was the head of the United House of Prayer for All People, with headquarters in Washington, D.C. For more than thirty-five years, he headed this organization, and his followers called him "Daddy." Rics Roberts, in the September 17, 1949, issue of the *Pittsburgh Courier,* wrote: "Rallying around their 'Sweet Daddy' are reputedly more than two million followers who are reverently certain that this man was chosen 'by appointment of God' to stand apart from all mortals."

Daddy Grace built his evangelistic movement on the technique of mixing pageantry, parades, music, uniforms, and open-door invitations. The Grace organizations reported 25,000 members in New York City; 25,000 in Newport News, Virginia; 10,000 at Norfolk, Virginia; 120,000 in thirty-one North Carolina cities; and 25,000 in Savannah, Georgia, where the Bishop owned a palatial summer home. The Bishop attracted public attention by employing assembly-line methods in baptisms. Fire department units drenched his converts with water under the blessed administration of Daddy Grace.

Bishop Grace was born in Portugal and spoke with pronounced Latin inflection. He made an unusual presence on the platform with his almost shoulder-length hair. Daddy was persuasive and sometimes began his messages by shouting, "If you want to know something that nobody can tell you, ask me. I'll tell you!" During his sermons, the Bishop often shed his coat as he warmed up. His sermons consisted mostly of shouting questions at his congregation, which replied in unison. At his Charlotte House of Prayer in North Carolina, an orchestra accompanied the singers who styled the old hymns with a swing tempo. The services were a mixture of preaching, music, and audience responses. Effective oratory and regard for money made Daddy Grace[6] rich and beloved. These impressions were formed by the author after attending the Bishop's services dozens of times while a student at Johnson C. Smith University at Charlotte, North Carolina.

The members of the House of Prayer always testified eloquently for a holy life expressed in terms of devotion to the Bishop. Sometimes the congregation replied to questions like this: What do you get from the teachings of the United House of Prayer? The members answered, "We're trying to find the right way, and Daddy Grace *knows* the way." In his sermons, the Bishop lashed out against smoking, drinking, war, and adultery with a stinging denunciation.

THE BLACK MUSLIMS

Since most people think of the Black Muslims as a religious cult, this Islamic movement is being considered here. Indeed black nationalism might be a synonym for this movement which symbolizes a minority people's search for first-class status in this country. The fountainhead of this movement is Elijah Muhammed, the Divine Messenger of Allah and Spiritual Head of the Lost Nation of Islam in the West. A detailed sketch of Mr. Muhammed is found in *The Black Muslims in America* (1961) by C. Eric Lincoln.

The threat of the Black Muslims developing a potential to create a political and racial crisis in the United States has been overshadowed lately by the civil-rights activities of CORE, Southern Christian Leadership Conference, and SNCC. Yet this possibility should not be overlooked, since Elijah Muhammed is the leader of the first movement of segregation since the American Civil War. Black Muslims practice "radicalism in reverse" because they have rejected white society in order to establish their own all-Negro province, which would be comparable in one way to Haiti. The proposed segregated province or state would be located within these United States instead of elsewhere. Whether the Messenger will make trouble remains to be seen.

The rise of Muhammed to leadership started in Sanderson, Georgia, where he was born on October 10, 1897, the seventh in a family of twelve children. Beginning his life on a farm, he married when he was twenty-two years old, migrated with his family to Detroit in 1923, served five years in prison for his nationalistic activities, and finally rose to the leadership of the Black Muslims with headquarters in Chicago. The registered membership is approximately 18,000 who attend services in some fifty temples across the nation; but, conservatively, Muhammed has a following of 50,000 nonregistered adherents.

Early in his career, Elijah Muhammed found that public speaking is a useful thing. Although his followers read printed materials, they rely mainly upon oral teaching, which is delivered in a series of proselytizing speeches. Instructional oratory teaches the officers to walk with rapid strides in and out of the temple. Through oratory, the Spiritual Head of Islam instructs registered members to refrain from dancing and gambling, stealing and extramarital sexual relations, and begin showing respect to women of the Negro race. The moral lectures show Mr. Muhammed as a leader who exhibits integrity and strong moral fiber. Although objecting to the social philosophy of Caucasians, Mr. Muhammed recommends their methods of operating big business as is evidenced by the chain of Muslim enterprises. These hum with enthusiasm and gusto.

When the Messenger rises to speak, followers see a man of light oriental complexion, five feet six inches, delicate in appearance, but in good health. Generally, he is attired in a black or striped suit, a bow tie, and wears a dark velvet fez. He is formal and carries himself with dignity on the rostrum, but at home he is a kind and devoted father and husband. As a public speaker, Mr. Muhammed's voice is firm, persuasive, sincere, and soft. His ethical appeal knows no boundary, inasmuch as he sets the example of industrious habits and is a good family man. This appeal is further manifested by ministers who go so far as to imitate Elijah Muhammed's body postures, walk, gestures, and speech.

Muhammed's oratory is used widely in membership recruitment and gaining nonregistered supporters for the purpose of expanding the principles and practices of the Black Muslim movement. These messages are referred to as "proselytizing rhetoric" that is both written and oral. The Messenger emphasizes the value of listening well and tells his followers that they can shout when they get home. Muhammed's hold upon his hearers is attributable to his visual directness, or eye contact, and friendly rapport. Prospective followers are wooed by his persuasion and the esoteric nature of the services and the movement. From time to time, he delivers special messages to specific assemblies at various temples. He often derides the Negro leadership and intelligentsia by saying that "politics will not solve the problems of the Negro anymore than it did for the Hebrews of Israel in Biblical times."

Footnotes, Chapter 14

1. Arthur Huff Fausett, *Black Gods of the Metropolis.*
2. "Second Front in Harlem," *Time* 40 (December 21, 1942): 74.
3. Edward Palmer, "Father Divine Is God," *Quarterly Review of Higher Education Among Negroes,* 13 (July, 1945): 257.
4. "Father Divine Divinely Human," *Chicago Defender,* October 5–15, 1965.
5. *Life,* November 27, 1944.
6. *Life,* October 1, 1944, 51–54.

15 / The New Revolt Period, 1954-1965

In one sense, the so-called new revolt is merely an extension of the earlier period of protest that came into focus during the 1930s. At that time, Negroes utilized protest literature, oratory, the Negro press, and court decisions to effect racial gains. The new revolt shifted from these techniques to those of sit-ins, demonstrations, Freedom Rides, marching movements, campus take-overs, and voting clinics.

This new movement engulfed the South, creating new problems for local law-enforcement agencies and politicians. Meanwhile, our two national political parties were faced at election time with the issue of endorsing these sit-ins and pledging stronger civil-rights platforms. This period also created certain problems for Negro presidents of state colleges in the South, because they could not discipline their students who were determined and courageous in the new civil-rights movement.[1]

But, equally powerful, was the determination of southern segregationists to bring matters under control through expulsion of picketing students. Thus, two insurmountable forces locked horns.

In just such a setting, new leaders, called "guerrilla chiefs," came to the fore, but they did not replace well-known leaders such as Roy Wilkins and A. Philip Randolph. The guerrilla chiefs have been largely identified with the new Negro revolt under the auspices of many organizations, including SCLC, SNCC, CORE, and VISTA. White segregationists were not without ingenuity, for they organized the Society for the Prevention of Negroes from Getting Everything, SPONGE. An epitome of the purposes of these organizations is given by John H. Britton in the June 24, 1965, issue of *Jet* magazine. Activities of professors, ministers, and students culminated in numerous civil-rights gains which cannot, however, be accounted for with complete accuracy. Certainly oratory had an indelible influence upon all the benefits that accrued.

All was not calm on the civil-rights battlefields of the South, because newspapers and television had a field day publicizing riots, violence encountered by the Freedom Riders, and federal marshals escorting James Meredith to the registration lines at the University of Mississippi in 1962. Finally, in 1964, Congress passed the historic Civil Rights Bill that made the Negro in fact a first-class citizen. The next year, the passage of the 1965 voting bill removed for the Negro all legal and illegal obstacles confronting him in the exercise of the ballot. These are just a few of the transitional events involving the freedom of the Negro and his welfare. And it must not be forgotten that these gains are owing in part to the guerrilla leaders.

FRED LEE SHUTTLEWORTH ("THE STONEWALL COLONEL")

The regular attacks upon Birmingham's vulnerable terrain earned for the Reverend Fred L. Shuttleworth the title of "Stonewall Colonel," because, as a leader of demonstrations, he landed in jail as often as he occupied his pulpit. CBS reporters heralded him as "the man most feared by Southern racists" as he was "the voice of the new southern militancy among Birmingham Negroes." Bombed twice and beaten by mobsters, he was involved in twenty-seven criminal and civil actions—seven of which came as a result of the Freedom Rides. His involvement with the courts yielded sentences totaling more than three years and $5,000 in fines. Shuttleworth has been sued for $3 million in *Time* magazine lawsuits along with three other Alabama ministers, and he lost an automobile and other property. Yet his courage did not wane. Once he was threatened by anonymous callers who vowed to get vengeance by harming his wife and children. This influenced him to move to Cincinnati, Ohio, and accept the pastorate of a church, but he commuted often to direct and lead his Birmingham followers to victory. His compatriots requested that he remain secretary of SCLC at Atlanta, Georgia, and he accepted. The South has not finished with Shuttleworth, nor has Shuttleworth finished with the South.

With the assistance of Martin Luther King, Jr., Shuttleworth and the leaders of the Alabama Christian Movement for Human Rights were able to reach a truce with Birmingham city officials, who agreed to desegregate lunch counters, rest rooms, drinking fountains, and fitting rooms in large downtown department stores within a period of ninety days.[2] Officials promised to inaugurate employment and promotion practices on a nondiscriminatory basis, as well as to release hundreds of jailed demonstrators on bond or their personal recognizance. The agreement also called for immediate establishment of a biracial committee which would set the timetable for integration. Many strategy meetings were held at the A. G. Gaston Motel in Birmingham.

Born in Montgomery County, Alabama, on March 18, 1922, Shuttleworth has lived there for thirty-nine of his forty-seven years. He received an A.B. degree, from Selma University in Alabama, a B.S. degree from Alabama State College. He has a wife and three children. The Reverend Shuttleworth has made a good leader, because he likes to talk. "My hardest job is to keep Fred Shuttleworth from talking," said an organization lawyer[3] to a reporter. Shuttleworth is one of the most articulate and fastest talkers in the Negro campaign for equality in the South. The Reverend C. K. Steele, Sr., himself an effective speaker and leader in the Tallahassee, Florida, demonstration crusades and sit-ins, said:

Rev. Fred Shuttleworth is a very unconventional speaker. When he begins, one is at once convinced that he will not be impressive at all. However, before he is through you are very much impressed. He starts with a low natural tone of voice that soon rises to a high pitch. He seems to have a gift for catchy sentences. For an example, when referring to Bull Connor, former police commissioner of Birmingham, Fred Shuttleworth remarked, "We have taken the Bull out of old *Bull* Connor and made a steer of him." He has kept the Alabama movement alive by the slogan, "The Movement Must Move."

The Alabama leader and orator is a tremendous "off-the-cuff" speaker in what, if done formally, would be called a "question-and-answer period." However, the speech critic would consider the forum feature a sort of nonfunctional appendage, which, if employed in a political campaign, rapidly becomes larger than the body of the main address. Although a civil-rights mass meeting in a church is not political, the leader must answer the questions directed to him from the congregation. While his speeches may lack some of the sonority and resonance of ancient oratory, his extemporaneous messages surge with enough fervor to rouse his audience to action. One recalls how Franklin Delano Roosevelt banished fear in 1933, how Charles de Gaulle saved France from collapse, and how Winston Churchill boosted morale during the crises in England during World War II. All three men delivered speeches that were calls to arms. In like manner, the Reverend Shuttleworth, during the civil-rights crisis, employed public speaking to recruit the race for overt action in the streets. It was a kind of "Whosoever will, let him come" call to freedom, and only a few people resisted the invitation. In issuing the call, Shuttleworth warmed up to his subject, then caught fire, becoming the noble essence of leadership. What more did he need to recommend him to the people?

A thin, intense man, Mr. Shuttleworth can play on the emotions of listeners at a meeting in a manner similar to Heifetz bowing and fingering the strings of a violin. In one address, Shuttleworth said to the congregation, "We're tired of waiting at these nightly meetings. . . . We're telling Bull Connor right here tonight that we are on the march and we're not going to stop marching until we get our rights." The congregation shouted the refrain, "Praise the Lord!" and "Pour it on, Reverend!" When the collection plates were passed, dollars showered into the treasury. Then, when the minister called for volunteers "to go to jail," the entire audience crowded down the aisles.

ROBERT WILLIAMS ("SATAN-SAINT" LEADER)

Most of the white residents of Monroe, North Carolina, knew Robert Williams only by a fiery letter entitled "The Crusader," which he sent to a newspaper editor. In 1961, community action and reaction against Williams were varied. Some white folks took him seriously, a few were impressed, others were infuriated, and the remainder ignored him. Now some eight years later, Negroes and whites are not agreed whether Robert Williams is devil or saint, foe or friend, insincere or sincere, a troublemaker or peacemaker, nonviolent or violent.

The conservative white power structure felt that Williams could have been an asset to the community and his race had he not proposed a revolutionary plan to organize "fire teams," an elite and well-established guerrilla force that would render impotent white people in American cities and rural areas. In his tactical scheme, the guerrillas would travel from city to city and start fires with lighted candles in order to bring destruction and desolation. Because Williams advocated destruction, he was branded a violent crusader.

The precipitating factors that forced the crusader to flee to Cuba were made manifest on August 27, 1961, when racial troubles erupted into physical violence in Monroe, North Carolina, a town of 11,000 inhabitants. Bottles and rocks were thrown, and two white policemen were shot. Williams and some confederates allegedly kidnapped a white couple. This forced him to flee with his family to Cuba. There he established an anti-Radio Free Dixie. His four associates, whom he left behind, were tried and convicted, but the North Carolina Supreme Court reversed the conviction. Immediately the defendants were charged a second time but they did not appear in court and forfeited their bond. The case is still pending.

Outspoken Williams kept an abundance of arms in his home for protection against threats and dangers from certain local whites. He warned that he would shoot any intruder. This statement was thereafter used to distort his public image as head of the Monroe Non-Violent Action Committee. Later, Williams told newspapermen in Cuba that he wanted to return to the United States if charges against him were dropped. If not, he said that he would move to Red China or North Vietnam.

Since the crusader's sojourn in Cuba, many of the reforms he advocated have been realized through law and community acceptance. For instance, Monroe is providing new jobs for Negroes in industry, recreation and school facilities are being desegregated, and federal laws have opened public accommodations to Negroes. Officials are very anxious to correct Monroe's mistakes as quickly as possible. City officials told newsmen they were greatly relieved by the untimely departure of Robert Williams. Through his stay in Cuba, Providence may be working to protect him from a fate similar to that of the late President John F. Kennedy and Medgar Evers of Mississippi.

The dynamics of Robert Williams were compelling, and many people supported him in his civil-rights activities. Many black people detested him for his lack of political acumen in the art of compromise, persuasion, and local strategy. Yet, he was effective as a speaker whose soft voice rendered resistance immobile by its persuasion. As a poet, he was able to set oral prose to music. When he was opposed by the Ku Klux Klan, Williams used his vocal art to express his virulent indignation and resentment. Although sincere in his motives, he often lacked tact and wisdom enough to think before speaking publicly. The subject matter of his speech reflected a hate brewed by racial fear and distrust.

Robert Williams's conversational mode of delivery entranced listeners and enabled him to establish an intimacy with his hearers. His delivery was clearly extempore; he prepared no manuscripts and never committed his speeches to memory, in toto. He presented a pleasing countenance to his audiences, but there was a lack of gaiety in his speeches, and he tended to be serious. Yet his audiences never objected, because the racial issue was never a fun show.

Williams held no claim to eloquent speechmaking, nor did he take specific training in public speaking. His bearing suggested dignity and earnest concern for the success of his efforts to convince folk to become adherents to his movement. He had an easy and graceful posture attuned to the quality and force of his voice, which was full and clear, and well modulated if not musical. He focused his efforts upon helping black people to gain first-class citizenship the best way he knew how.

Inasmuch as Robert Williams was many things to different people before he fled the United States, his leadership cannot be easily assessed. For the last five years, he has been too far removed from his hometown in North Carolina to make any impression upon his contemporaries. His leadership in America has been reduced to a matter of inconsequence. In a sense, Williams is in a position similar to that of an exiled and battle-scarred military general whose troops are scattered and defenseless, but yet hopeful that he can return to rally them to the colors. But now there is no urgent need for the return of Williams since the passage of the 1964 Civil Rights Bill. The civil-rights fever seems to be subsiding. To change the civil-rights laws into action, however, will take a long time, and this will be the greatest challenge that leaders like Robert Williams will ever face.

JAMES FARMER ("WONDER BOY OF CIVIL RIGHTS")

A well-known civil-rights guerrilla chief is James Farmer, former director of CORE, which was established in 1942 and became very potent in 1960. Farmer has been labeled the "Wonder Boy of Civil Rights" by Simeon Booker in his book entitled *Black Man's America* (1964), and the staging of Freedom Rides by CORE increased his prestige.

The former CORE executive director is an educated minister who never has served a pastorate. Without relying solely upon oratory, Farmer led members of the movement right into the heat of the civil-rights fray where he became a formidable foe of segregation. In 1961, he led a group of seventeen trainees in Freedom Rides from Washington, D.C., into the far South and tested transportation policies by using rest-room facilities and sitting integrated. One bus went up in smoke, while a second vehicle was damaged near Anniston, Alabama. Another Freedom Ride "fizzled out" in Birmingham when bus drivers walked off their jobs.

Although James Farmer is an eloquent speaker, he has seldom used oratory to promote civil-rights programs. But he has the necessary qualities of a finished orator and has demonstrated them during telecasts connected with his activities under the auspices of CORE. During television discussion with newsmen, Farmer's remarks are convincing and logical and his diction is superbly clear. The former CORE leader has always been convinced of his mission and the truth behind it. In his CORE activities, he spoke as one having authority, and his belief in the movement made his voice ring with sincerity.

In a television discussion of racial issues, Farmer is very much at home. His voice has unusual flexibility, range, and a slight vibrato. Farmer is a logician whose language and words are strictly for the intellectual public. Yet, it would be comparatively easy for him to adapt his language and vocabulary in a manner that would arouse the masses on account of his ethical and persuasive appeal. People are convinced that his words and actions are one and the same thing. With him persuasive oratory has not been imperative, since he has utilized most effectively the medium of militant and intelligent action. Those who have heard him speak know that, as he proceeds, his voice becomes more vibrant and resonant, more convincing and dynamic—the necessary requisites of an orator to drive home his ideas.

James Farmer is a doer and believes in an "organizing, evolving, constellating, centering ground" for democracy—the evidence for which is a certain measure of order and predictability in things like antidiscrimination and first-class citizenship. No matter how much an orator affirms that he is anti-this or anti-that, he can get to the simple heart of things if he speaks and works for first-class citizenship. Although James Farmer is not working under the auspices of CORE at present, he feels that an all-out effort in the direction of the so-called "black power" theory will only set the Negro up for the biggest fall in civil-rights history.

Since leaving CORE, James Farmer has tried to interest state, local and federal agencies in funding housing experiments for Negroes in New York City and the surrounding area. One of the best ideas conceived by Farmer has fallen upon the deaf ears of those who could help. Maybe the officials in office think Farmer's program is unsophisticated or oversimplified, but Farmer is interested in this concept: "The point in my proposed housing experiment is to get the lowest common denominator, in order to place the culturally deprived in the best housing at an economical cost." It is just as simple as that, for he realizes that Negroes intend to remain in this country and enjoy the rights available to all, including better housing. Hence, the exodus of Negroes elsewhere does not appeal to him, since he feels that when the white man gives North America back to the Indians—then Negroes will go back to Africa. And God knows that this will never happen.

MABEL FULLER

Not all activists are leaders in the sense that they go out into the streets to lead demonstrations and marches. This is the kind of labor chief embodied in Mabel Fuller, codirector of education of the Undergarment and Negligee Worker's Local 62, ILGWU, in New York City. In November, 1963, she embarked upon a six-week trip to Japan as an American specialist selected by the Departments of Labor and State for the labor-exchange program of the United States and Japan.

When the undergarment industry was unionized, Mabel Fuller, then sixteen years of age, was elected chairman of the local's organizational meeting. In 1937, she was elected a member of the local's executive board, and, in 1946, went on to become a staff organizer. In her present office as codirector of education, she assists in the planning of direct educational programs for the local membership of 18,000. It has often been said that public speaking is a gateway to leadership. It was Mabel Fuller's ability to speak in public that influenced the local union members to select her as presiding officer at their organizational meeting. When she was elected a member of the staff and organizer in 1946, it was evident that she was an effective public speaker who was capable of carrying the message of uniondom to workers in the undergarment industry.

As codirector of education for the membership of her union, Mabel Fuller realizes that only education and training can inspire a female worker to lift herself up by her own bootstraps. Her growth in experience and power to express herself effectively have transcended objections on the part of prospective members who probably would be contented to mark time.

This has made her a symbol of emulation to the Negro members of the union who hope that their children may also become a leader in the field of labor. Her persuasive powers are dependent upon her personal conviction regarding whatever may raise the status of female workers regardless of race. Mabel Fuller's voice will not fade upon the breezes of the desert air, and it never was meant to be unheard. Instead, her vocal platform talents reach out in behalf of all women, especially those in the ranks farthest down.

GLORIA RICHARDSON ("CIVIL-RIGHTS JOAN OF ARC")

Unknown and like "a root out of dry ground," Gloria Richardson by fate's good fortune rose from oblivion into the national limelight as a civil rightist. Leadership in Cambridge, Maryland, hinged upon her. In the fight to make the Negroes first-class citizens in their local communities, Mrs. Richardson is without peer. In her hometown, she led Negroes in demonstrations that dramatized the minority people's need for better jobs, improved job training, adequate housing, improved educational instruction and facilities, and accommodations in public facilities. A woman of extreme intensity, she unsmilingly and passionately drove hard bargains in making demands of the Cambridge white power structure.

From June to July, 1963, were her days of triumph, when power and fame were hers, when she was a household word and object of widespread admiration and "when she was the St. Joan of the civil-rights movement," according to Robert A. Liston, writing in the *Saturday Evening Post*.[4] During Richardson's period of leadership, the Negro crime rate decreased in Cambridge, where the citizens were caught up in a movement against discrimination. She told Murray Kempton of the *New Republic* in November, 1963: "It's funny, but during the whole time we were demonstrating actively, there was almost no crime. . . . Now they have gone back to fighting each other again. They have been thrown back to carrying a chip on their shoulders."

The persistent pressure directed against the officials of Cambridge caused white leaders to propose a special election in which citizens could vote on an amendment to the town's charter which would make it illegal to refuse service to Negroes in restaurants, motels, and other places of public accommodation. During preelection activities, white ministers preached brotherly love, to which Gloria Richardson turned a deaf ear. She advised Negroes not to go to the polls and vote, while she stayed at home during the election and made no effort by word or deed to gain passage of the very legislation for which she fought so hard. Strange to say, opposition to the proposed amendment came mainly from a white citizens' association and Gloria Richardson, chairman of the Cambridge Non-Violent Action Committee.

Gloria Richardson cannot be placed in a definite mold, for she followed the dictates of her own mind. She argued that Negroes shouldn't have to vote for rights guaranteed by the Constitution, but her opponents said that it made little sense to use such reasoning to destroy a troubled community's rare opportunity to advance in a very practical way toward improved race relations. However, the proposed amendment was lost because only 48 per cent of the registered Negro voters turned out at the polls. At once, certain persons set about to heal the rift between Gloria Richardson and other Negro leaders in early October, 1963, because she threatened to resign her position with the local Non-Violent Action Committee. The bickerings led Mrs. Richardson to sever her relations with the Cambridge civil-rights movement, but the next year the passage of the 1964 Civil Rights Bill achieved the goals for which Negroes fought bravely in the face of great odds.

It is too early for an exact evaluation of the work and leadership of Gloria Richardson. It is known that she has a personality that begets loyalty and demands respect from her followers. Her ethical appeal is almost without comparison, and her voice is persuasive enough to conscript a host of adherents who listen to what she tells them. Richardson's personal magnetism is significantly enhanced by her consuming sincerity, as well as an overwhelming faith in the importance of the work she is commissioned to do. The clear voice of God speaks to this woman. Something splendid had to happen because she dared to believe something within her was superior to circumstances existing in Cambridge, Maryland. She was not guilty of doing one thing and saying another, nor of what Ralph Waldo Emerson once said: "What you *are* thunders so loud I can't hear what you say."

Gloria Richardson had to do considerable speaking before Negro groups in her hometown, and she made her words marvelously simple and they understood. In conference with city officials, she used intellectual language that was logical, often critical and, by embellished innuendos, made the listeners read between the lines of her discourse. The speaker often drew parallelisms with language so exquisite that her enemies were impelled to listen. And yet their obstinacy prevented much success at the conference table. Once she said something to this effect: "Intelligence keeps both eyes open, and wants to know; but *wisdom,* which is rare and more necessary, often keeps its eyes half-closed and averts its head from sights it can neither accept nor reject."

Gloria Richardson considered speechmaking something that required concentration, very much like hitting a baseball. The batter has to be sharply alert with every muscle and nerve in tight coordination. When speaking, Gloria Richardson "felt her body and brain move into high gear." She learned how to control her material, herself, and her audience. Her remarks were clear and pointed, and she did not permit her content to become entangled in a maze of oratorical byways. Thus she kept on the right rhetorical highway. The subject matter of her speeches flowed from within, and this gave her a distinct advantage. Each speech had a purpose, and she geared her persuasion to this goal.

Racial pacificists wanted her to accept illogical compromises. Since they couldn't justify the proposed compromises, they wrung their hands in horror, vainly hoping to bring their idealism to the attention of the racial combatants. Gloria Richardson, realizing that nothing much is gained from either deploring or passing resolutions or compromising, accepted the fact that the civil-rights struggle is within us, inasmuch as humanity has not developed basically beyond the primitive stage where might makes right. Consequently, this orator decided to bank her hopes of winning first-class citizenship upon vigorous social action.

RUBY HURLEY ("THE EAGER DYNAMO")

Mrs. Ruby Hurley, Southeast Regional NAACP director with headquarters in Atlanta, Georgia, is an "eager dynamo." This designation is an epitome to her whole being. She is especially gifted in putting gusto into an NAACP meeting when the program officials have crowded too many activities in a single session without considering the time limits of the meeting. This opportunity comes whenever it is time to make an appeal to the audience for finances. In this role, Ruby Hurley gives orders for everybody to stand for a minute, stretch, and yawn. When the audience is seated again, she talks to the listeners in an off-the-cuff style. As the major-domo, she directs the ushers to guide everyone by the collection table so that each person may rid himself of some dollars he begrudgingly holds in his pocket, and from which he will not part if a collection plate is passed.

Once in Raleigh, North Carolina, the author witnessed Ruby Hurley in action as she commanded the ushers to guide everybody into the collection line. The author found that no one, himself included, could escape making a significant contribution if he valued his self-respect. While the audience marched to the table, Ruby Hurley and some members of the audience engaged in a kind of slapstick humor and quick repartee. For instance, she gave out lines like this: "Talk is cheap, but it takes greenbacks to get things done! Let's have those fives, tens, and twenties, brother. It takes money to make the civil-rights gospel march!" In response, a listener might reply, "I like the way you got those cheapskates covered, madam!"

Ruby Hurley, who received her college education at Miner Teacher's College, is a product of the District of Columbia public schools and the Robert H. Terrell Law School. She was once employed by the Industrial Bank of Washington, and later her work with the Washington Youth Council brought recognition from the national office and resulted in her appointment as NAACP youth secretary in 1943. Youth chapters increased from 86 in 1943 to more than 280 units with more than 25,000 members. During 1951, Ruby Hurley was sent to Birmingham on a temporary assignment to coordinate NAACP chapters in Alabama, Georgia, Florida, Mississippi, and Tennessee. Subsequently, the Southeast region was established and then expanded to include North and South Carolina. It then included more than 300 branches with nearly 35,000 members. The headquarters of the Southeast region is presently located in Atlanta, Georgia, from which Mrs. Hurley coordinates the work of the organization. She travels thousands of miles annually investigating numerous cases related to mob violence and open hostility.

Invitations to speak pour in by the hundreds to Ruby Hurley each year. The officials of the Twentieth Annual Convention of the North Carolina NAACP branches, for example, invited her to speak as a keynoter when it convened in Charlotte, North Carolina, from June 10 to 13, 1963. In September, 1965, the regional director spoke in Raleigh, North Carolina, and delivered what a *Carolinian* staff writer labeled a "charged-up" message in the First Baptist Church. She said that "Raleigh is something else; there seems to be a feeling of complacency, and that we have arrived. Not only in Raleigh, but in other areas of North Carolina, you find the counterparts of Mississippi." During June, 1965, Ruby Hurley was guest speaker at a Spartanburg, S.C., NAACP rally at which the "Woman of the Year" was honored. In the fall of 1965, the orator spoke in Winston-Salem, North Carolina, and said that North Carolina Negroes were a long way from freedom despite the outward appearance. Although the occasion honored the Reverend Pitts, pastor of Shiloh Baptist Church and president of the General Baptist State Convention, who received an award, the audience was very small. The speaker remarked, "I get frustrated in this state. I've read so long about how great North Carolina is. I have read about moderation and good race relations. . . . North Carolina is not defiant; it is cagey. This state is devious. It lulls the Negro to sleep."

As an orator, Ruby Hurley can adapt her words to suit the occasion. In clear diction, she moves an audience with measured passion and arouses listeners to give active support to the movement for civil rights. She is aware that persuasive public speaking is not enough to place Negroes in good jobs, but, nevertheless, she uses oratory in the service of people by inspiring their thoughts and stimulating them to become activists. Her subject matter is arranged on the principle of pyramidal construction. Her ideas rise to a point, but slowly and symmetrically from a colossal base. The diction is simple and the vocabulary conversational. Upon an occasion like the memorialization of the passage of the 1954 Supreme Court decision, or the enactment of the 1964 Civil Rights Bill, her platform delivery is adaptable and sets the proper mood to the fullest. Somehow she finds the magic words that appeal to the emotions of the rank and file. At the climax of an address, Ruby Hurley lets loose a tempestuous roar of passion which swiftly subsides to a neutral vocal key.

MEDGAR EVERS

Not all guerrilla chiefs escape the bullets of the enemy, and such was the tragic fate of Medgar Evers, state NAACP leader in Mississippi, who was cut down in his prime on June 12, 1963, by an anonymous assassin's bullet just as he was getting out of his car to enter his home. Like the fallen John F. Kennedy, Medgar Evers represented for the Negro all that is good and best in his quest for equality for Negroes in his state. On one occasion, Medgar Evers appeared on an NBC telecast during which he recounted the nature of his work in Mississippi. He impressed television viewers with his modesty regarding some of the gains that he had helped black Mississippians to achieve. Medgar Evers was effective in his voter-registration campaigns through his calm attitude, which was different from that of his boastful brother who took his place in the NAACP fight.

The best tribute that could be paid the deceased leader, a Freedom Rider of the Mississippi backwater country, was the memorial service held for him at his grave site in Arlington National Cemetery in Washington, D.C., in June, 1963. It was a kind of rerun of the activities of the fallen chief who had risked all for freedom through the long night of the pilgrimage for justice. It was, in a sense, a narrative of the struggle against strong opposition from the various local Mississippi agricultural planters and certain of the white power structure. Delivering the eulogy was Clarence Mitchell, lobbyist and director of the NAACP Washington Bureau. The eulogist cited the deceased hero for his courage in refusing to operate in secrecy as did the Ku Klux Klan and other "purveyors of discord." Continuing, Mitchell stated that Medgar Evers was "a part of the American heritage stemming from the history of revolts, and [black] Mississippians, like other brave men, had resorted to constitutional weapons instead of violence in waging war against second-class citizenship."

Medgar Evers made speeches that were instructional in nature. First, he had to instruct the rural masses in how to deal with their fears of the wealthy white farmers, thugs, and businessmen. Second, he urged them to lay aside their fears of repercussions should they go to the voter-registration centers. Third, he had to teach the people the basic and rudimentary facts about the United States Constitution and Bill of Rights in order that they might pass successfully the punitive and rigid Mississippi voter's test. His messages were factual and appealed in a direct way to the minds of the common people, many of whom could scarcely read. Last, he challenged the people as Jesus Christ did when he said, "If any man will come after me, let him deny himself, and take up the cross, and follow me."

Working in Mississippi could easily have caused Medgar Evers to develop a negative and pessimistic attitude in his speeches, but he preferred optimism by indicating some of the good things in the state where the people were born and reared. He urged folks to take a panoramic view of the beautiful forests and landscapes, the promise of cities by industrialization, the magnificent shores on the Gulf of Mexico, and the future prospects of Negroes who were trained in the technical skills, engineering, professions, and businesses of all kinds. These opportunities were called by the speaker "the gifts of God which should be enjoyed by all citizens in Mississippi."

As an orator, Medgar Evers was deadly serious and convinced of the righteousness of the battle for civil rights. His vocal delivery was inclined to be theological in nature, but not of the fire-and-brimstone mold. Like the great prophets of old, Medgar Evers talked to the Negroes of Mississippi about their sins of *omission* rather than those of *commission*. He implied that it was what the Negro had not done about the ballot that kept him so far behind in the state and elsewhere. His wonderful personal control and temperament did not permit him to say anything that he would regret later or that would retard his mission in the state. In an appealing conversational voice, the NAACP leader used wisdom in training Mississippi citizens in what they should know about voting legislation in order to qualify to vote.

EVALUATION OF THE ORATORY OF THE PERIOD

In assessing the quality of oratory in a particular period, critics often employ criteria involving the eloquence of men who determined public opinion, stimulated crusading movements, and influenced parliamentary and congressional legislation. Today one does not expect to hear oratory like that of our colonial period, because our culture and the electronic age have demanded the conversational mode of oral expression. Yet this fact does not justify the mediocrity of public speaking so prevalent in our churches, Congress, courts, and classrooms. Using the pattern of the times, our guerrilla orators, for the most part, lack the showmanship of our musical groups, dancers, and singers. This lull in eloquent and stimulating public address has been traced by Raymond Motley under the title "Raise Our Sights" in *Newsweek* for January 31, 1961. Motley laments the fact that the present oral discourse "consists of flagrant appeals to the stomach and pocketbooks, demagogic attacks upon business for its sins committed years ago, irrelevant lint-picking and canned ghost-written speeches— all clothed with jargon which only partially covers the stark nakedness of thought."

Like their white counterparts, the Negro Congressmen of this period, with few exceptions, are dull speakers. This becomes readily evident when one reads their addresses printed in the *Congressional Record*. Many of these addresses are written by assistants, and they include embellishments of voluminous insertions of matter clipped from newspapers. This type of drivel cannot compare with the discourses that used to dignify the House and Senate Chambers when delivered by such giants as Webster, Calhoun, and Clay. There is considerable lack of vitality in legislative speaking today, for we have no constitutional verities as expressed by a Borah, no hard and factual reasoning as exhibited by Taft, and few carefully prepared arguments such as those once given by LaFollette.

Impassioned speaking of a kind has been frequently stimulated by the movement for civil rights, and such orators have been mostly either Negroes or segregationist demagogues whose ranting often destroyed vocal effectiveness. Part of this trend can be traced to a decline in the latent talents and capabilities of the men who enter politics and public office. Our better speakers are found in other careers, such as in the fields of radio and television. So far as the Negro is concerned generally, there is little emphasis upon training in public speaking and debating. This is a challenge to our educational institutions to give the type of speech training that will help Negroes to say effectively *how* they want to find a way out of the racial dilemma, when no way is clear, certain, or easy.

Footnotes, Chapter 15

1. "The Sit-in Demonstrations and the Dilemma of the Negro College President," *Journal of Negro Education* 30 (Winter, 1961): 1–3.
2. *The New York Times,* May 11, 1963, p. 8.
3. Ibid.
4. Robert A. Liston, "Who Can We Surrender To?," *Saturday Evening Post,* 226 (October 5, 1963): 78–80.

16 / Study in Contrast:
Malcolm Little and
Whitney Young

The NAACP led by Roy Wilkins, the SCLC directed by Martin Luther King, Jr., and the National Urban League led by Whitney Young have dominated powerfully the activities designed to aid minority groups to achieve democratic equality in all areas of American life. Each one of these organizations is headed by a leader, deserving the rank of a four-star general in the civil-rights battle. Sociologists have chosen to call these leaders "The Big Three." However, the author chooses not to use this classification for Whitney Young.

Malcolm Little belonged to the Black Muslim movement, and, according to some scholars, he should be discussed in the context of religious cults. However, in terms of the man's philosophy, Malcolm X transcends the preoccupation of the religious cults, and he vacillated between nationalism and a constructive approach to a solution of the racial problems of the rank and file. His activities goaded his followers into wakefulness and kept their morale high. His was a leadership that appeared to give his followers little to do, while he was trying to resolve his inward struggles into a clear-cut direction of what would be his purpose in life. For these reasons, the author refused to include Malcolm X in the chapter on cults. The purpose of this chapter is to present Malcolm Little and Whitney Young in two sharply different profiles, so that readers can evaluate in their own terms the dynamics of both men.

MINISTER MALCOLM LITTLE ("MALCOLM X")

Any movement having considerable prestige is bound to attract brilliant adherents like the late Malcolm Little, widely heralded as "Malcolm X," protester, panelist, Muslim minister, and orator "profundo." Numerous articles have been written about this controversial figure who was sometimes identified as a smooth, oily ex-convict. However, as the spokesman of Black Muslimism, Malcolm X was worthy of comparison with Gamaliel of the Hebrews and Plato and Aristotle of the Greeks. It was rumored once that Minister Malcolm X was next in line to receive the office of Messenger of Allah.

At the peak of his career, Malcolm X separated himself from the Black Muslim movement and launched his own faction, only to be assassinated while speaking from the stage of a Harlem ballroom in mid-afternoon on February 21, 1965. It was reported that his slaying was an act of revenge by active members of the Black Muslim sect. At the trial in January, 1966, the government claimed that three men had stationed themselves in the audience. Two of them started a fight to distract attention, while a third disciple, Thomas "15-X" Johnson, shot Malcolm in the chest with a sawed-off shotgun—after which, the other two men rushed to the stage and fired bullets into the prone body of Minister Malcolm.

Malcolm's untimely death ended his career before he was able to develop the guidelines that, in essence, recognized the Negro as an integral part of the United States, a distant cry from Elijah Muhammed's doctrine of black separation. Because of a marked change in 1964, Minister Malcolm decided to break with Elijah Muhammed and his pronouncements. It is alleged by Alex Haley in his epilogue to *Autobiography of Malcolm X* (1964) that Malcolm's death was the result of his break with Allah Elijah Muhammed, and that Muhammed had commissioned three Black Muslims to take his life.

The public remembers Malcolm X as an eloquent Muslim minister and philosopher whose trail led from a dingy prison cell to the Mount of Olives. During this time, he developed himself into an eloquent orator and street-corner spellbinder. People enjoyed his speaking, whether or not they agreed with what he said, because he made public speaking an appealing art. The author, who heard Minister Malcolm speak in New York three times, observed that he was a favorite with audiences. Yet this did not mean that he was not heckled a good deal. The vocal style of Malcolm caught forcefully the fancy of numerous "avenue hangbys," loafers who frequently followed him to his several speaking stations.

When Malcolm X was considering how he might best project his new movement into the hearts and minds of people, he found his natural talent for public speaking a useful tool. His persuasive oratory brought him a large following of both blacks and whites. It was this contact with whites in the course of his meteoric rise to national prestige that brought about a change in his attitude toward whites—they were not all the devils he had once thought they were. He received numerous invitations to speak at student forums in eastern universities where he was always respectful and responsive to the reactions of his listeners. It is thought that the knowledge of certain secular practices at the headquarters of Elijah Muhammed's headquarters shocked him. This knowledge, along with his reconversion, gave Malcolm the needed conviction to sway prospective converts to his new movement.

Malcolm X opposed the doctrine of nonviolence advocated by Martin Luther King, Jr. as an approach to a solution of the persistent racial problem. As a Black Muslim, he said that we are never the aggressor, but if anyone attacks us, "we will lay down our lives." He said that he would never start a fight, never look for trouble, never stir up confusion, but yet he would never condone the doctrine of nonviolence. The leader never tired of saying, "Get the white man off my back." This kind of speaking made enemies, to be sure, but audiences were convinced that Malcolm X was no "turn-the-other-cheek man."

Malcolm was effective as both an organizer and a speaker in the Black Muslim movement. His speaking activities were not limited to the temples of the Muslims and street-corner audiences, since he was a participant in radio and television panel discussions. His skill in speaking was remarkable for one with only an eighth-grade education, but he had read widely and acquired an abundance of knowledge after he affiliated with the Black Muslims. Reading good literature had enlarged his vocabulary and refined his language style. Minister Malcolm demonstrated his powers when, during a telecast in 1963, he was interviewed by James Baldwin about his connection with the Black Muslim movement. Malcolm X excelled in rapid-fire give-and-take. It has been said that he was interviewed more than any other Negro leader from 1961 to 1963. All the interviews featuring Malcolm X revealed his personal magnetism as an orator and public speaker. He had a graceful vocal inflection appropriate to the meaning of what was said.

In telecasts, Minister Malcolm was self-assured, used dignified gestures, and maintained proper platform style. Tall and trim for a man of forty-odd years, with his professor's beard and soapbox oratory, he did a fine job of proselyting even when challenged by hecklers. He exhibited marvelous mental powers, a storehouse of words, and an ability to make his audiences go home and think. The way the minister carried himself behind the lectern impressed his audiences. Knowing many people's dislike of all Black Muslims and the orator's ostentatiousness, the hostility he aroused is understandable. His speeches redeemed souls, in spite of his personal vanity. But certain Negro leaders, in spite of being hostile to the Islamic religion, heard him with approbation and applause.

The basis for Malcolm's eloquent public speaking may be traced to his facility for writing prose that was both poetical and rhythmic. The soul or basis of his oratory was the strikingly simple and concrete idea. Allah's Minister had a well-modulated voice, and spoke within a narrow band of pitch that gave him great reserve whenever he needed it. It was with his honey-toned voice that he coped with the harassment of the rabble and controlled his temper. "Mr. Muslim," as he was often called, was an active, vigorous orator who sometimes pounded the lectern with his first. His marvelous vocal mechanism was in its full perfection and strength, and hearers, swayed by the lure of the Muslim doctrine, were compelled to surrender themselves to the magnetic pull of his proselytizing rhetoric. Some listeners resisted his persuasion, but they never forgot his dedicated passion.

What about the man himself? Malcolm's life did not follow the fairy-tale "happy ever after" ending, nor was it the typical success story of "from rags to riches." When he was imprisoned in 1947, he met Elijah Muhammed, from whom he learned about the religion of Islam. Then the Spirit carried him, as it were, upon the Mount in order for him to make the greatest decision of his life. When he descended from the Mount of Temptation with the Devil there was no doubt about his mission and what he must do. His battle with the satan of his unconscious mind restored his morale and gave him a new commitment for living. The experience made him manly and reconstructed his integrity. Yet his struggles to eke out a living in a big city during his youth and his term in prison left him without any feelings of humanity for Caucasians. He blamed his struggles and youthful delinquency on white people who made it difficult for a black man to earn a decent living. There was no earthly Galilean to say to him, "Go and sin no more, thy sins are forgiven." His life was a paradox that had to be solved by himself alone.

Near the end of his life, a complete change came as a result of the truth he learned in Mecca. The experience led him to remark that his friends did not include just Negroes and Muslims, but men of all races and political beliefs—agnostics, Christians, Uncle Toms, moderates, and radicals. As a leader, Minister Malcolm could not be dismissed lightly. Louis E. Lomax once remarked, "No sane man, black or white, dares a mass program in Harlem without including Malcolm X. For if it comes to a showdown, Malcolm can muster more people than Adam Powell, A. Philip Randolph, Martin Luther King, Jr., and Roy Wilkins all put together."[1] Some men are forgotten when they die. What greater tribute could be paid this orator, who was unexpectedly called to his reward, than to say that he commanded the hearts and ears of eager listeners. When the fatal shots rang out, Malcolm's talents were soaring on the climax of a public speech. His language was bold, fierce, and strong, and his faith was certain.

WHITNEY YOUNG, JR. ("THE DEAN")

When the National Urban League, which was organized in 1910, wanted an inspiring and efficient leader in October, 1961, it called Whitney Young, Jr., former dean of the Atlanta School of Social Work, to take over the helm and leadership. "The Dean," as he is often called, had the necessary background that seemed to set him apart as something special for the job. He was a premedical student at Kentucky State College in Frankfort, where he received the bachelor's degree when he was eighteen years old. Changing his academic major, he earned the master's degree in social work at the University of Minnesota. As dean of the Atlanta School of Social Work, Young had earned security and an academic reputation.

The call to head the National Urban League was a bid to stand upon the corners of time and help minority groups to get job training and placement suitable for their skills. It was a bid, as we have seen later, to devise a "Marshall Plan" for

Negroes whereby they can be the beneficiaries of preferential treatment as an indemnity for injustices they have endured for more than three hundred years.

Whitney Young accepted a heavy responsibility when he became executive director of the National Urban League. This gave him the opportunity to enlarge the League's efforts to seek new opportunities for Negroes in industry as it once did in assisting Negro migrants during the early part of this century. The position Young now fills makes him a key man in bringing the employer and employees together around the table in a beneficial way. He must, therefore, carry on a tradition which has been practiced by the National Urban League for more than fifty years in behalf of employment of the man farthest down the ladder.

Just what is the nature of the National Urban League and why does it rank among the "Big Three Organizations" that are operating to advance the cause of Negroes in this country? The National Urban League has sixty-five local chapters located across the nation, and it does not consider itself a social or civil-rights organization or agency. It has 100,000 members who pay dues to support its program. There are 232 college-trained social workers on its staff, and it has 6,000 active volunteers, a large number of whom are white. Although it is not a civil-rights organization, it does at times act as troubleshooter to ease racial tensions in specified areas. Lawrence Lynch, a *Wall Street Journal* reporter, once called the NUL a kind of "Skills Bank" in which Whitney Young works to keep it solvent.

In carrying out NUL national policies, Mr. Young once remarked that its representatives act intelligently, shunning picketing and demonstrating. For this stand, the NUL has drawn significant criticism from militant Negroes, but the organization does not hesitate to use the climate created by direct-action protests of others and thus extract concessions at the bargaining table.

As a writer and public speaker, Young came to the attention of the public in August, 1965, with his proposal for a Marshall Plan for Negroes that would give them preferential treatment as an indemnity for past injustices. At that time, he urged the federal government to undertake an immediate, dramatic, and tangible crash program to close the intolerable economic, social and educational gap that separates most Negro citizens from the American majority. In a television speech made on Sunday, June 9, 1963, Young estimated that this program would cost the federal government about $14 billion annually. The orator concluded that the "program for restoration of our [racial] losses might take the form of a law of restitution to correct, as far as possible, the effects of slavery and segregation." Prior to assuming the directorship of the National Urban League, Young sensed the implications of the Negro revolution. In addressing the eighty-eighth Annual Forum of the National Conference on Social Welfare on May 28, 1962, Young said in his peroration that "our Revolution at this point with American Negro citizens is a Revolution of Expectation that seeks only a birthright for them as American citizens. May we move with speed, perception, and intelligence to assure the success of this revolution, and to justify the heritage which is ours as social workers."

Whitney Young travels extensively over the nation making speeches before members of various units of the NUL and other interested groups. In this capacity, he never misses the opportunity to call the attention of Negro youth to the challenging positions on the NUL staff. Aside from this digression, the speaker organizes skillfully the content of his addresses. His ideas unravel as smoothly as a ball of quality yarn. There is an urgency in his voice as he challenges the League leadership and membership to new horizons of activity by an intelligent approach to the solutions of many community problems. The *great imperative* is to him like "carrying the Message to Garcia," or "speeding the good news from Ghent to Aix."

Following the passage of the 1964 and 1965 civil-rights bills, it has become imperative for Negro leaders to make first-class citizenship an actuality. Young is doing his part to bring to full circle his work in this direction. He considers oratory more than a communicative skill, since an effective leader must speak with some degree of eloquence. Although he is not a phrase-maker of spellbinding proportions, Young finds every opportunity to advance the Negro's cause by what he can give in his discourses. The NUL director makes his speechmaking incidental. He did not come to establish a system of oratory but to lead a crusade, and to think more daringly and more divinely in order to explain to the world his service to mankind.

Whitney Young is no fanatic, and he does not rouse his audiences on the streets to sing songs. He does not need yells and cheers to set the mood for audiences to engage in what we label "speaker-and-audience talk-back" participation. Rather than the hoopla of demonstrations, followed by telecast scenes of rioting, he presents to his hearers cold, startling facts that often shock their sensibilities. When Young opens his mouth, his words do not spout from "a half-cocked gun," nor does he use bombast or oratorical flourishes. His platform decorum is gentlemanly, intelligent, and poised, and his subject matter convinces people that the best way to settle differences is at the conference table. In conference sessions with employers and management, his voice is articulate and adequately loud and flexible in tone. The convincing character of Mr. Young's voice and speeches is traceable to his powerful intellect and intense study. His powers of abstraction and discrimination are tremendous, and he has a lively fancy and enthusiasm that are overwhelming. Listeners are persuaded by his mental gifts, his courage, and his honest approach. He employs these gifts to keep his hearers pleasantly expectant rather than motivated to creating disorders. Whereas other men, like the guerrilla chiefs of civil rights, seek to make their eloquence ornamental, Young aims at substance rather than grace. He pays strict attention to the art of arranging sentences so that they will achieve the greatest effect and audience response. Consequently, his delivery has harmony and cadence while his oral composition is consistently logical in structure.

Young does not have at his disposal the "circus techniques" employed by the eminent Billy Graham, and he depends upon the soundness of truth to catch and hold his audience. He has a frankness that precludes any suspicions on the part of the listeners. His messages come straight from an honest heart. While some critics may think that Young is too dignified, grave, and forcible in his platform delivery, there is also an admixture of politeness, urbanity, ease, and subtle gaiety. Finally, clearness and copiousness of argument and illustration are the chief excellencies for which his public speeches are noted.

Footnotes, Chapter 16

1. Louis E. Lomax, *The Negro Revolt,* p. 177.

17 / Martin Luther King, Jr.

"The Nonviolent Prophet"

No other leader has been written about as much as Martin Luther King, Jr., unless it was Booker T. Washington. It was the Montgomery bus boycott that ushered him upon the American scene as a formidable Negro leader, and thereafter his platform skills developed into those of a topflight orator. He came forth like the Biblical "root out of dry ground" and offered a nonviolent approach to the solution of the racial problems in the United States. Afterward, his prestige grew until he became the one leader who was willing to leave the pulpit and lead civil-rights marches in order to lift up the downtrodden and underprivileged from the mire of second-class citizenship.

King's nonviolent movement led his followers to regard him as the "Saviour of First-Class Citizenship" while men of high calling ventured to label him America's Gandhi. Dedicated nonviolent adherents would brook no attack on their idol, even in the face of such criticism as outlined by George S. Schuyler, formidable newspaper columnist, who once took Martin Luther King to task thus:

Since the reverend clergy followed the Pied Piper, Dr. Martin Luther King, Jr., into the Southern Christian Leadership Conference a half decade ago, and have loudly claimed the leadership of the race, they can now go all out to head drives for Negroes to improve themselves through their own efforts.

Regardless of the many viewpoints concerning Doctor King, it is almost impossible to evaluate accurately the orator and his work, since he moved with such rapidity to many places. However, a decade from now, after several years of reflection, an objective appraisal can possibly be made.

BIOGRAPHICAL SKETCH

The biography of Martin Luther King, Jr., has been published in several books by reputable authors, and King himself delineated the activities of the Montgomery bus boycott in *Strides Toward Freedom* (1958). One of the best biographies of King was published by L. D. Reddick in *Crusader Without Violence* (1959), which dealt with the life and times of the orator. In the *Negro Revolt* (1960), Louis E. Lomax evaluated the work of at least a dozen leaders, including Dr. King; the revolt against certain Negro leaders is amply discussed by Lomax in the June, 1960, issue of *Harper's* magazine. The life of Dr. King by Lerone Bennett, Jr., has been published by Pocket Books, under the title of *What Manner of Man.*

One catches the essence of the dramatic quality of Dr. King's early work in Alabama in the new spirit engendered among Negroes when the Montgomery bus boycott was won. This new spirit was a magnificent idea that took hold of the black man and shook him to his depths, turned him inside out, and made him feel the grandest creature upon the face of the earth. This shocked and even frightened some white people in the South. Winning the bus boycott indicated that

Negroes were not as complacent as some people had thought they were. A most dramatic way of describing this characteristic of the new Negro was revealed in a conversation with a middle-aged black woman who said: "Lord, chile, we colored people ain't nothing but a bundle of resentment and suffering going somewhere to explode." Almost equally as concrete was a second comment found in *Strides Toward Freedom,* authored by Martin Luther King, Jr. When asked what she thought and felt about having to walk instead of riding buses in Montgomery, the woman replied, "My feet is tired but my soul is rested."

King's nonviolent victory at Montgomery was the stimulant for the evolution of a new racial tactic. By 1963 nonviolence had become a magnanimous weapon that cut without wounding and made noble the man who wielded it. Black citizens felt that it was a sword that healed and won victories. Four years later, blacks were willing to risk martyrdom in order to arouse the social conscience of the nation.

In 1965, "Mr. Civil Rights" went to Oslo, Norway, to receive the Nobel Peace Prize. Wherever he traveled, audiences sang "We Shall Overcome!" King played a leading role in James Meredith's Mississippi march in 1966 and was active in the open-housing confrontation in Chicago. In 1967, he took time out to rest so that he might rethink his civil-rights strategy.

It was in 1968 that Dr. King laid plans for a Poor People's March on Washington; as a preliminary, he engaged in demonstrations in Memphis, Tennessee. Then, on April 4, 1968, King met an untimely death at the hands of an assassin at the Lorraine Motel in Memphis, Tennessee. The story of James Kay and the conspiracy to kill Martin Luther King, Jr., is told by William Bradford Huie's series of exclusive reports beginning in the November 12, 1968, issue of *Look.*

Two weeks later, the *Afro-American* epitomized the bitter end in these words: "Doctor King was the last of the apostles of nonviolence, and with his death this philosophy died. It was not the black people that killed it. It was white violence and racism. It put the lid on in Dallas and nailed it down in Mississippi."

BOYCOTT KEYNOTE SPEECH

After seamstress Rosa Parks was arrested on a bus because she violated one of Montgomery's segregation laws, a preliminary meeting was called to decide what action should be taken by the local Negro citizens. The strategy chiefs selected Martin Luther King, Jr., to make the keynote address at a mass meeting held in Holt Street Church. King said:

Without notes and manuscript, I told the story of what happened to Mrs. Parks. Then I reviewed the long history of abuses and insults that Negro citizens had experienced on the city buses. "But there comes a time," I said, "that people get tired. We are here this evening to say to those who have mistreated us so long that we are tired of being segregated and humiliated, tired of being kicked around by the brutal feet of oppression." [The congregation met this statement with fervent applause.] "We had no alternative but to protest," I continued. "For many years, we have shown amazing patience. We have something which has given our white brothers the feeling that we like the way we were treated. But we come here tonight to be saved from the patience that makes us patient and with anything less than freedom and patience!" [Again the audience interrupted with applause.]

Briefly, I pointed out our actions, both morally and legally. Comparing our methods with those of the White Citizens Councils and Ku Klux Klan, I pointed out that while "these organizations are protesting for the perpetuation of injustice in the community, their methods led to violence and lawlessness. But in our protest there will be no cross burnings. No white person will be taken from his home and beaten by a hooded Negro mob and brutally murdered. There will be no threats and intimidation. We will be guided by the highest principles of law and order.

"Our reactions must be guided by the deepest principles of our Christian faith. Love must be our regulating ideal. Once again we must hear the words of Jesus echoing across the centuries: 'Love your enemies, bless them that curse you and despitefully use you.' If you fail to do this, our protest will end up as meaningless as a drama on the stage of history, and its memory will be shrouded with the ugly garments of shame. In spite of the mistreatment that we have confronted we must not become bitter and end up by hating our white brothers. As Booker T. Washington said, 'Let no man pull you so low as to make you hate him.' " [Once more the audience responded enthusiastically.]

Then came the closing statement: "If you will profess courageously, and yet with Christian love, when the history books are written in future generations, the historians will have to pause and say, 'There lived a people—black people—who injected new meaning and dignity into the veins of civilization. This is our challenge and our overwhelming responsibility.' " [As Doctor King took his seat, the people rose to their feet and applauded.]'

Dr. King was thankful afterwards that he had gotten across the message of how to combine the militant and the moderate. Furthermore, the people had been just as enthusiastic when he urged them to love their enemies as they were when he condoned their right to protest.

SPEECH PREPARATION

Leadership in the nonviolent movement catapulted Martin Luther King, Jr. into the national limelight. From then on, he rode upon wings of forceful eloquence and oratory. Realizing that brilliant oratory was an asset to him, King spent considerable time in preparing his sermons and speeches. L. D. Reddick, a biographer, said that the Reverend King was methodical in preparing his speeches for almost every occasion. "He likes to read up on his topic for a couple of days, outline it, then write what he wants to say. He will then lay the manuscript aside, going back to it a few hours before it is delivered. When he has gone through this process, he does not need to use either script or notes when he stands up to make his speech."[2] However, after he became heavily involved in the nonviolent movement, King could hardly afford the luxury of elaborate preparation. Conversely, as pastor of the Dexter Avenue Baptist Church, King admitted he had been "spending a minimum of fifteen hours a day for preparation, even to drafting his speeches in longhand."

Through the study of world history, King learned that it paid for a leader to have a good voice and that it must be trained religiously. Because he was not born with vocal eloquence, he took his normal speech mechanism and improved it with vigorous practice to make himself articulate in oral communication. When his training was complete, he expounded his theories with ease and fluency. As a youth, King participated in many speaking activities. For example, during his senior year in high school, he won a local Elks oratorical contest in the Georgia state finals at Valdosta. Thus he learned to speak effectively through practice.

Dr. King liked to discuss or debate his speech subjects with someone before actually delivering them. Often his wife served as a sounding board in these preparations, but she did not write her husband's speeches. His chief administrative staff in the Southern Christian Leadership Conference, Atlanta, Georgia, ranked high on his list of critical advisers for he could always count on constructive and sympathetic criticism from them.

While studying theology, the Reverend King had learned the teachings of ancient Greek and Roman rhetoricians concerning forensic oratory. He learned that for a speech to contain beauty and dignity of composition, there were three things necessary: first, it must please; second, it must convince; and, third, it must persuade. For the first effect, the orator must speak gracefully; for the second, he must talk plainly; and for the third, he must express himself with great ardor and fervency.

Martin Luther King's theological education taught him the tradition of cultivating the oratorical art and voice. The ancient Greek and Roman orators took speech training seriously under the instruction of famous rhetoricians. Greek actors, for example, practiced vocal exercises in the mornings before breakfast, since they felt that the voice was more flexible before eating. They were strictly temperate in food and drink. Cicero remarked that Roman actors and orators spent hours practicing before mirrors. Arduous practice was imperative for Greek actors, because they were obliged to use "the pure Athenian" without a trace of dialect or foreign accent. Since they performed in huge outdoor theaters, they sought to develop strong vocal projection. The Greeks and Romans were without peer in oral delivery, but they did not win their fame the easy way. This knowledge impressed Martin Luther King, Jr., in a significant way.

PLATFORM DELIVERY

Someone whose identity has since been lost labeled Martin Luther King, Jr., "the man with the gavel voice." Whatever nervousness King felt at the beginning of his addresses wore off as he warmed up to his subject. If he was applauded enthusiastically when he rose to speak, this reduced some of his nervousness.

The SCLC civil-rights general was an orator almost without peer in his times. One biographer[3] remarked that King had a magnetic, powerful, and rich baritone voice comprising a wide range. "King had a semi-soft musical voice which he used without oratorical tricks," remarked Art Carter of the *Afro-American*. The *California Eagle*'s Almona Lomax stated that she was impressed very much with Doctor King's forceful delivery, charm, and gentleness.

In 1958 the author heard King speak at the Institute of Religion in Raleigh, North Carolina, at the large Needham Broughton High School. Since the Broughton auditorium could not seat everybody, 1,500 people had to be accommodated in the educational building of the First Church of Christ, where they heard the orator over the loudspeaker. Dr. King first outlined the progress of Negroes in the United States and said, "We have come a long way, but there is still a longer road we must travel to first-class citizenship." It was always his purpose to sear the American conscience by a program of nonviolence in which Negroes could meet hate with love. A middle-aged white woman who sat in front of the author was so moved with King's message that she wept as King described the indignities suffered by black citizens. The truth of his words swayed the emotions of the author until they swelled his spirit with both joy and indignation. King had to gesticulate sparingly since a microphone pinned him close to the lectern within a small area, but the force of his words needed no large gestures to emphasize his message.

King made great use of his nasal resonators, which enriched his vocal tones. These tones were slightly flat, because of his failure to make more oval the openings of his vocal outlets. But this did not matter, since the power of his ideas transcended his technique. The message was overpowering and carried his audience safely through the whirlpools of emotion and frustration with injustice. When King concluded his hour-and-a-half address, three curtain calls were demanded before the applause subsided into silence. And this silence was filled with recollections of his narrative and poetic cadence, so vivid and alive just a few minutes earlier.

Doctor King became a sitter-in and demonstrator to promote the idea of nonviolence, and this gave his followers even greater confidence in his speeches. This practice had its root in an idea expressed by the Reverend John Pharr, recruitment representative for Johnson C. Smith University, in a sermon at the Trinity United Presbyterian Church, Tallahassee, Florida, in December, 1965. Speaking on the subject "The Divine Sit-In," Pharr talked about "leader identification." He described how Ezekiel sought to help his people, the Israelites, by living with them in order to know their problems at first hand. In Ezekiel 3 : 15 the prophet spoke sympathetically: "Then I came to them of the captivity at Talabib, that dwelt by the river of Chebar, and I sat where they sat, and remained there astonished among them seven days." At the end of seven days, Jehovah commissioned Ezekiel to sojourn among the people to help them gain their freedom from the foreign power.

Likewise, Doctor King, through his grass-roots identification with the Negro, staged a kind of "divine sit-in." He demonstrated and went to jail with his followers. He lived in a lower-middle-class Atlanta residential area. It was apropos that King shared the sit-in experience along with the people. He was a leader who walked in the path of the downtrodden that he might sit where they sat.

MARCH-ON-WASHINGTON ORATION

The triumphant March on Washington for jobs and freedom on August 28, 1963, was a two-decade dream come true to a host of Negro leaders, and especially A. Philip Randolph who first conceived of this idea during World War I. The 1963 occasion was momentous and impressive, since between a quarter to a half million Negroes assembled at the Washington Monument. The exact number involved in the March cannot be ascertained, since the news media were in wide disagreement in their reports. But what was even more impressive was the decorum of this massive crowd, in spite of the predicted confusion and pandemonium. A detailed account of the March, its planning, coordination, and its sponsors was reported in the September and October issues of *Ebony* magazine in 1963, the October issue of *Crisis,* and the October 7 issue of the *Pittsburgh Courier,* not to mention every important daily newspaper.

The program, which was televised nationally, featured speakers who were headliners, including A. Philip Randolph, Roy Wilkins, Walter Reuther, Whitney Young, the Reverend Eugene Carson Blake, Matthew Ahmann, and Rabbi Joachim Prinz. The final orator was the eloquent star, Martin Luther King, who stepped before the microphone and began speaking on the subject, "I Have a Dream Today," a well-prepared speech, destined to become the classic oration for Negro civil rights and freedom. The statement, "America has given its colored citizens a bad check, a check that has come back marked insufficient funds," hung on the listening ears and hearts and minds of those persons present.

The author, who heard the address over television, was moved with tremendous pride in the ideals of his race and by the rhythmic cadence of the speaker. The total effect on King's hearers must have been comparable to the experience of the disciples of Jesus Christ upon the Mount of Transfiguration. Then, in silence, the hearers and himself were carried down, as it were, to the River Jordan to be baptized in the Spirit.

It was this oration that made King the immortal idol of his adherents; certainly for him and the occasion, it will be remembered in the same manner as Lincoln's Gettysburg Address, Wendell Phillips' oration "Toussaint L'Ouverture," William Jennings Bryan's "Cross of Gold" speech, and Robert G. Ingersoll's "Funeral Oration at His Brother's Grave."

William G. Nunn, Sr., a journalist, called the March-on-Washington oration "the rallying cry for 20 million black Americans, delivered by a twentieth-century Messiah, because the words squeezed the pulsating hearts of millions of Americans." Carried away, Nunn added: "The majestic and magnetic and compelling voice of the Rev. Martin Luther King, Jr., was picked up by radio and television as it thundered across the hills, mountains, dales, and the valleys of America. It was flung into the deep recesses of foreign climes by the seeing 'eyes and ears' of Telstar." Woody Taylor, in the *Pittsburgh Courier* of September 3, 1963, summarized the oration thus: "This historic speech by the chief exponent of nonviolent action in the fight for civil rights was a fitting climax to the many events leading up to and after the famous March on Washington for Jobs and Freedom."

P. L. Prattis, a former executive editor of the *Pittsburgh Courier,* after he heard King speak on August 28, 1963, during the culmination of the great March, told the author:

Doctor King maintained what I call *poise.* He didn't speak with distracting gestures of either hands or arms. Next, he transfixed his audience with colorful imagery. This may be a bit overdrawn, but it was the kind of imagery people liked. But colorful and logical was his *totalling* up the debt the United States owes American Negroes. His elucidation here was in terms all people could understand. Without notable changes in voice or manner, but with intense passion which could be felt by those who listened, he moved into the *peroration* and gave more than 200,000 people a message of hope. He made the slogan "We shall overcome" ring in their ears. I would say that the tremendous impression he made on everybody was because of his elementary reasoning, his picturesque language and image symbols, and his dignity. He was one of the greatest speakers on the program, supported by one of the greatest messages to the human spirit and mind.

OCCASIONAL SPEAKING

Probably no other man in the United States filled a more crowded schedule of addresses in response to invitations than Dr. King, unless it was Booker T. Washington and the Presidents of the United States. If he had been money-minded, he could easily have been a millionaire with fees earned from speaking engagements. The orator was invited to give an address before the National Press Club in Washington on July 26, 1962. Part of this address called attention to the church as a segregated institution. Thus spoke King:

More and more the voice of the church is being heard. It is still true that the church is the most segregated major institution in America. As minister of the gospel, I am ashamed to have to affirm that eleven o'clock on Sunday morning, when we stand to sing "In Christ There Is No East or West" is the most segregated [moment] of the week. But in spite of these appalling facts, we are beginning to shake the lethargy from our souls. Here and there churches are courageously making attacks on segregation among their congregations. Several parochial and church-related schools in the South are throwing off the traditional yoke of segregation. As the church continues to take a forthright stand on this issue, the transition from a segregated society to an integrated society will be infinitely smoother.

Dr. Martin Luther King, Jr., talked unceasingly about disobeying unjust laws, and many of his enemies felt that he should be put in jail for a long period. Nevertheless, the Apostle literally rid himself of the specter of a long jail term. Right and justice and mercy all prevailed, except for short stays in many city jails. Yet, there was another great host that considered the openness of King's actions (which made him exceedingly vulnerable to arrest and jail sentences) downright stupidity. This criticism did not bother the Reverend King, since he felt that "right the day must win."

RHETORICAL FIGURES

Rhetorical figures of speech made Dr. King's speeches vibrant through comparison and contrast. One is struck by his descriptive figures of speech—similes, metaphors, allegories, and personifications. In Chicago, during the summer of 1965, King told one audience in Winnetka that the price Americans must pay for the oppression of Negroes is self-destruction, and that "the clock is ticking, and we must act before it is too late." He added, "We must work to get rid of segregation because it scars the soul." Another time, Dr. King said,

"Segregation is on its deathbed" and the only question remaining is how costly segregationists will make the funeral. Newspaper reports of his speeches list figures like these: "We must meet physical force with soul force," "the iron feet of oppression," "clouds floating in our mental skies," and "although laws may not change the hearts of men, they do change the habits of men." On another occasion, the orator remarked, "The stone of separate but equal has been rolled away, and justice rose up from the dark and gloomy grave." During the commencement exercises of six high schools in a combined program in Charlotte, North Carolina, in June, 1965, Dr. King said, "We must keep loving them and wear them down by our capacity for suffering."

LEADERSHIP APPRAISAL

What kind of appearance did Dr. King make on the platform? Louis E. Lomax succinctly stated that King was a Baptist preacher "who was well read in philosophy and theology, of medium height and size and girth, brown-skinned, with a moustache and interesting eyes that slanted slightly upward."

Some black leaders felt that King should stay out of those cities where local leaders did not welcome his help. Many whites associated him with physical violence between the races even though his gospel was nonviolence. In this connection, Will Herberg, professor of moral theology at Drew University, charged the civil-rights leader with deliberately trying to undermine the foundations of internal order in the nation. Others holding this point of view are too numerous to mention. Except for indirect influence, King was not at fault for these racial outbreaks since the disturbances were often caused by "fringe" white hoodlums. Much of the trouble could have been avoided if his followers had been conditioned and schooled in nonviolent techniques. Many of the black adherents had no real idea of what it was all about. Still others began to question the effectiveness of demonstrations, on the grounds that they were no longer imperative.

Taking a critical look at the small-time black civil-rights leaders who tried to imitate King, J. B. Harren, a columnist for *The Carolinian* of Raleigh, North Carolina, said:

> Today, too many of our so-called civil-rights leaders are going off "half cocked" like a gun, with the results that aimed-at goals of gaining certain civil rights advancement are slipping through their fingers while they strut around making a lot of noise like the geese they emulate with a loss of confidence from the people by their inadequate general planning.

Harren believes that Negroes can bargain intellectually through the strength of their ballot.

The small-time guerrilla chiefs were bad enough but some critics alleged that Martin Luther King was just as much at fault. For example, King took one summer to make a "people to people" tour that included six metropolitan cities, among them Chicago and New York. In no uncertain terms, Chicago leaders told him to go home because they did not need his help. The orator did not take the hint, and after two days of marathon speaking in July, had to go to bed and sleep.

Not all of King's ventures were as successful as was the Montgomery bus boycott. There were defeats and even catastrophes. In Albany, Georgia, the demonstration flopped, and the city bus line went bankrupt. In Selma, Alabama, the economy suffered on account of a boycott. This happened in many other communities. Rather than acquiesce to King's demands, St. Augustine, Florida, lost much of its tourist business.

The nonviolent movement in Birmingham had better luck than in other places. In the meantime, a church was bombed and four Negro children were killed. Dr. King, who had been to Birmingham several times before, immediately dispatched himself to the scene and rendered all the help he could. At the funeral of the children, he spoke bluntly, "The bombing of a

Negro church won't defer our efforts to desegregate Birmingham and all Alabama." The bombing also aroused many newspaper editors, most notably Eugene Patterson of the *Atlanta Constitution,* who wrote in an editorial on September 16, 1963: "The Sunday School play is ended. With a weeping mother, we stand in the bitter smoke and hold a shoe. If our South is ever to be what we wish it to be, we will plant a flower of nobler resolve for the South now upon these four small graves."

Although some of King's marches fizzled, his oratory seared the American conscience and engendered among Negroes the urge to cast their ballots. For instance, the number of Negroes registered to vote in eleven southern states rose from about 600,000 in 1948 to 1.2 million in 1956 and 2.2 million in 1964. There is no statistical way to figure out the influence of Dr. King upon the voting habits of Negroes, but it is known that he set the climate for this change in their behavior.

ORATORY MADE KING'S MOVEMENT CLICK

As we have seen, the leadership of Martin Luther King cannot be separated from his public speaking. Each reinforced and underpinned the other. Without speechmaking the nonviolent movement would have gone to pieces, and without leadership there would have been no need for persuasive oratory. Don McKee, Associated Press newsman, stated it this way: "But the striking feature, and perhaps the major factor in King's success, is not seen but heard. It is his oratory that stirs the mass meetings and staid university halls." Ralph Abernathy, an SCLC official, said pretty much the same thing. "It's his ability to communicate, to place in words the longings, the dreams, the hopes and aspirations of an oppressed people." Numerous speakers did this, but King said it in a novel way.

Dr. King considered that the goal of the speaker is to influence the listeners. Experience taught him how much the audience can contribute to the success of a speech—more, in fact, than most people realize. Through visual directness, King analyzed and played by ear the responses of his listeners. He found that paying close attention to their attitudes could be both disturbing and beneficial. When one section of the audience did not respond to his speaking, he did quick mental editing and changed what he planned to say, making himself more intelligible to the audience.

Audiences these days tend to be more analytical and comprehending than in the past. The task of the newspaper is to present facts, evolve ideas, combine ideas into judgments, compare truths or contrast them, so that readers may draw conclusions. When the press does this, it develops an informed audience for the orator. The press, therefore, has not usurped the place of the public speaker, but it has given him a new task and responsibility. Because of this, the Reverend King realized that audiences are tougher and will assess a speaker more rigidly, even though Negro hearers are also anxious to assist the leader in his efforts to help them and himself.

The multiplicity of writers trying to assess Dr. King as a leader created some controversial news stories about him. While the pros and cons waxed hotter, the nonviolent Reverend King became more articulate and eloquent. His voice grew indescribably sweeter and more musical each year to the man farthest down. Very few orators were ever listened to with greater delight and reverence.

FULL-TEXT SPEECHES

Love, Law, and Civil Disobedience

Members of the Fellowship of the Concerned of the Southern Regional Council, I need not pause to say how very delighted I am

Source: Delivered by Dr. Martin Luther King, Jr., to the delegates of the Fellowship of the Concerned of the Southern Regional Council on November 16, 1961.

to be here today, and to have the opportunity to be a little part of this very significant gathering. I certainly want to express my personal appreciation to Mrs. Tilly and the members of the Committee, for giving me this opportunity. I would also like to express just a personal word of thanks and appreciation for your vital witness in this period of transition which we are facing in our Southland, and in the nation, and I am sure that as a result of genuine concern, and your significant work in communities all across the South, we have a better south today and I am sure will have a better South tomorrow with your continued endeavor, and I do want to express my personal gratitude and appreciation to you of the Fellowship of the Concerned for your significant work and for your forthright witness.

Now, I have been asked to talk about the philosophy behind the student movement. There can be no gainsaying the fact that we confront a crisis in race relations in the United States. The crisis in 1954 outlawing segregation in the public schools has been precipitated on the one hand by the determined resistance of reactionary forces in the South to the Supreme Court's decision. And we know that at times this resistance has risen to ominous proportions. At times we find the legislative halls of the South ringing loud with such words as interposition and nullification. And all these forces have developed into massive resistance. But we must also say that the crisis has been precipitated on the other hand by the determination of hundreds and thousands and millions of Negro people to achieve freedom and human dignity. If the Negro stayed in his place and accepted discrimination and segregation, there would be no crisis. But the Negro has a new sense of dignity, a new self-respect and new determination. He has reevaluated his own intrinsic worth. Now this new sense of dignity on the part of the Negro grows out of the same longing for freedom and human dignity on the part of the oppressed people all over the world. Now we must say that this struggle for freedom will not come to an automatic halt, for history reveals to us that once oppressed people rise up against that oppression, there is no stopping-point short of full freedom. On the other hand, history reveals to us that those who oppose the movement for freedom are those who are in privileged positions who very seldom give up their privileges without strong resistance. And they seldom do it voluntarily. So the sense of struggle will continue. The question is how will the struggle be waged.

Now there are three ways that oppressed people have generally dealt with their oppression. One way is the method of acquiescence, the method of surrender; that is, the individuals will somehow adjust themselves to oppression, they adjust themselves to discrimination or to segregation or colonialism or what have you. The other method that has been used in history is that of rising up against the oppressor with corroding hatred and physical violence. Now, of course, we know about this method in western civilization, because in a sense it has been the hallmark of its grandeur, and the inseparable twin of western materialism. But there is a weakness in this method because it ends up creating many more social problems than it solves. And I am convinced that if the Negro succumbs to the temptation of using violence in his struggle for freedom and justice, unborn generations will be the recipients of a long and desolate night of bitterness. And our chief legacy to the future will be an endless reign of meaningless chaos.

But there is another way, namely the way of nonviolent resistance. This method was popularized in our generation by a little man from India, whose name was Mohandas K. Gandhi. He used this method in a magnificent way to free his people from the economic exploitation and the political domination inflicted upon them by a foreign power.

This has been the method used by the student movement in the South and all over the United States. And naturally whenever I talk about the student movement I cannot be totally objective. I have to be somewhat subjective because of my great admiration for what the students have done. For in a real sense they have taken our deep groans and passionate yearnings for freedom, and filtered them in their own tender souls, and fashioned them into a creative protest which is an epic known all over our nation. As a result of their disciplined, nonviolent, yet courageous struggle, they have been able to do wonders in the South, and in our nation. But this movement does have an underlying philosophy, it has certain ideas that are attached to it, it has certain philosophical precepts. These are the things that I would like to discuss for the few moments left.

I would say that the first point or the first principle in the movement is the idea that means must be as pure as the end. This movement is based on the philosophy that ends and means must cohere. Now this has been one of the long struggles in history, the whole idea of means and ends. Great philosophers have grappled with it, and sometimes they have emerged with the idea, from Machiavelli on down, that the end justifies the means. There is a great system of thought in our world today, known as Communism. And I think that with all of the weakness and tragedies of Communism, we find its greatest tragedy right there, that it goes under the philosophy that the end justifies the means that are used in the process. So we can read or we can hear the Leninists say that lying, deceit, or violence, that many of these things justify the ends of the classless society.

This is where the student movement and the nonviolent movement that is taking place in our nation would break with Communism and any other system that would argue that the end justifies the means. For in the long run, we must see that the end represents the means in process and the idea in the making. In other words, we cannot believe, or we cannot go with the idea that the end justifies the means because the end is preexistent in the means. So the idea of nonviolent resistance, the philosophy of nonviolent resistance, is the philosophy which says that in history, immoral destructive means cannot bring about moral and constructive ends.

There is another thing about this philosophy, this method of nonviolence which is followed by the student movement. It says that those who adhere to or follow this philosophy must follow a consistent principle of noninjury. They must consistently refuse to inflict injury upon another. Sometimes you will read the literature of the student movement, and see that, as they are getting ready for the sit-in or stand-in, they will read something like this, "If you are hit do not hit back, if you are cursed do not curse back." This is the whole idea, that the individual who is engaged in a nonviolent struggle must never inflict injury upon another. Now this has an external aspect and it has an internal one. From the external point of view it means that the individuals involved must avoid external physical violence. So they don't have guns, they don't retaliate with physical violence. If they are hit in the process, they avoid external physical violence at every point. But it also means that they avoid internal violence of spirit. This is why the love ethic stands so high in the student movement. We have a great deal of talk about love and nonviolence in this whole thrust.

Now when the students talk about love, certainly they are not talking about emotional bosh, they are not talking about merely a sentimental outpouring; they're talking something much deeper, and I always have to stop and try to define the meaning of love in this context. The Greek language comes to our aid in trying to deal with this. There are three words in the Greek language for love, one is the word *eros*. This is a beautiful type of love, it is an aesthetic love. Plato talks about it a great deal in his Dialogue, the yearning of the soul for the realm of the divine. It has come to us to be a sort of romantic love, and so in a sense we have read about it and experienced it. We've read about it in all the beauties of literature. I guess in a sense Edgar Allan Poe was talking about eros when he talked about his beautiful Annabel Lee, with the love surrounded by the halo of eternity. In a sense Shakespeare was talking about eros when he said "Love is not love which alters when it alteration finds, or bends with the remover to remove: O, no! it is an ever-fixed mark that looks on tempests and is never shaken; it is the star to every wandering bark. . . . " (You know, I remember that because I used to quote it to this little lady when we were courting; that's eros.) The Greek language talks about *Philia* which was another level of love. It is an intimate affection between personal friends, it is a reciprocal love. On this level you love because you are loved. It is friendship.

Then the Greek language comes out with another word which is called the *agape*. Agape is more than romantic love, agape is more than friendship. Agape is understanding, creative, redemptive, goodwill to all men. It is an overflowing love which seeks nothing in return. Theologians would say that it is the love of God operating in the human heart. So that when one rises to love on this level, he loves men not because he likes them, not because their ways appeal to him, but he loves every man because God loves him. And he rises to the point of loving the person who does an evil deed while hating the deed that the person does. I think this is what Jesus meant when he said "love your enemies." I'm very happy that he didn't say like your enemies, because it is very difficult to like someone bombing your home; it is pretty difficult to like somebody threatening your children; it is difficult to like congressmen who spend all of their time trying to defeat civil rights. But Jesus says love them, and love is greater than like. Love is understanding, redemptive, creative, goodwill for all men. And it is this whole ethic of love which is the idea standing at the basis of the student movement.

There is something else; that one seeks to defeat the unjust system, rather than individuals who are caught in that system. And that one goes on believing that somehow this is the important thing, to get rid of the evil system and not the individual who happens to be misled, who was taught wrong. The thing to do is to get rid of the system and thereby create a moral balance within society.

Another thing that stands at the center of this movement is another idea: that suffering can be a most creative and powerful social force. Suffering has certain moral attributes involved, but it can be a powerful and creative social force. Now, it is very interesting at this point to notice that both violence and nonviolence agree that suffering can be a very powerful social force. But there is this difference: violence says that suffering can be a powerful social force by inflicting suffering on somebody else; so this is what we do in war, this is what we do in the whole violent thrust of the violent movement. It believes that you achieve some end by inflicting suffering on another. The nonviolent say that suffering becomes a powerful social force when you willingly accept that violence on yourself, so that self-suffering stands at the center of the nonviolent movement and the individuals involved are able to suffer in a creative manner, feeling that unearned suffering is redemptive, and that suffering may serve to transform the social situation.

Another thing in this movement is the idea that there is within human nature an amazing potential for goodness. There is within human nature something that can respond to goodness. I know somebody's liable to say that this is an unrealistic movement if it goes on believing that all people are good. Well, I didn't say that. I think the students are realistic enough to believe that there is a strange dichotomy of disturbing dualism within human nature. Many of the great philosophers and thinkers through the ages have seen this. It caused Ovid, the Latin poet, to say, "I see and approve the better things of life, but the evil things I do." It caused even St. Augustine to say "Lord, make me pure, but not yet." So that there is in human nature, Plato, centuries ago said that the human personality is like a charioteer with two headstrong horses, each wanting to go in different directions, so that within our own individual lives we see this conflict and certainly when we come to the collective life of man, we see a strange badness. But in spite of this there is something in human nature that can respond to goodness. So that man is neither innately good nor is he innately bad; he has potentialities for both. So in this sense, Carlyle was right when he said, that "there are depths in man which go down to the lowest hell, and heights which reach the highest heaven, for are not both heaven and hell made out of him, ever-lasting miracle and mystery that he is?" Man has the capacity to be good, man has the capacity to be evil.

And so the nonviolent resister never lets this idea go, that there is something within human nature that can respond to goodness. So that a Jesus of Nazareth or a Mohandas Gandhi can appeal to human beings and appeal to that element of evil within them, and a Hitler can appeal to the element of evil within them. But we must never forget that there is something within human nature that can respond to goodness, that man is not totally depraved; to put it in theological terms, the image of God is never totally done. And so the individuals who believe in this movement and who believe in nonviolence and our struggle in the South, somehow believe that even the worst segregationist can become an integrationist. Now sometimes it is hard to believe that this is what this movement says, and it believes it firmly, that there is something within human nature that can be changed, and this stands at the top of the whole philosophy of the student movement and the philosophy of nonviolence.

It says something else. It says that it is as much a moral obligation to refuse to cooperate with evil as it is to cooperate with good.

Noncooperation with evil is as much a moral obligation as the cooperation with good. So that the student movement is willing to stand up courageously on the idea of evil disobedience. Now I think this is the part of the student movement that is probably misunderstood more than anything else. And it is a difficult aspect, because on the one hand the students would say, and I would say, and all the people who believe in civil rights would say: Obey the Supreme Court's decision of 1954 and at the same time, we would disobey certain laws that exist on the statutes of the South today.

This brings in the whole question of how can you be logically consistent when you advocate obeying some laws and disobeying other laws. Well, I think one would have to see the whole meaning of this movement at this point by seeing that the students recognize that there are two types of laws. There are just laws and there are unjust laws. And they would be the first to say obey the just laws, they would be the first to say that men and women have a moral obligation to obey just and right laws. And they would go on to say that we must see that there are unjust laws. Now the question comes into being, what is the difference, and who determines the difference, what is the difference between a just and an unjust law?

Well, a just law is a law that squares with a moral law. It is a law that squares with that which is right, so that any law that uplifts human personality is a just law. Whereas that law which is out of harmony with the moral is a law which does not square with the moral law of the universe. It does not square with the law of God, so for that reason it is unjust, and any law that degrades the human personality is an unjust law.

Well, somebody says that that does not mean anything to me; first, I don't believe in these abstract things called moral laws, and I'm not too religious, so I don't believe in the law of God; you have to get a little more concrete, and more practical. What do you mean when you say that a law is unjust, and a law is just? Well, I would go on to say in more concrete terms that an unjust law is a code that the majority inflicts on the minority that is not binding on itself. So that this becomes difference made legal. Another thing that we can say is that an unjust law is a code which the majority inflicts upon the minority, which that minority had no part in enacting or creating, because that minority had no right to vote in many instances, so that the legislative bodies that made these laws were not democratically elected. Who could ever say that the legislative body of Mississippi was democratically elected, or the legislative body of Alabama was democratically elected, or the legislative body even of Georgia has been democratically elected, when there are people in Terrell County and in other counties, because of the color of their skin, who cannot vote? They confront reprisals and threats and all of that; so that an unjust law is a law that individuals did not have a part in creating or enacting because they were denied the right to vote.

Now by the same token, a just law would be just the opposite. A just law becomes saneness made legal. It is a code that the majority, who happen to believe in that code, compel the minority, who don't believe in it, to follow, because they are willing to follow it themselves, so it is saneness made legal. Therefore the individuals who stand up on the basis of civil disobedience realize that they are following something that says that there are just laws and there are unjust laws. Now, they are not anarchists. They believe that there are laws which must be followed; they do not seek to defy the law, they do not seek to evade the law. For many individuals who would call themselves segregationists and who would hold on to segregation at any cost seek to defy the law, they seek to evade the law, and their process can lead on into anarchy. They seek in the final analysis to follow a way of uncivil disobedience, not civil disobedience. And I submit that the individual who disobeys the law, whose conscience tells him it is unjust and who is willing to accept the penalty by staying in jail until that law is altered, is expressing at the moment the very highest respect for law.

This is what the students have followed in their movement. Of course there is nothing new about this; they feel that they are in good company and rightly so. We go back and read the Apology and the Crito, and you see Socrates practicing civil disobedience. And to a degree academic freedom is a reality today because Socrates practiced civil disobedience. The early Christians practiced civil disobedience in a superb manner, to a point where they were willing to be thrown to the lions. They were willing to face all kinds of suffering in order to stand up for what they knew was right even though they knew it was against the laws of the Roman Empire.

We could come up to our own day and we see it in many instances. We must never forget that everything that Hitler did in Germany was "legal." It was illegal to aid and comfort a Jew, in the days of Hitler's Germany. But I believe that if I had the same attitude then as I have now I would publicly aid and comfort my Jewish brothers in Germany if Hitler were alive today calling this an illegal process. If I lived in South Africa today in the midst of the white supremacy law in South Africa, I would join Chief Luthuli and others in saying, break these unjust laws. And even let us come up to America. Our nation in a sense came into being through a massive act of civil disobedience, for the Boston Tea Party was nothing but a massive act of civil disobedience. Those who stood up against the slave laws, the abolitionists, by and large practiced civil disobedience. So I think these students are in good company, and they feel that by practicing civil disobedience they are in line with men and women through the ages who have stood up for something that is morally right.

Now there are one or two other things that I want to say about this student movement, moving out of the philosophy of nonviolence, something about what it is a revolt against. On the one hand it is a revolt against the negative peace that has encompassed the South for many years. I remember when I was in Montgomery, Alabama, one of the white citizens came to me one day and said—and I think he was very sincere about this—that in Montgomery for all of these years we have been such a peaceful community, we have had so much harmony in race relations and then you people have started this movement and boycott, and it has done so much to disturb race relations, and we just don't love the Negro like we used to love him, because you have destroyed the harmony and the peace that we once had in race relations. And I said to him, in the best way I could say and I tried to say it in nonviolent terms: We have never had peace in Montgomery, Alabama, we have never had peace in the South. We have had a negative peace, which is merely the absence of tension; we've had a negative peace in which the Negro patiently accepted his situation and his plight, but we've never had true peace, we've never had positive peace, and what we're seeking now is to develop this positive peace. For we must come to see that peace is not merely the absence of some negative force, it is the presence of a positive force. True peace is not merely the absence of tension, but it is the presence of justice and brotherhood. I think this is what Jesus meant when he said, "I come not to bring peace but a sword." Now Jesus didn't mean he came to start war, to bring a physical sword, and he didn't mean, I come not to bring positive peace. But I think what Jesus was saying in substance was this, that I come not to bring an old negative peace, which makes for stagnant passivity and deadening complacency, I come to bring something different, and whenever I come, a conflict is precipitated between the old and the new, whenever I come, a struggle takes place between justice and injustice, between the forces of light and the forces of darkness. I come not to bring a negative peace, but a positive peace, which is brotherhood, which is justice, which is the Kingdom of God.

And I think this is what we are seeking to do today, and this movement is a revolt against a negative peace and struggle to bring into being a positive peace, which makes for true brotherhood, true integration, true person-to-person relationships. This movement is also revolt against what is often called tokenism. Here again many people do not understand this, they feel that in this struggle the Negro will be satisfied with tokens of integration, just a few students and a few schools here and there and a few doors open here and there. But this isn't the meaning of the movement, and I think that honesty impels me to admit it everywhere I have an opportunity, that the Negro's aim is to bring about complete integration in American life. And he has come to see that token integration is little more than token democracy, which ends up with many new evasive schemes and it ends up with new discrimination, covered up with such niceties of complexity. It is very interesting to discover that the movement has thrived in many communities that had token integration. So this reveals that the movement is based on a principle that integration must become real and complete, not just token integration.

It is also a revolt against what I often call the myth of time. We hear this quite often, that only time can solve this problem. That if we will only be patient, and only pray—which we must do, we must be patient and we must pray—but there are those who say just do these things and wait for time, and time will solve this problem. Well, the people who argue this do not themselves realize that time is neutral, that it can be used constructively or destructively. At points the people of ill will, the segregationists, have used time more effectively than the people of goodwill. So individuals in the struggle must come to realize that it is necessary to aid time, that without this kind of aid, time itself will become an ally of the insurgent and primitive forces of social stagnation. Therefore, this movement is a revolt against the myth of time.

There is a final thing that I would like to say to you: This movement is a movement based on faith in the future. It is a movement based on a philosophy, the possibility of the future bringing into being something real and meaningful. It is a movement based on hope. I think this is very important. The students have developed a theme song for their movement, maybe you've heard it. It goes something like this: "We shall overcome, deep in my heart, I do believe, we shall overcome," and they go on to say another verse, "We are not afraid to day, deep in my heart, I do believe, we shall overcome." So it is out of this deep faith in the future that they are able to move out and adjourn the councils of despair, and to bring new light in the dark chambers of pessimism. I can remember the times that we've been together, I remember that night in Montgomery, Alabama, when we had stayed up all night, discussing the Freedom Rides, and that morning came to see that it was necessary to go on with the Freedom Rides, that we would not in all good conscience call an end to the Freedom Rides at that point. And I remember the first group got ready to leave, to take a bus for Jackson, Mississippi, we all joined hands and started singing together. "We shall overcome, we shall overcome." And something within me said, now how is it that these students can sing this, they are going down to Mississippi, they are going to face hostile and jeering mobs, and yet they could sing, "We shall overcome." They may even face physical death, and yet they could sing, "We shall overcome." Most of them realized that they would be thrown into jail, and yet they could sing, "We shall overcome, we are not afraid." Then something caused me to see at that moment the real meaning of the movement. That students had faith in the future. That the movement was based on hope, that this movement had something within it that says somehow even though the arc of the moral universe is long, it bends toward justice. And I think this should be a challenge to all others who are struggling to transform the dangling discords of our Southland into a beautiful symphony of brotherhood. There is something in this student movement which says to us, that we shall overcome. Before the victory is won, some will lose jobs, some will be called Communists and Reds, merely because they believe in brotherhood, some will be dismissed as dangerous rabble-rousers and agitators merely because they're standing up for what is right, but we shall overcome. That is the basis of this movement, and as I like to say, there is something in this universe that justifies Carlyle in saying no lie can live forever. We shall overcome because there is something in this universe which justifies William Cullen Bryant in saying truth crushed to earth shall rise again. We shall overcome because there is something in this universe that justifies James Russell Lowell in saying, truth forever on the scaffold, wrong forever on the throne. Yet that scaffold sways the future, and behind the dim unknown standeth God within the shadows, keeping watch above His own. With this faith in the future, with this determined struggle, we will be able to emerge from the bleak and the desolate midnight of man's inhumanity to man, into the bright and glittering daybreak of freedom and justice. Thank you.

I Have a Dream Today

I am happy to join with you today in what will go down in history as the greatest demonstration for freedom in the history of our nation.

Five score years ago, a great American, in whose symbolic shadow we stand today, signed the Emancipation Proclamation. This momentous decree came as a great beacon of hope to millions of slaves, who had been seared in the flames of withering injustice. It came as a joyous daybreak to end the long night of their captivity.

But one hundred years later the colored American is still not free. One hundred years later the life of the colored American is still sadly crippled by the manacle of segregation and the chains of discrimination.

One hundred years later the colored American lives on a lonely island of poverty in the midst of a vast ocean of material prosperity. One hundred years later, the colored American is still languishing in the corners of American society and finds himself an exile in his own land. So we have come here today to dramatize a shameful condition.

In a sense we have come to our Nation's Capital to cash a check. When the architects of our great republic wrote the magnificent words of the Constitution and the Declaration of Independence, they were signing a promissory note to which every American was to fall heir.

This note was a promise that all men, yes, black men as well as white men, would be guaranteed the inalienable rights of life, liberty, and the pursuit of happiness.

It is obvious today that America has defaulted on this promissory note insofar as her citizens of color are concerned. Instead of honoring this sacred obligation, America has given its colored people a bad check, a check that has come back marked "insufficient funds."

But we refuse to believe that the bank of justice is bankrupt. We refuse to believe that there are insufficient funds in the great vaults of opportunity of this nation. So we have come to cash this check, a check that will give us upon demand the riches of freedom and security of justice.

We have also come to this hallowed spot to remind America of the

---

Source: This full text of "I Have a Dream Today," which Dr. Martin Luther King, Jr., delivered at the Lincoln Memorial, Wednesday, August 28, the day of the March on Washington, was printed in the September 7, 1963, issue of *The Chicago Defender*. Every newspaper of any consequence carried the full text of this speech.

fierce urgency of *Now.* This is no time to engage in the luxury of cooling off or to take the tranquilizing drug of gradualism.

Now is the time to make real the promise of democracy.

Now is the time to rise from the dark and desolate valley of segregation to the sunlit path of racial justice.

Now is the time to lift our nation from the quicksands of racial injustice to the solid rock of brotherhood.

Now is the time to make justice a reality to all of God's children.

It would be fatal for the nation to overlook the urgency of the moment and to underestimate the determination of its colored citizens. This sweltering summer of the colored people's legitimate discontent will not pass until there is an invigorating autumn of freedom and equality. Nineteen sixty-three is not an end but a beginning. Those who hope that the colored Americans needed to blow off steam and will now be content, will have a rude awakening if the nation returns to business as usual.

There will be neither rest nor tranquillity in America until the colored citizen is granted his citizenship rights. The whirlwinds of revolt will continue to shake the foundations of our nation until the bright day of justice emerges.

But there is something that I must say to my people who stand on the threshold which leads into the palace of justice. In the process of gaining our rightful place we must not be guilty of wrongful deeds.

Let us not seek to satisfy our thirst for freedom by drinking from the cup of bitterness and hatred.

We must forever conduct our struggle on the high plane of dignity and discipline. We must not allow our creative protest to degenerate into physical violence.

Again and again we must rise to the majestic heights of meeting physical force with soul force. The marvelous new militancy which has engulfed the colored community must not lead us to a distrust of all white people, for many of our white brothers, evidenced by their presence here today, have come to realize that their destiny is tied up with our destiny and their freedom is inextricably bound to our freedom.

We cannot walk alone.

As we walk, we must make the pledge that we shall always march ahead. We cannot turn back. There are those who are asking the devotees of civil rights, "When will you be satisfied?"

We can never be satisfied as long as the colored person is the victim of the unspeakable horrors of police brutality.

We can never be satisfied as long as our bodies, heavy with the fatigue of travel, cannot gain lodging in the motels of the highways and the hotels of the cities.

We cannot be satisfied as long as the colored person's basic mobility is from a smaller ghetto to a larger one.

We can never be satisfied as long as our children are stripped of their selfhood and robbed of their dignity by signs stating "for white only."

We cannot be satisfied as long as a colored person in Mississippi cannot vote and a colored person in New York believes he has nothing for which to vote.

No, no we are not satisfied and we will not be satisfied until justice rolls down like waters and righteousness like a mighty stream.

I am not unmindful that some of you have come here out of your trials and tribulations. Some of you have come straight from narrow jail cells. Some of you have come from areas where your quest for freedom left you battered by storms of persecutions and staggered by the winds of police brutality.

You have been the veterans of creative suffering. Continue to work with the faith that unearned suffering is redemptive.

Go back to Mississippi, go back to Alabama, go back to South Carolina, go back to Georgia, go back to Louisiana, go back to the slums and ghettos of our modern cities, knowing that somehow this situation can and will be changed.

Let us not wallow in the valley of despair. I say to you, my friends, we face the difficulties of today and tomorrow.

I still have a dream. It is a dream deeply rooted in the American dream.

I have a dream that one day this nation will rise up and live out the true meaning of its creed. We hold these truths be be self-evident that all men are created equal.

I have a dream that one day out in the red hills of Georgia the sons of former slaves and the sons of former slaveowners will be able to sit down together at the table of brotherhood.

I have a dream that one day even the state of Mississippi, a state sweltering with the heat of oppression, will be transformed into an oasis of freedom and justice.

I have a dream that my four little children will one day live in a nation where they will not be judged by the color of their skin but by their character.

I have a dream today.

I have a dream that one day down in Alabama, with its vicious racists, with its governor having his lips dripping with the words of interposition and nullification; that one day right down in Alabama little black boys and black girls will be able to join hands with little white boys and white girls as sisters and brothers.

I have a dream today.

I have a dream that one day every valley shall be engulfed, every hill shall be exalted, and every mountain shall be made low, the rough places will be made plains, and the crooked places will be made straight, and the glory of the Lord shall be revealed and all flesh shall see it together.

This is our hope. This is the faith that I will go back to the South with. With this faith we will be able to hew out of the mountain of despair a stone of hope.

With this faith we will be able to transform the jangling discords of our nation into a beautiful symphony of brotherhood.

With this faith we will be able to work together, to pray together, to struggle together, to go to jail together, to climb up for freedom together, knowing that we will be free one day.

This will be the day when all of God's children will be able to sing with new meaning "My country 'tis of thee, sweet land of liberty, of thee I sing. Land where my fathers died, land of the Pilgrim's pride, from every mountainside, let freedom ring!"

And if America is to be a great nation, this must become true. So, let freedom ring from the hilltops of New Hampshire. Let freedom ring from the mighty mountains of New York.

Let freedom ring from the heightening Alleghenies of Pennsylvania.

Let freedom ring from the snow-capped Rockies of Colorado.

Let freedom ring from the curvacious slopes of California.

But not only that, let freedom ring from the Stone Mountain of Georgia.

Let freedom ring from very hill and molehill of Mississippi and every mountainside.

When we let freedom ring, when we let it ring from every tenement and every hamlet, from every state and every city, we will be able to speed up that day when all of God's children, black men and white men, Jews and Gentiles, Protestants and Catholics, will be able to join hands and sing in the words of the old spiritual, "Free at last, free at last? Thank God Almighty, we are free at last."

Footnotes, Chapter 17

1. Martin Luther King, Jr., *Strides Toward Freedom*, pp. 61–63.
2. L. D. Reddick, *Crusader Without Violence*, p. 11.
3. Ibid., p. 8.

18 / Radio and Television Speaking

Prior to the 1954 Supreme Court decision outlawing segregation in public schools, Negro speakers rarely made use of radio and television facilities. The few exceptions were politicians who gave campaign speeches in large metropolitan centers on programs paid for by the big political parties. There were also numerous weekly religious broadcasts by preachers who appeared on the air on weekday evenings or for Sunday worship services. There are several reasons why Negroes have made limited use of the radio and television media for speaking before 1950. First, large organizations like the NAACP, National Urban League, Alpha Kappa Alpha Sorority, Kappa Alpha Psi Fraternity, and Negro American Labor Council have not conducted public relations programs by means of broadcasts. Negro organizations rarely purchase broadcast time, even though various civil-rights activities have received a lot of publicity. They have accepted gratis spot announcements which follow the format of "brotherhood" pleas prepared and submitted by such organizations as the Federation of Jewish Philanthropies. The speaking we have heard from Negro orators over radio and television comes to the public as free service in the interest of the people. Often on the news program of Walter Cronkite, televised scenes of speeches given at civil-rights demonstrations have been shown. But these news spots did not cost civil-rights groups a cent.

In the second place, there are only a few radio and television stations which are owned and operated by Negro stockholders; and, therefore, few employment opportunities have been made available to Negroes in announcing and newscasting. Radio station WERD, owned by a Negro company in Atlanta, Georgia, is one of the rare exceptions.

Third, white-owned radio and television stations before 1950 seldom featured broadcasts with Negroes participating in panel discussions, occasional public speaking, and news broadcasts. But after 1960, civil-rights activities, sit-ins, demonstrations, and Freedom Rides ushered in the golden age for Negro radio and television participation and oratory. Nonviolent activities by Negroes on city streets were brought to public notice with the practice by police of water-hosing and setting dogs on demonstrators. These events made national and international news which broadcasting networks were anxious to put on the air. Each year after 1960, there has been an increase in interviewing, radio speaking, and news presentations involving Negroes and speechmaking. The public has seen and heard on television James Farmer, Fred Shuttleworth, Gloria Richardson, Whitney Young, Ruby Hurley, A. Philip Randolph, Malcolm X, Roy Wilkins, and Medgar Evers.

GOODWILL AMBASSADORS

One can count on the fingers of one hand instances of Negroes speaking over the radio and television to promote racial goodwill. Two examples were W. W. Lambert of Mt. Vernon, Ohio, and the Reverend S. J. Nathaniel Tross of Charlotte, North Carolina. In 1942, W. W. Lambert, who now resides in California where he and his wife have established a church and home for aged people, originated an interracial program which he named "The Old Colored Hostler" and broadcast once each week on Fridays at 1:00 P.M. in Mansfield, Ohio, over radio station WMAN. This program ran for three years, and Lambert paid for the broadcast time from the income earned working at a part-time extra job. "The Old Colored Hostler" program consisted of a weekly five-minute radio speech discussing the achievements of Negroes in America and citing examples of the spirit of brotherhood. Usually Lambert's opening statement called attention to the place "where the rivers of right and justice meet, and the spirit of Lincoln walks the shoreline." Many of the programs commemorated holidays, but they always included the Negro. In his Christmas program in 1942, for example, Lambert concluded:

We may rest assured that there cannot be peace on earth until we are willing to recognize the God-given rights to all men and see to it that men of every race, creed, and color, are treated as ourselves. Then, and only then can we honestly lead the world in singing, "Joy to the World, the Lord is come, Let earth receive her king."

After three consecutive years of broadcasting, Lambert discontinued "The Old Colored Hostler" and no Negro organization offered to sponsor its continuance.

Dr. S. J. Nathaniel Tross, formerly editor of church school literature of the AME. Zion Church, broadcast for twelve years an interracial program over radio station WBT, of Charlotte, North Carolina, on Sunday mornings at 9:45 o'clock. This program won the Variety Award for being the best of its kind in the nation. In his broadcasts, Tross did not harangue his listeners. He made appeals only to the human race. When presenting the evils of the community, he merely stated the facts without placing blame on any one race. He emphasized how the undesirable condition could be corrected through community cooperation and enterprise. Then he tried to do something to remove the evil. To him action spoke louder than words. A new automobile was presented to him in May, 1950, on the program's tenth anniversary as a gift from the white citizens to show their appreciation of his efforts to promote interracial goodwill. The presentation took place in the studios of Station WBT, and at that time Dr. Tross was referred to as "the Ambassador of Goodwill." During the spring of 1951, he was a candidate for a position on the Charlotte School Board. His enemies called him a "time-is-not-ripe" Uncle Tom who catered to the wishes of white people. This allegation led Tross to challenge two of his critics to a public debate on civic and racial issues, but they declined. Although he polled several thousand votes, Tross was not elected.

RELIGION BY RADIO

Negro ministers have been broadcasting sermons and church services to millions of Americans weekly. They reach more people than any other group of Negroes through a communicative medium. Radio audiences have been built up mainly through the showmanship of preachers and the musical talent of their choirs. The advent of television added to the popularity of these broadcasts. The ministers have ranged all the way from well-educated, dignified, and intellectual pastors of well-established denominations to self-ordained, loud-shouting faith healers in storefronts. A detailed account of broadcasting by these ministers and their choirs has been published in the July, 1947, issue of *Ebony* magazine.

An earlier chapter on religious cults and sects revealed the popularity of preachers like the Elder Solomon Michaux whose inspiring services and choirs attracted large radio audiences each week. Some of these ministers emphasized that Christianity was in trouble in a world of moral decay where sin is rampart. Today, they are urging men to get right with God. Viewers who tune in on these services note how the emotional fervor becomes a catharsis that siphons off the frustrations of the religious adherents. On the other hand, the educated clergy endeavor to get their congregations to internalize intellectually what emotional members would feel. Their sermons help the church in helping men and women to meet the humble Christ, in having the freedom to question old forms of the church, and in recognizing the demands of the present age in order to achieve unity between those within and without the church for the purpose of testing the resilience of the church.

In Texas, the Reverend R. E. Ranger, a Negro preacher, aired a program from his Wayside Christ in the Church over NBC from coast to coast from 1940 to 1950. The Reverend Singleton Chambers, head of Evangelist Temple, gave two broadcasts weekly in Kansas City and Little Rock near mid-century. It is reputed that he healed more than 14,000 persons by telephone conversation, while 200,000 listeners heard him for almost twenty years. About 1950, a dynamic radio minister whose services appealed to 75,000 radio listeners was the Reverend Clayton Russell, leader of the Independent Church of Christ in Los Angeles, California. More than eleven thousand persons tuned in weekly to station KFOX to hear the Reverend Russell since he was a compelling speaker. Sometimes he entered political campaigns in support of civil rights, labor, and the welfare of war veterans.

No other radio personality in Negro circles is more widely known than the Reverend William Borders of Atlanta. He has conducted radio appeals for funds over station WGST to improve racial relations in Georgia. For instance, Borders raised $10,000 to bury the victims of the Monroe lynchings and move their families to the North. Offended white people, who heard his militant addresses at the height of his popularity, suggested that he move away from Georgia. Borders was graduated from Northwestern University in Illinois, and some years later he published a book entitled *Seven Minutes at the Mike in the Deep South* while pastor of the Wheat Street Baptist Church in Atlanta with 6,000 interracial members.

Virginia, during the decade prior to 1965, was noted for two radio programs conducted by the Reverend Richard B. Martin of Norfolk and the Reverend Charles Lawrence Evans of Richmond. Martin, who was at the time Rector of Grace Protestant Episcopal Church, preached over station WTAR on the "Daily Church of the Air." Before becoming a cleric, he was a teacher at Morris College in Sumter, South Carolina. He often urged men not to make God's word synonymous with a fixed list of taboos. Evans, who has been executive secretary of the 50,000-member Virginia Baptist Association, once delivered a sermon each Sunday over station WRNL in Richmond. The sermons of the series emphasized our fake world of undesirable motives. He especially urged Negroes to seek techniques for gaining personal confidence, peace of mind, and freedom from worry. While he was conducting his radio program, the Reverend Evans was a columnist for the *Journal and Guide* of Norfolk, Virginia.

The deep South was abundantly supplied with a host of radio preachers from 1920 to 1950. The Reverend John W. Goodgame broadcast one hour each Sunday from the Sixth Avenue Baptist Church in Birmingham, Alabama. At the time, the Reverend D. E. Holloway preached in Jacksonville, Florida, each Sunday morning over station WIVY under the auspices of the National Educational and Religious Council. Thousands of listeners in Miami, Florida, tuned in to hear Archbishop Ernest L. Peterson, often mistaken for Caucasian, speak on station WMIBM for about twenty years prior to 1954. A citizen of the Virgin Islands, Peterson was a machinist by trade before coming to the United States to become a cleric. He was graduated from Howard University and once served a church in Cuba. Next, he became the first Negro Primate of the American Catholic Church in 1941.

This discussion has not included every minister who has

had a radio program. The situation is comparable to the occasion when the Apostle Paul wrote a letter to the early Hebrew churches. He narrated the deeds of the great Jewish religious heroes by name. Then, running out of time, Paul said: "And there were others!" To include all of the Negro radio ministers would be impossible, since there has often been at least one preacher broadcasting radio services in every important city in the United States of America.

19 / Lecturing Activities of Negroes

With the advent of the electronic age, standing in front of the microphone became the vogue among public speakers appearing before huge audiences in auditoriums and outdoors. Political orators, fearing misquotations by newspapers, began reading their speeches rather than trusting their memory. This type of speaking is a hindrance to eloquent oratory as we once knew it. The microphone confines the speaker behind the lectern, which also makes it convenient to read from manuscripts. This confinement also checks expansive body movement which was once the artful technique of great speakers. Besides, the reading of speeches also renders the content cut and dried and devoid of liveliness and vibrancy. This new type of vocal delivery, which has been practiced for decades by numerous speakers, has made it difficult for us to distinguish between lecturing and oratory. And yet the great teachers of the past like Plato and Aristotle no doubt gave unemotional lectures for instructional purposes. Selected students who had a thirst for knowledge sat at the feet of their instructors and listened eagerly. It was communication for information only, as has been the case of high governmental officials lecturing to television audiences.

The term "lecturing" in its original sense meant the act of reading an instructional discourse to an audience of interested persons. As presently conceived, "lecturing" connotes an instructional discourse delivered formally before a university class, an educational or religious convocation, or an audience that is intellectually and culturally inclined. The appeal of the lecturer is generally made to the intellect. Almost every person communicating by radio and television these days makes no pretense of eloquence and contents himself with merely reading from a manuscript, to wit: commencement speeches, congressional addresses, campaign speeches in political circles, and sermons in churches.

CHAUTAUQUA ERA

From the turn of the century up to the 1920s, lecturing under the sponsorship of the Redpath Lyceum Bureau, Incorporated, was a profitable profession in this country. Tent circuits spangled the forty-eight states. In the peak year, 1924, "an estimated 30,000,000 Americans sat in brown tents pitched on nearly 12,000 main streets and enjoyed lectures, music, drama, and other cultural items making up the typical Chautauqua week of offering."[1] During his youth, the author witnessed these pitched tents in Chester, South Carolina, his hometown, but could not attend because of his color.

The roster of "talent" was made up of the "Who's Who" of the era. Until his death in 1915, Booker T. Washington was the only Negro lecturer whose popularity would make a chautauqua booking successful and profitable. But Washington never lectured under the management of any bureau.[2] He was invited to speak on the chautauqua circuit on occasion, but he was never under management. Washington avoided even the appearance of exploiting his own name for personal profit. He did lecture, however, on subjects dealing with all phases of racial relations and with his work at Tuskegee. These two subjects were broad enough to include any aspect of Negro and American life. Whenever he received an honorarium, it was accepted in the name of Tuskegee Institute.

The absence of Negro lecturers on Southern Redpath Lyceum circuits was partly owing to the same reason that banned Negro patrons from the audiences attending the performances. It could not be blamed entirely on the lack of speaking talent and learned lecturers for, during Booker T. Washington's times, there were easily a dozen Negro leaders of distinction and speaking ability. However, singers, mostly college groups, were sometimes employed by the chautauqua to give concerts. Usually they were accompanied by a faculty member who gave a short speech during one of the intermissions.

ORGANIZATIONS AND LECTURING BUREAUS

Negro organizations and agencies use lecturing as a propaganda and educative device, but they have not generally employed lecturers on a full-time basis for this purpose. It is true, however, that James Weldon Johnson, William Pickens, Walter White, and Roy Wilkins—all of the NAACP—have given hundreds of lectures while touring the United States to establish NAACP branches. Yet lecturing with them was a part-time affair, compared with the other duties they had, or have, to perform. The same can be said about Lester Granger, who represented the National Urban League. When organizing the Universal Negro Improvement Association, Marcus A. Garvey lectured in thirty-eight states to raise funds for his "Back-to-Africa" movement. In this capacity, he could hardly be termed a professional lecturer. To create a public image, industry, political parties, and other organizations have advertising and public relations budgets amounting to billions of dollars. To sell an idea today involves a vast machinery of propaganda and expense. Negro leaders have failed to use the advertising media to advance their movements and the civil-rights program.

Negro organizations are functioning presently without definite programs designed to give the black man a good and respectable image, in spite of evidence provided by industry to indicate the imperative of good public-relations and propaganda devices aimed at selling ideas and goods. When the author polled certain leading organizations operating in fraternal, employment, labor, and educational areas, it was reported that they had not conducted professional public-relations programs or made systematic use of advertising media. These are startling facts, and yet the Negro college sororities and fraternities, fraternal organizations, churches, and civil-rights groups have not seen fit to provide annual budgets for this purpose. The National Broadcasting Company, for example, said in 1965 that "aside from spot announcements of a public nature, Negro organizations and civil-rights groups do not purchase broadcast time."

Among the few well-known concert and lecture management bureaus scheduling Negro artists, musicians, and lecturers are: International Lectures, Inc., Independence, Missouri; Giesen Management, Inc., New York City; Arts Program Association of American Colleges, New York City; and W. Colston Leigh, Inc., New York City. Ray Moseley, director of International Lectures, stated that his bureau had never had any Negro speakers on its circuit. Since some of the speaking tours, scheduled by W. Colston Leigh, dated back to the 1930s, B. R. Grand prepared the following list of black lecturers from memory: Countee Cullen, Walter White, Zelma George, Langston Hughes, Zora Neale Hurston, and Simeon Booker. The director of Arts Program Association of American Colleges stated that some speaking tours included Roland Hayes, lecturer and singer; John Akar, lecturer from Sierre Leone; and Dr. Zelma George. The Giesen Management of the Columbia Lecture Bureau, Inc., did represent Dr. William Hansberry, but he died before he could fill his engagements.

LECTURING FEES

Negro educators, ministers, authors, and labor experts have given lectures under the auspices of local and state organizations. As has been emphasized, they have not generally traveled under lyceum management for fees, except when they entered temporary contracts to speak on the college lyceum series. They have received honoraria sufficient to pay their expenses, ranging from $50 to $250, depending upon the distance traveled and the prestige of the speaker. If he chose, Dr. Martin Luther King, Jr., could easily have had contracts to lecture under the auspices of various bureaus. Critics have accused him of "capitalizing" upon his prestige in order to fill his pockets. Apparently, this accusation is untrue, because King placed his living expenses at $10,000 to $12,000 a year. He earned no salary from the SCLC, since he would not accept it. His church paid him $4,000 per year and supplemented this with $2,000 for parsonage allowances. King added $5,000 to $6,000 to this salary from speaking engagements, but 90 percent of the income from his lectures and writing was contributed to the movement, the church, and Morehouse College. Doctor King felt that wealth would destroy his effectiveness, in spite of the fact that he could have legitimately earned from $100,000 to $200,000 annually from speaking engagements and writing. He consciously avoided making money.

Management bureaus have paid Negro lecturers an average of $300 to $600 per engagement. If the Redpath Lyceum Bureau had been active in his day, Dr. King would have earned a fee matching that paid the great orator, Wendell Phillips, who demanded at the height of his career $1,000 per lecture during the antislavery period. Since he was a wealthy man, Phillips, a Caucasian, deposited the money from his lectures in the treasury of the Abolition Society.

When colleges and universities began to receive federal grants for science and mathematics institutes, antipoverty programs, Upward Bound, and other educational projects, Negro consultants were paid handsome fees for their services and lectures in the amount of $75 to $100 a day plus expenses. Famous medical men, like the late Dr. Charles Drew, could very well command a daily fee of $500 and up if he were alive.

PROMINENT LECTURERS

Between 1925 and 1950, a galaxy of stars appeared on the lecture platform and soared, as it were, upon an intellectual firmament. During this time, Professor Ira DeA. Reid, sociologist, was a most productive lecturer and writer. Lecturing at numerous colleges and forums, Reid intrigued his listeners by pouring out a vast storehouse of knowledge on the social aspects of the Negro. A contemporary of Dr. Reid was the Harvard graduate, Dr. Rayford Logan, professor of history at Howard University. Logan was best known for his editorship of *What the Negro Wants* and the vigorous challenge he presented when lecturing about underprivileged people in Africa, India, and elsewhere. During this period, the late Dr. E. Franklin Frazier became an authority on the Negro family and lectured widely upon this subject. His graphic, factual approach startled his audiences. Whenever one mentions Fisk University in Nashville, Tennessee, the name Charles S. Johnson is brought to mind. It was reputed that Professor Johnson knew more about the racial problem than any Negro living at the time. Among his prolific writings were *Negro College Graduate* and *Preface to Racial Understanding*. Because of his training in sociological research, Johnson lectured in unemotional tones and skillfully described cases he had seen. He supported a step-by-step program of racial progress rather than a sweeping revolution in racial relations.

LECTURING ARTISTS

Many Negro musicians, dancers, dramatists, and poets have presented cultural lectures covering various phases of the fine arts on college lyceum programs. At one time, nearly ninety so-called Negro colleges scheduled lectures in addition to musical and dramatic performances featuring Negro talent. The popular headliners before midcentury were philosophers like Alain Locke and the Reverend Howard Thurman, poets with the commanding stature of James Weldon Johnson, Claude McKay, and Melvin Tolson, and pioneer playwrights in the educational theater like S. Randolph Edmonds and James W. Butcher, Jr. A number of writers have established some degree of fame, including Gwendolyn Brooks, Ossie Davis, Ralph Ellison, and James Baldwin. To be sure, a host of other artists have upon occasion filled lecture engagements.

Zora Neale Hurston, an anthropologist, produced before her death many works on Negro folk literature. To collect material for talks on this subject she traveled widely in Louisiana and Florida, her home state. Hurston rose to popularity with two novels, *Jonah's Gourd Vine* and *Their Eyes Are Watching God,* and a travel book on Haiti and Jamaica. For several years, she toured colleges and universities lecturing and reading from her works.

A writer who held his own from 1930 until his death was Langston Hughes, whose literary fame began when he first published poems in *Opportunity* magazine. In 1925, Vachel Lindsay read three poems by Hughes at the Little Theatre of the Wardman Park Hotel in Washington, where the poet Hughes was a busboy. This brought national attention to his writings. He wrote hundreds of poems, nearly twenty plays, numerous radio scripts, and weekly newspaper columns. For more than thirty-five years, Langston Hughes lectured upon literature and racial problems and read his poems. His first full evening program was given in Washington for an interracial audience in 1925 at the M Street Playhouse. Dr. Alain Locke presided. The poet's first appearance in New York was in 1926 at the Shipwreck Inn near Columbia University in honor of the publication of his first poems, *The Weary Blues.*

The first cross-country lecture tour took place from September, 1931, to June, 1932, and was underwritten by the Julius

Rosenwald Fund. In July, 1932, Hughes embarked on a trip around the world. After his return to the United States, he booked his own lectures from 1925 to 1940. After this time, the poet lectured under the management of W. Colston Leigh, Inc., 521 Fifth Avenue, New York City. During Negro History Week, he always had a full schedule of lectures. Audience reactions were cordial and occasionally enthusiastic. When he participated in a "Town Meeting of the Air" radio program, he spoke well enough in his prepared speech, but the audience was challenged by his unrehearsed and impromptu answers to questions from the floor, and the solid deliberation and brilliant repartee of the man became manifest.

Hughes said that social poets often get themselves into trouble. In 1926, for instance, he was invited to give a program of his poems in an Atlantic City church. During the program, he read some of his blues about hard luck and hard work. A deacon approached the pulpit with a note which the poet placed on the rostrum beside him. But he did not read it until he had finished and acknowledged the applause of the audience. The note read, "Do not read any more blues in my pulpit." It was signed by the minister. That was the first experience that Langston Hughes had with censorship, and opposition to his poems prevented his appearing in public programs on several later occasions. The poet has discussed glaring examples of this sort of thing in an essay, "My Adventures as a Social Poet."

Footnotes, Chapter 19

1. Headquarters, 80 Boylston, Room 1159, Boston, at that time.
2. According to the Department of Records and Research, Tuskegee Institute.

Appendices

THE AUTHOR'S LIST OF LEADING ORATORS BASED UPON
FOLLOW-UP STORIES OF SPEECHES IN NEWSPAPERS
OVER A FIVE-YEAR PERIOD

EDUCATION

Mary McLeod Bethune
Charlotte Hawkins Brown
Mordecai Wyatt Johnson

Booker T. Washington
Charles Wesley
Benjamin E. Mays

FRATERNALISM

J. Finley Wilson

RELIGIOUS EDUCATION

Nannie Burroughs

GENERAL CULTURE

James Weldon Johnson
Paul Robeson
Mary Church Terrell

SOCIAL REFORM

Channing Tobias
Walter White
Martin Luther King, Jr.

LABOR

A. Philip Randolph

Willard Townsend

POLITICS

Archibald James Carey, Jr.   Adam Clayton Powell, Jr.
Arthur Mitchell   Patrick B. Prescott, Jr.

RELIGION

Charles S. Morris, II   Channing Tobias
George A. Singleton   Benjamin E. Mays
          Martin Luther King, Jr.

WOMEN ADVANCEMENT

Mary Church Terrell

LIST OF ORATORS TABULATED FROM QUESTIONNAIRES, 1945–1950

GENERAL CULTURE

James Weldon Johnson   Mordecai Wyatt Johnson
Charlotte Hawkins Brown   Channing Tobias
Charles Wesley   Mary Church Terrell
Paul Robeson   Charles H. Brown
          Charles S. Morris, II

FRATERNALISM

J. Finley Wilson   Charles Wesley

SOCIAL REFORM

James Weldon Johnson   Paul Robeson
Mary Church Terrell   Channing Tobias
Mordecai Wyatt Johnson   W. E. B. DuBois
Booker T. Washington   Walter White
Mary McLeod Bethune   A. Philip Randolph

Benjamin E. Mays
Adam Clayton Powell, II
Lillian Wheeler Smith

Charlotte Hawkins Brown
Patrick B. Prescott
Homer Brown

LABOR

A. Philip Randolph

Willard Townsend

CULTISTS

Elder Michaux
Prophet James F. Jones
Father Divine
Bishop Grace

Bishop D. W. Nichols
Rev. Utah Smith
Rev. Charles Beck

To prepare this list, the author distributed 150 questionnaires to 100 professors of American history, 20 newspaper editors, 5 news commentators, 20 public speaking professors, and five well-known laymen.

Bibliography

BOOKS:

Altgeld, John P. *Oratory and the Public*. Chicago: n.p., 1915.

Baird, A. Craig. *American Speeches, 1944–45*. New York: H. W. Wilson Company, 1945.

Barlett, Robert M. *They Work for Tomorrow*. New York: Fleming H. Revell, 1943.

Bennett, Winfred DeWitt. "A Survey of American Negro Oratory." Master's thesis, George Washington University, 1935.

Berle, Adolphe A. *The American Republic*. New York: Harcourt, Brace and World, Harvest ed., 1965.

Bond, Horace Mann. *Negro Education in Alabama*. Washington, D. C.: Associated Publishers, 1939.

Bontemps, Arna. *One Hundred Years of Freedom*. New York: Mead and Company, 1963.

Booker, Simeon. *Black Man's America*. Englewood Cliffs, N. J.: Prentice-Hall, 1964.

Brawley, Benjamin. *Negro Builders and Heroes*. Chapel Hill, N. C.: University of North Carolina Press, 1937.

———. *Social History of the American Negro*. New York, 1941.

———. *The Negro in Literature and Art*. New York: Duffield Company, 1918.

Brigance, William, Ed. *History and Criticism of American Public Address*. New York: McGraw-Hill Book Company, 1943.

Brisbane, Robert H., Jr. "The Rise of Protest Movements Among Negroes Since 1900." Ph. D. dissertation, Harvard University, 1949.

Brown, Ina Corine. *The Story of the American Negro*. New York: Friendship Press, 1936.

Bullock, Ralph W. *In Spite of Handicaps*. New York: Association Press, 1927.

Case, Victoria, and Case, Robert C. *We Call It Culture*. New York: Doubleday and Company, 1948.

Daniels, Sadie. *Women Builders*. Washington, D.C.: Associated Publishers, 1931.

Du Bois, W. E. B. *The Souls of Black Folk*. Chicago: McClurg Company, 1903.

Embree. Edwin R. *13 Against the Odds*. New York: Viking Press, 1945.

Everett, Faye Philip. *The Colored Situation*. Boston: Meader, 1936.

Fausett, Arthur Huff. *Black Gods of the Metropolis*. Philadelphia: University of Pennsylvania, 1944.

Franklin, John Hope. *From Slavery to Freedom*. New York: Alfred A. Knopf, 1947.

Frazier, E. Franklin. *The Negro in the United States*. New York: Macmillan Company, 1949.

Goode, Eslanda. *Paul Robeson*. London: Victor Gollancz, 1930.

Gosnell, Harold F. *Negro Politicians.* Chicago: University of Chicago Press, 1935.

Hardwicke, Henry. *History of Oratory and Orators.* New York, 1896.

Hartshorn, William N. *Era of Progress.* Boston: Priscilla Publishing Company, 1910.

Hickey, Neil, and Edwin, Ed. *A. C. Powell and the Politics of a Race.* New York: Fleet Publishing Co., 1965.

Holt, Rackham. *Mary McLeod Bethune.* Garden City, N. Y.: Doubledy and Company, 1964.

Holtzclaw, William H. *The Black Man's Burden.* New York: Neale Publishing Co., 1915.

Johnson, Charles S. *The Negro in American Civilization.* New York: Henry Holt and Company, 1930.

Johnson, James Weldon. *Along This Way.* New York: Viking Press, 1933.

————. *Black Manhattan.* New York: Alfred A. Knopf, 1930.

————. *Negro Americans, What Now?* New York Viking Press, 1934.

Kerlin, Robert. *The Voices of the Negro.* New York: E. P. Dutton, 1930.

King, Martin Luther, Jr. *Strides Toward Freedom.* New York: Harper & Brothers, 1958.

Loggins, Vernon. *The Negro Author.* New York: Columbia University Press, 1931.

Logan, Rayford, Ed. *What the Negro Wants.* Chapel Hill, N. C.: University of North Carolina Press, 1944.

Lomax, Louis E. *The Negro Revolt.* New York: Harper & Brothers, 1962.

McClorey, John. *The Making of a Pulpit Orator.* New York: Macmilliam Company, 1934.

McKay, Claude. *Harlem Metropolis.* New York: E. P. Dutton Company, 1940.

Markmann, Charles, and Sherwin, Mark. *John F. Kennedy: A Sense of Purpose.* New York: St. Martin Press, 1961.

Martin, Fletcher. *Our Great Americans.* Chicago: Gamma Corporation. 1953.

Mays, Benjamin E., *The Negro Church.* New York: Institute of Social and Religious Research, 1933.

Monroe, Alan H. *Principles and Types of Speech.* Brief ed. New York: Scott, Foresman and Company, 1945.

Moton, Robert R. *Finding a Way Out.* New York: Doubleday and Company, 1920.

Muehl, William. *The Road to Persuasion.* New York: Oxford Univerisity Press, 1956.

Ottley, Roi. *Black Odyssey.* New York: Charles Scribner's Sons, 1948.

————. *New World A-Coming.* Boston: Houghton Mifflin Company, 1943.

————. *The Lonely Warrior.* Chicago: Henry Regnery Co., 1955.

Platz, Mabel. *The History of Public Speaking.* New York: Noble and Noble, 1935.

Powell, Adam C., Jr. *Marching Blacks.* New York: Dial Press, 1946.

Reddick, L. D. *Crusader Without Violence.* New York: Harper & Brothers, 1959.

Richardson, Ben. *Great American Negroes.* New York: Thomas Y. Crowell Company, 1945.

Spero, Sterling D. *The Black Worker.* New York: Columbia University Press, 1931.

Thurman, Howard. *The Creative Encounter.* New York: Harper & Brothers, 1954.

Turpin, Edna L. H., Ed. *The New South and Other Addresses.* New York: Marynard, Merrill and Co., 1904.

Walls, William J. *Joseph Charles Price.* Boston: Christopher Publishing Company, 1943.

White, Walter. *A Man Called White.* New York: Viking Press, 1948.

Woodson, Carter G. *Negro Orators and Their Orations.* Washington, D. C.: Associated Publishers, 1925.

Wright, Richard. *Twelve Million Black Voices.* New York: Viking Press, 1941.

Wynn, David W. *The NAACP Versus Negro Protest.* New York: Exposition Press, 1955.

Yoakim, Doris. "Women's Introduction to the American Platform." In *History of American Public Address* edited by N. Brigance. New York: McGraw-Hill Book Company, 1943.

PERIODICALS:

Afro-American, March 4, 1950.

"Alabama Bomb Victims Buried." *St. Petersburg* (Florida) *Times,* September 19, 1963.

"American Orators, New Style." *Literary Digest,* August 5, 1916, p. 307.

Anderson, Trezzvant W. *Pittsburgh Courier,* April 5, 1951.

Annals of the American Academy of Political Science 140 (November, 1923): 15.

"A. Philip Randolph: Man Behind the March on Nation's Capital." *Jet,* September 5, 1963, p. 14.

Bibb, Joseph D. *Pittsburgh Courier,* November 25, 1944; November 23, 1946; May 6, 1950; October 21, 1950; February 3, 1951.

"The Big Man Is Martin Luther King, Jr." *Newsweek* 62 (July 29, 1963): 30.

"Biggest March in History." *Ebony* 19 (November, 1963): 29–31; 35–40; 42–46.

Boulware, Marcus H. "The Approaching Death of James Crow." *Negro Digest* 11 (July, 1962): 38–39.

Brown American (Fall and Winter, 1944–1945), p. 9.

California Eagle (Los Angeles), September 7, 1945.

Capital Times (Madison, Wisconsin), September 3, 1949.

Carter, Elmer A. A discussion of A. Philip Randolph. *Opportunity* 15 (October, 1937): 299.

Carter, Michael. "Meet Adam Powell." *Afro-American Newspapers,* November, 1944.

Cayton, Horace. "Carey, the Republican." *New Republic* 69 (October 18, 1948): 10.

Cayton, Horace. *Pittsburgh Courier,* April 17, 1948; July 1, 1950.

Charlotte (North Carolina) *Observer,* March 17, 1951.

Chicago Daily News, June 17, 1928.

Chicago Defender, October, 1932 (no day indicated); April 24, 1948; October 30–November 5, 1965.

Cox, Oliver C. "The Crises in Leadership Among Negroes." *Journal of Negro Education,* 19 (Fall, 1950): 459–465.

Current Biography, March, 1941; June, 1942; January, 1948.

Daily Worker, June 3, 1932.

Edson, Arthur. "Dirksen and Senate Made for Each Other." *St. Petersburg Times,* January 27, 1965.

"Father Divine." *Spoken Word* 3 (April 24, 1937): 6.

"Father Divine Divinely Human." *Chicago Defender,* October 5–15, 1965.

Fayetteville (North Carolina) *Observer,* July 1, 1965.

Ferguson, Elizabeth A. "American Slave Insurrection Among Negroes." *Journal of Negro Education* 7 (January, 1938): 32.

Fowlkes, William. Magazine Section, *Pittsburgh Courier,* October 21, 1950.

Frazier, E. Franklin. "Garvey: Mass Leader." *Nation* 123 (August 18, 1926): 147.

Granger, Lester B. "Phylon Profile, II; Willard S. Townsend." *Phylon* 5 (4th Quarter, 1944): 333.

Graves. Lem. *Pittsburgh Courier,* July 23, 1949.

————. "Negroes in the Halls of Congress." *Pittsburgh Courier,* July 30, 1949.

————. "Washington Notebook." *Pittsburgh Courier.* November 12, 1949.

Hancock, Gordon. Editorial, *Dayton (Ohio) Forum,* February 21, 1941.

Harren, J. B. *The Carolinian* (Raleigh, N. C.), January 1, 1966.

High, Stanley. "Black Omen's." *Saturday Evening Post,* 210 (June 4, 1938): 38.

Interracial Review 23 (September, 1950): 131.

Journal and Guide (Norfolk, Virginia), July 28, 1944.

Knight, C. A., ed. Editorial, *Charlotte (North Carolina) News,* June 7, 1950.

Kreuger, E. T. "Negro Religious Expression." *American Journal of Sociology* 38 (July, 1932): 22–25.

Ledbetter, J. S. *Missionary Review of the World* 59 (June, 1936): 315–316.

Life, October 1, 1944; November 27, 1944; August 13, 1945.

Liston, Robert A. "Who Can We Surrender To?" *Saturday Evening Post* 226 (October 5, 1963): 78–80.

Literary Digest 123 (March 6, 1937): 8.

McKenzie, Marjorie. "Challenge on Legal Tactics." *Pittsburgh Courier,* July 7, 1961.

Maryland State Bulletin, vol. 1, no. 1, (October, 1937).

Mays, Benjamin E. "My Views." *Pittsburgh Courier,* October 19, 1963.

"Mordecai Johnson's Charter Day Address." *Afro-American Newspapers,* August 13, 1949.

"Mystery Man of Race Relations [Channing H. Tobias]." *Ebony* 6 (February, 1951): 15.

Negro History Bulletin, 2 (October, 1938): 1.

News and Observer (Raleigh, North Carolina), January 23, 1966.

New York Times, May 11, 1963; October 23, 1950.

"Nix Blasts Southern Solons for Double Talk Hypocrisy." *Jet,* September 16, 1965, pp. 8–9.

Nunn, William S., Sr. *Pittsburgh Courier,* September 3, 1963.

Opportunity 2 (May, 1924): 155.

Palmer, Edward. "Father Divine Is God." *Quarterly Review of Higher Education Among Negroes* 13 (July, 1945): 257.

Pittsburgh Courier (National Edition), November 25, 1944–October 19, 1963.

Public Speaking Review, November, 1911.

The Pulpit, June, 1944.

Ragland, J. Farley. "Southern Highlights." *Journal and Guide* (Norfolk, Virginia), August 4, 1945.

"Religious News Magazine." *St. Petersburg (Florida) Times,* October 16, 1965.

Rowan, Carl T. "Has Paul Robeson Betrayed the Negro." *Ebony,* October, 1957.

"Second Front in Harlem," *Time* 40 (December 21, 1942): 74. *The Sign,* 29 (October, 1949): 9.

"The Sit-in Demonstrations and the Dilemma of the Negro College President." *Journal of Negro Education* 30 (Winter, 1961): 1–3.

Spike, Robert. "Our Churches Sin Against the Negro." *Look,* May 18, 1965, p. 36.

"Ten Who Deliver." *Fortune,* November, 1946.

Thomas, V. P. "Mr. Booker T. Washington in Louisiana." *Crisis* 10 (June, 1915): 144–46.

"Three Men." *Commonweal,* August, 1940, p. 325.

Tuskegee Messenger, March and April, 1936.

Wish, Harvey. "American Slave Insurrections." *Journal of Negro History* 23 (July, 1937): 299–320.

"Who's Who Among the Big Elks." *Color* 3 (January, 1947): 8–13.

Young, P. B., Sr., "The Passing Scene." *Journal and Guide* (Norfolk, Virginia), January 20, 1951.

Index